T0369122

Three Little Birds

FAITH, HOPE, AND LOVE

JACQUELINE McDANIELS MARTIN

WESTBOW·
PRESS
A DIVISION OF THOMAS NELSON
& ZONDERVAN

Scriptures taken from the Holy Bible, New International Version®, NIV®. Copyright © 1973, 1978, 1984, 2011 by Biblica, Inc.™ Used by permission of Zondervan. All rights reserved worldwide. www.zondervan.com The "NIV" and "New International Version" are trademarks registered in the United States Patent and Trademark Office by Biblica, Inc.™

WestBow Press books may be ordered through booksellers or by contacting:

WestBow Press
A Division of Thomas Nelson & Zondervan
1663 Liberty Drive
Bloomington, IN 47403
www.westbowpress.com
1-(866) 928-1240

Because of the dynamic nature of the Internet, any web addresses or links contained in this book may have changed since publication and may no longer be valid. The views expressed in this work are solely those of the author and do not necessarily reflect the views of the publisher, and the publisher hereby disclaims any responsibility for them.

Cover illustration by Marie Houtz.

ISBN: 978-1-4908-0814-7 (sc)
ISBN: 978-1-4908-0813-0 (hc)
ISBN: 978-1-4908-0815-4 (e)

Library of Congress Control Number: 2013916480

Printed in the United States of America.

WestBow Press rev. date: 03/10/2014

To "Sweet Baby James"

*Our love for you has been reserved in a
special place in our hearts.*

And

*Frick, Frack, Pop Pop, The Bird Family, Doc Mission, My Partners in Crime,
Doc Optimistic, Nurse Heart of Gold, St. Giles Presbyterian Saints, Palmetto
Bank, Palmetto Presbyterian Saints, Prayer Warriors,
and MUSC Caregivers.*

*And now these three remain: faith, hope and love.
But the greatest of these is love.*
1 Corinthians 13:13

CONTENTS

INTRODUCTION

*If you have a song of faith in your heart, it will be
heard by the look on your face.*

L iving life as a Christian means, "living life to a higher calling."
When we face trials and tests of our faith during our lives, how
do we continue to live this higher calling lifestyle, especially
during the darkest days one could experience in life? How do you
continue to remain faithful to God during hardships and "live a life
worthy of your calling" as the Apostle Paul wrote and encouraged the
Ephesians and Christians to do in the Book of Ephesians?

For some, living life to the fullest, according to God's desires at
times, seems difficult. When tragedies occur in a family or relationships,
at times attempting to just get up out of the bed every day may seem
impossible. Depression and anxiety may set in and at times can attempt
to take over your life—especially during tragedies. *Three Little Birds:
Faith, Hope and Love* is proof that living a full life during hardships
is possible by utilizing the gifts God provides us. Even when the

hardships of life seem overbearing, God's greatest gifts: faith, hope and love, shine and remain in our lives no matter how stormy the days become and how dark the nights seem. During these trials, faith, hope and love always glitter specks of light upon us. They shine and brighten our days during dark times. If you just open your eyes, lean on a friend, or simply ask for help in order to continue living. God faithfully provides for our needs. Our job is to just make sure our eyes as well as hearts are open wide and willing to receive these gifts.

My vision of a "higher calling" came unexpectedly, seven months ago on May 17, 2011,with the birth of my third child, James Robert Martin. As I have and continue to endure one of the toughest trials of my life, I strive to live faithfully as a Christian. I hope my story of the Three Little Birds will bring strength and comfort to those enduring their own journey and trials. *Three Little Birds: Faith, Hope and Love*, is a true story that transcends four months of "bird-chirping" or God's songs of praises, promises, and suffering. This is my reflection along a personal pursuit of trying to live life to a higher calling or simply put, as a Christian. My life's passion and mission is to improve the world "one baby step at a time," through serving others and local charities that support families of children who are chronically ill. I believe through God's grace, support, and love from His followers we can continue living life to a higher calling through trials and tests of faith, even if it is one baby step at a time.

I truly believe with the support and love of God, we all are able to help other families in need, while continuing to spread God's gifts of faith, hope, and love. Even during stormy nights, I charge you to remain faithful to God. Never give up hope and always continue to love yourself as well as others during storms. May your hearts be nurtured and healed through love from the community of God as well as God's grace. I hope this story will help you hear the birds chirp daily in your walk with God as well as your walk to live life to a higher calling.

Blessings to you for journeys full of birds chirping, songs of faith, hope, and love!

Jacqueline
"Nurse Mom"

Part 1

FAITH

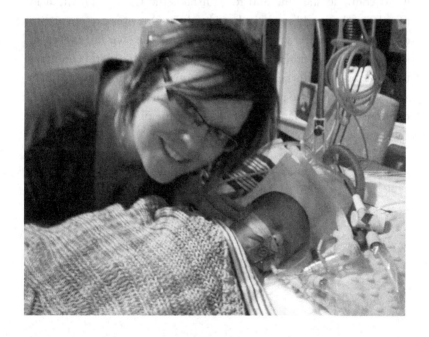

Faith is a bird that feels dawn breaking and sings while it is still dark.
—Rabindranath Tagore

F aith is a belief or trust in somebody or something, especially without logical proof. Faith is what you hold on to when you do not have anything else to grasp tightly through tough times and trials. Faith is what you lean upon when your child is born prematurely with a congenital heart defect, and you are thrown unexpectedly into a life of charity.

One guarantee in life is everyone endures hardships and receives a test of faith. This test of faith enables us to continue to count and remember our blessings. This test of faith seems to hide the world's beautiful colors and silence the chirping and singing of birds. Nature feels hidden during these difficult times. But in that darkness, faith continues to shine brightly.

During difficult times, community and help from others allow us to continue standing and to withstand the trials. With the help of others, the world's colors shine brightly. Our eyes are opened to different experiences, trials, and journeys in our own life as well as in the journeys of others. If only we can see how the world continues to shine bright with faith. If only we can accept the help of others and embrace the love and community God provides. If only we can continue to remain faithful to God and remember, God is good, all the time!

CHAPTER 1

In the Beginning

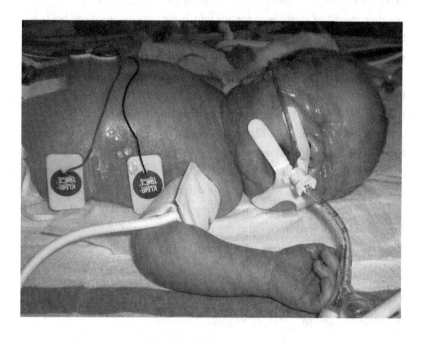

In his heart a man plans his course, but the Lord determines his steps.
Proverbs 16:9

Delivery Day ~Nurse Mom
Tuesday, May 17, 2011, 7:46 p.m.

Happy birthday, James! I woke up at 5 a.m. to my cell phone beeping "low battery." Both my hands were numb, I was sick to my stomach, and had a throbbing headache. I woke up J. J., my husband, and we decided to go to Greenville Memorial Hospital. It was also Frack's (James's sister) seventh birthday Happy birthday Frack! Frick, James's older brother, and Frack went with us to the hospital, where our family friend Mama Peacock picked them up.

After checking into the Triage unit on the sixth floor, the doctors discovered my blood pressure was high. Lab work showed elevated enzymes, which meant my liver function was becoming affected. I was admitted to the high-risk area, thinking we would be waiting a few days before we delivered Baby James. The original plan was to try to get another round of steroids, a forty-eight-hour process, into my body to help mature James's lungs. I had already had a series of shots when I was admitted to the hospital in April for several days as a precaution.

Around 5 p.m., "Doc Delivery" was concerned because my headache was not going away. I had received tons of medicine throughout the day to knock out the throbbing pain in my head, but it wasn't going away. Doc Delivery decided we would deliver James on this day because he was concerned I might have a stroke. The operating room was prepped, J. J. was prepared, and baby James was delivered via C-section at 7:46 p.m., weighing approximately five pounds and fifteen ounces. He was seventeen inches long. Happy birthday to my sweet, beautiful baby I had been carrying for seven months, with almost two months on bed rest. I love you, James!

Day of Days ~Dad
Wednesday, May 18, 2011, 9:30 p.m.

The echocardiogram (echo), an ultrasound of the heart, was delayed from 9:30 a.m. until 2 p.m. today. The enlarged heart was a concern, but James's heart rate was stable. At 12:30 p.m., the echo was processed due to concerns over rising lactic acid levels that indicated a lactic acid buildup in the blood. James was having problems getting oxygen to his tissues. The echo showed his heart had not one but two major abnormalities. The valves on both sides of his heart were severely underdeveloped and could not effectively pump blood forward through the lungs and out to the body. Because these valves wouldn't close, blood pumped back and forth between chambers in the heart and back into his lungs, increasing the amount of pressure on his lungs.

The doctors at Greenville Memorial Hospital contacted the Medical University of South Carolina (MUSC) in Charleston, South Carolina, to see about getting a helicopter or airplane to airlift James to Charleston from Greenville. The earliest James can get on a plane to Charleston will be 9 p.m. To add injury to insult, our neighbor just called and informed me that our family cat, Max (who was a part of our family for fifteen years) had been attacked and killed by dogs in the front yard.

In the meantime, Jacqueline, James's mom and my wife, is still suffering from high blood pressure, preeclampsia, toxemia, MRSA, and HELLP syndrome (a complication of the preeclampsia). She is still recovering from the C-section and barely able to get out of the bed. She is suffering a high level of anxiety from the narcotics, not to mention James's declining condition. This is probably the worst day of my life.

Settling In ~Dad
Monday, May 23, 2011, 3:56 p.m.

James has one major primary problem: the valves in his heart. We have to get James's other organs strong enough to sustain an initial surgery called a hybrid. This hybrid surgery requires a stint to be placed into his ductus and bands to be placed around his aorta. In order for James to sustain this surgery, he has to make progress with three critical organs: the lungs, the kidneys, and the liver.

The lungs are probably the most critical piece of James's recovery, because the primary function of the heart is to deliver oxygen to the organs. The lungs have a direct link to the functionality of both the kidneys and the liver. The first indicator that needed to be improved was his blood gas level. This is a measure of lactic acid buildup in the blood. The morning we arrived in Charleston, James's lactic acid level was 13.7 and rising. They already expected liver and kidney damage and did not know if he would make it until his mother could get to Charleston from Greenville.

As soon as James arrived at MUSC, the doctors put a larger tube down his trachea and paralyzed him with medicine so he could not

5

move. James was put on 100 percent oxygen and given almost fifty breaths per minute. In other words, James was not doing any breathing on his own. By paralyzing him, he could make better use of the oxygen his heart was getting out to the body. But it wasn't until after Jacqueline arrived that the lactic acid levels began to decrease. Sometimes you just need your mama! With her arrival, we saw the lactic acid level decline to 9.9 and then 7.9.

Over the course of three days, James's blood gas numbers declined to 2 percent, which is normal. During the last three days, the doctors gave James diuretics to drain fluid out of his lungs. His ventilator is now producing 30 percent of his oxygen. His number of breaths was reduced from almost fifty to twenty-four. This all means his lungs are getting stronger and require less and less assistance. In the meantime, they took him off the paralyzing medicine and his lactic acid levels remained constant. This is a big win for us.

When we first arrived, we anticipated damage to the kidneys based on the lactic acid level. We had to pump James full of several different medicines to help his lungs deliver oxygen. Unfortunately, the kidneys could not sustain the necessary levels. The doctors wanted to start giving diuretics but were concerned about James's blood pressure. Even still, the doctors gave him diuretics, and praise God, James's blood pressure remained constant. As the doctors increased the diuretics over the course of two days, James's urine output grew. Additionally, he was able to come down off some of the medicines, which resulted in drainage of fluid from his lungs. This in turn helped his oxygen levels. Last but not least, the doctors were able to decrease the amount of diuretics and maintain kidney function, which meant James's kidneys are doing better than when we first arrived. This was a step in the right direction!

We don't know as much about the liver yet. It still could have some damage, but we supported James with vitamin K, which helps with blood clotting. He responded well, and this part of the problem appears to be solved. However, James's bilirubin count was high, so he had black lights all around him to assist the liver and reduce the bilirubin level. The liver was working, but it is a more difficult organ to assess because of all the other complications. However, early indications were that we are going to be okay. We just need a little time to mature and grow.

We can't proceed to step two—the hybrid surgery—until these organs are strong enough to handle the surgery. It is probably going take two or three weeks to get to that point. We ask that everyone keep us in his or her prayers.

Small Blessings ~Nurse Mom
Monday, May 23, 2011 11:30 p.m.

Today was a great day. I walked all day and did not need the wheel chair to get around. J. J. and I have a ten-minute walk from the Ronald McDonald House to the hospital. We enjoyed each other today by walking and spending time with James. Today was so special to me, because this morning I read James one of my favorite books, *The Kissing Hand*. If you are not familiar with this story please check the book out and read it. At the end of the story I kissed James's hand and made his left hand the kissing hand. He grips everything with his left hand so I left him a kiss (like Mama Raccoon in the story) in his left hand so he could be brave in the hospital when we are not there. I read James lots of books during the day and talk to him about everything. The Ronald McDonald House has a library so I am able to have access to lots of wonderful books to share with him.

We were able to give James a bath but the great news is that he opened his eyes tonight. This is the first time I have seen his eyes open. He was so sleepy but opened and shut his eyes several times tonight. Plus, James's nurse, Nurse God-Send, is so sweet. She told me tonight that I could bring in blankets for James's bed. You would have thought someone had given me $1 million the way this news excited me. I am so afraid of germs that I have hesitated bringing anything into James's room, especially his bed. So, late tonight, J. J. and I went out and purchased James a few blankets. I was also able to find Frick a surprise he has been talking about for weeks.

I miss Frick and Frack so much. Frick is our eight-year-old-son, and Frack, our seven-year-old-daughter. I talked to them on the phone today. They have another week of school and then they will be here with me in Charleston. They are coming up this weekend on Friday after they get out of school. I am excited to see them as soon as possible.

James continues to make small baby steps each day, so I ask you friends to please continue to pray for him. God is hearing your prayers. We will find out tomorrow morning about James's jaundice level, as he has been under a black-light lamp for a day now. Please pray the levels are reduced and James soon will not have to "lamp bathe" in his room. Blessings to you all. P. S. To James, I love you!

A Step Back ~Dad
Tuesday, May 24, 2011 10:59 a.m.

This morning, Jacqueline and I arrived at the hospital to find that James had incurred a couple of setbacks. He had a couple of blood gas tests that showed elevated lactic acid levels again. They had to put him back on the morphine and the paralyzing agent to keep him still. They also noticed some issues with his left lung. The doctors are performing Chest Physical Therapy (CPT) to James, which is equivalent to a mama patting James on the back to help loosen up the congestion and fluids in his left lung. It's a step back, but we're foolish to think we won't have these throughout this process. The folks in the hospital know what they're doing.

Jacqueline and I continue to pray really hard. We continue to read books to James, hold his hand, talk with him, and provide support to the doctors and nurses in any way we can.

A Hard Day for Mom ~Nurse Mom
Tuesday, May 24, 2011 12:25 p.m.

When I arrived at the hospital a few hours ago J. J.'s face told me all I needed to know: today was going to be a rough day. I entered the unit and noticed the black light lamp was off of James, so I have to admit I was a tad bit happy until I walked into the room. James's gas levels increased from two to 5.2 in his body, and I think his lungs have a little bit of fluid that will need to be displaced.

So, what can I do as Mom to help improve this situation and continue to be faithful? I am going back to the Bible now and searching for God's comfort. I am going to my favorite book in the Bible, of course James, to read about faith and wisdom. This is the word of God. Thanks be to God.

After rereading this passage, James II in the Bible, I am thinking how I can have endurance and ask God for wisdom. So, to give you a bit of background information, I have not been able to talk to any of the doctors and barely the nurses. I get extreme anxiety when the doctors walk in and I have to walk out. Instead, J. J. gives me updates.

This morning when the doctor walked into the room, I asked God to give me strength to have faith and endurance to talk to the doctor. I asked for wisdom from the doctor so I can know how to ask others to pray. Here goes: friends, I need you to pray for James's tricuspid valve to improve. The doctor thinks the echo test performed this morning may have shown a slight improvement. In order to make sure, they will do another echo this afternoon to check. If the valve has a small improvement, this gives us proof of God's healing and that James is slowly improving. In order for James to be a candidate for surgery, one of his valves has to improve—as three of the four are damaged.

Here is a good example of wisdom. I was able to talk to the doctor today and actually ask more questions than J. J! How about the wisdom God gave me to keep going today? This afternoon another echo is going to take place. Please friends, gather together and pray for improvement in the tricuspid valve as well as James's gas levels to decrease. The paralytic has been put back on to see if this is why James's levels increased last night. It was so priceless to see him open his eyes, but if it takes him sleeping I will have to continue to be faithful and understand so he may heal. The Bible states that we must ask God in prayer for what we need. Please go to prayer and ask God for us. Blessings to you!

James II

*My brothers and sisters whenever you face trials of any kind, consider it
nothing but joy, because you know the testing of your faith produces endurance;
and let endurance have its full effect, so you may be mature and complete,
lacking in nothing. If any of you is lacking in wisdom, ask God, who gives
to all generously and ungrudgingly, and it will be given to you. But ask in
faith, never doubting, for the one who doubts is like a wave of the sea, driven
and tossed by the wind: for the doubter, being double-minded and unstable
in every way, must not expect to receive any-thing from the Lord. ~*

Prayer Vigil Scheduled ~Nurse Mom
Tuesday, May 24, 2011 3:51 p.m.

St. Giles will meet in prayer on Sunday, May 29, at 6 p.m. in the
fellowship building to pray for those in our congregation with special
needs. We will most especially lift up sweet baby James Robert Martin.
Please join us for this brief, 20-30 minute prayer vigil if you are able.
St. Giles is located at 1021 Hudson Road in Greenville, South Carolina.
Everyone is invited to attend.

~

If you believe, you will receive whatever you ask in prayer.
~ Matthew 21:22

CHAPTER 2

In the Woods & Wilderness

Faith is to believe what we do not see, and the reward
of faith, is to see what we believe.
Saint Augustine

Endurance ~Dad
Wednesday, May 25, 2011 11:06 a.m.

Today we met with "Doc Hope." He gave us a good report on James. His lactic acid levels are back down between two and three and he has responded well to some of the changes in medications. Doc Hope explained that a lot of James's treatments are going to be trial and error and we need to anticipate setbacks along the way. The big picture is to take more baby steps forward than backward. A lot of this is trial and error to see what James can tolerate and what he can medically endure. The doctor described it as, "We're not out of the woods. We're still well in the woods, but we're stable in the woods which are a lot more than we could say a week ago."

The respiratory therapist on the plane ride with me was here today. I spotted her in the elevator. I found out today when we landed in Charleston, James had an episode before they could get him off the plane. She told her partner, "We're not going to let anything happen to that baby with his father standing right there on the tarmac." Fortunately, they were able to get him going again and get him to the hospital. I was never aware of anything distressful, thankfully. I don't think I could have taken it. After she dropped off her current patient, the therapist came and visited us for a few minutes. She was very happy we were still here. She made me realize each day is a blessing. Each day we all need to improve ourselves in some way, shape, or form. We all have setbacks along the way and it's okay. As long as by the end of the week, we've moved in the right direction, we'll eventually get back to where we need to be. It may be a long distance, but you have to stay the course and just take things one day at a time. Be thankful for the day. Make use of the day. And don't let these setbacks get you off course. Stay with it. Endure.

Our Daily Bread ~Dad
Thursday, May 26, 2011 11:13 a.m.

This morning we received a very good report on James. He remained stable throughout the night without the paralytic. This is a huge step for our little guy. Two days ago, we put him back on the paralytic because he couldn't sustain the carbon dioxide levels in his body. His lactic acid level went back up to five so he had to go back on the medicine. He has performed better over the past two days, which indicates his organ functions have improved and he is able to metabolize more efficiently. This is a bona fide measure of improvement. As a reward, they are going to give him his first cc of "Mom's world-famous, homemade breast milk!" This is huge—not only for James—but for Jacqueline. Upon hearing the news, she was so excited she actually clapped like one of those monkeys with the brass symbols. It is good to see her smile like that. That's a smile only a child can bring out of the mother.

Because of this, Jacqueline is having a good day. One of the keys to James's success is that he hasn't been over stimulated. They want him to remain very peaceful. So instead of reading to him and talking to him, Jacqueline's quietly reading the Bible (James of course). We are thankful for the day, and the good news that greeted us this morning. We're looking forward to Frick and Frack arriving today. We miss them. Hopefully we can spend a little time with them and do something fun. I'm not a big gamer, but the Ronald McDonald House has a Wii and some games. Maybe Frick and Frack can teach me how to play a couple of the games tonight. I'm also looking forward to seeing my mom and dad.

On a separate note, Jacqueline apparently has started me on a weight-training routine. On the walk over to the hospital this morning, I felt like the bags weighed twice as much as they normally do. I couldn't understand why I was feeling it so much this morning when I hadn't in days past. When we arrived at the hospital I realized she had packed half of a library in those bags! Normally, I might be mad, but she told me she could see the benefits and that it was working. How can you get mad at that?

One thing that is good for us is the short walk to the hospital from the Ronald McDonald House every day. With the sunshine and a little breeze on the way, we talk. We also laugh and cry. We hold hands—something we haven't done in years. We carry our bags. We carry each other, figuratively, not literally. The books she reads to James are heavy enough!

Tonight, the doctors will discuss James's hybrid surgery. They meet on Thursdays to discuss who is or isn't a candidate. According to Nurse Awesome, James is on the calendar for discussion. But, based on what I know of James's situation and in my discussion with doctors, I don't believe him to be a candidate—yet. We still need to see improvement in certain areas, particularly his tricuspid valve. We need for this valve to work more in order for James to be a candidate. I am hopeful, though. We have enough good news to get us through the day already.

Last but not least, I want to thank all of those who visit our CaringBridge.org site and leave notes in the guestbook. We go through and read each one. I can't stress enough how good it makes us feel to have that love and support that our friends and family provide. Jacqueline and I were talking about a few of you that we need to do something really nice for. It didn't take long for us to realize there is an army of you out there. The amount of love and support we've received is far greater than we could repay. But please know the notes of encouragement and prayers are needed, felt and appreciated more than we could show. I just want to say thank you.

Learning Appreciation ~Nurse Mom
Thursday, May 26, 2011 5:11 p.m.

I am sitting here with James and J. J. waiting on Frick and Frack to arrive. I have missed them so much and am glad I will see them today. Frick wants to play video games and Frack will keep me busy in the library reading books. Plus, there is a playground outside where we can all swing and play.

J. J. and I have a whole new perspective on appreciating our children. We are realizing we need to cherish every day God gives Frick, Frack and James to us. Life becomes busy very quickly. Sometimes as parents we forget to enjoy our children—especially when siblings fight. The last time Frick and Frack were down visiting they started to fight about who was going to push me in the wheelchair. J. J. and I laughed. Things had returned to normal. Frick and Frack were once again showing their love to each other by fighting. Since they are only twenty-one months apart, they are very close to each other but seem to enjoy fighting or shall I say arguing.

James is peacefully resting today and we are trying to keep stimulation low. It is so hard for me not to hold his hand, rub his head and kiss his head. J. J. says, "I want to kiss this baby all over. His lips look so perfect." We are being patient and learning God has a plan, so we are following all the orders from the nurses and doctors even if it means we can't kiss James.

The doctors and nurses here at MUSC in Charleston are amazing and gifted as well as blessed with and abundance of knowledge from God. There is a conference call tonight with all the doctors to discuss the cases here in the PCICU and James is on the agenda since he has improved from admission. I am amazed the doctors consult with one another across other healthcare facilities. Doc Hope met us this morning and told us James's improvement from a week ago was good. J. J. and I joked around in a joyful way as Doc Hope told us James was quite a case and was very different and unusual with his condition. Wouldn't it be just like J. J. and I to have an unusual condition? Blessings to you!

Risk is a Relative Term ~Dad
Friday, May 27, 2011 1:44 p.m.

I met with the head of cardiology, "Doc House," today for about ten minutes. His first words were he was glad to finally meet me. He was very happy we "were still here." He first heard about James a week ago when James's case was presented in the weekly conference. At that time, the decision was made to treat James medically, to see if they could keep him alive for a day or two, and go from there. Today, James is ten days old, lying on his stomach, trying to take some fluid from his lungs. He is otherwise pretty stable. His improvement is tremendous and his organs are functioning better than what was originally thought possible. He looks remarkably comfortable and at ease.

When the doctor looks at his pictures compared to what James looked like in those first hours, he can hardly believe it's the same child. He is, "surprised we are still here." Still, he has no preconceived notions we are out of the woods, not by a long shot. James is still very sick and surgery presents what he referred to as, "a very high risk." My response to him was simple: at one point in time, we didn't know if James would live long enough for his mother to be transported from Greenville Memorial Hospital to Charleston by her two Partners in Crime (two amazing ladies whom are friends from church) three hours away. We almost lost him twice (to my knowledge). From my standpoint, God has already graced us with days we could have very well missed out on if not for the surgical team and The Great Cardiology Physician in heaven.

If you think about it, each day is a gift from God. I'm sad it took such a traumatic event for me to understand what this means. Still, I'm happy to learn the lesson—even if it was the hard way. I look at James, lying on his belly with his knees tucked underneath him. His little rear end points to the air (well maybe not so little, he is a Martin after all), sleeping, and things feel almost normal for a moment. I think back to how Frick and Frack used to sleep the exact same way. I realize I am lucky to have three beautiful children and whatever time we get with each of them is a gift. I need to appreciate each moment.

My kids hound me about going to the beach, going to the playground, going to the game room, and it occurs to me that I am blessed to be in such high demand. A fleeting thought also crosses my mind that one day James will be just as eager. One day he, too, will beg to go to the beach, the playground, or the game room. I quickly banish that thought. I squash it. I can't afford to think that positively. His situation is too dire. He's too fragile. To think about his future is too risky. I don't want to open myself to that kind of optimism. But still, he's here. Doctors didn't give him much of a chance to get to this point. From the beginning, he didn't have much of a chance. So when the doctor told me today that surgery is on the table but it will be a "very high risk", I'm okay with that. Because what I'm hearing is there IS a chance. Maybe it's a small chance, but it's a chance. Given where we were a week ago, I'll take it. I will take it as good news that we are considering surgery, even if it's high risk. Just a week ago, James's fate was almost sealed, not once, but twice. The fact we have a possible option on the horizon is a huge positive, even if the chips are down and the chances are small. We're still here. We have a chance.

Getting Rid of the Guilt ~Nurse Mom
Friday, May 27, 2011 8:08 p.m.

Today has been an action-filled day with lots of "Daddy, Daddy," and "I want" from the kids. J. J. is in high demand from Frick and Frack. As for me, I feel like my "youth" is missing. Imagine that? When J. J. announced this morning it was time to leave to "have fun," I felt extremely sad and started to cry. How can I enjoy myself and have fun while James is in the hospital fighting for his life? I found myself sitting on the bench at the park watching everyone play, riding in the car feeling numb and carrying loads of guilt. For once in my life I had zero desire to go to the beach. I felt so much guilt. Guilt is such a terrible load to carry. If I could have only carried James a little bit closer to term; laid in the bed more without complaint; been a bit more patient with life, I am sure this is normal for a mother to feel this way, and I have been begging God all day to place peace in my heart and heal James. Don't get me wrong, today has been a good day, but I definitely feel the toll of being here in Charleston a little over a week watching over a sick child.

As I type, the kids are "ganging" up on J. J. here in our room at the Ronald McDonald House. Boy, are they being loud. I feel sorry for the person underneath us. J. J. has so much patience with the kids and has not lost his "youthful" play yet. Tomorrow is another day, and hopefully James will continue to grow and stay stable. Please continue to pray for James. Knowing you all are praying for him provides me comfort. The prayers allow me to make it through each day as I try to unload my guilt.

I'm off to see James, read him a book, say his prayers and tuck him in for the night. These are all the normal things a Mom does at night for her baby, except I am with him in the ICU. I hope you all have a great holiday weekend and please stay safe.

CHAPTER 3

Unfamiliar Paths

Along unfamiliar paths I will guide them.
Isaiah 42:16

Finding Peace ~Nurse Mom
Saturday, May 28, 2011 7:34 a.m.

Good morning family and friends. Today is a beautiful day in Charleston and my crew is still sleeping. It was a late night for us last night. We visited James and found him on his tummy sleeping very peacefully with his little arms pulled up around his face, just like how he used to sleep inside my belly. Oh how this brings me comfort to see him sleeping like this. I had ten ultrasounds while I was pregnant and during most of the ultrasounds, James was found with his arms up next to his face.

In yesterday's entry I mentioned asking God to fill my heart with peace and help remove any guilt. This morning I woke up bright and early (of course) to continue the "milk production" and found a devotion book a dear friend left me last weekend when she visited. I decided to open it and start reading. Wouldn't you know, the first devotion topic discussed lasting peace. Plus, the title of the book is *Finding Peace*. Wow! God really knows how to answer my prayers!

~

Be of good comfort, be of one mind, live in peace; and the
God of love and peace will be with you.
2 Corinthians 13:11

18

Every time I start feeling down God lifts me. Finding the devotion book on my nightstand this morning was a perfect way to start my day and fill my heart with joy. I am praying this morning for James's health of course as well as for God to fill my day with lots of joy and peace. Maybe I will be able to make a trip to the beach today with the family without feeling any guilt. Also, with the help of another Saint we found a church congregation to worship with tomorrow. It brings me happiness to tell you I am going to be able to worship again tomorrow. It has been a while since I have been able to attend worship due to the bed rest and pregnancy sickness. Praise God for all our blessings.

Now it is time to wake everyone so we can enjoy the beautiful day God provides. Blessings to you all for a safe and happy holiday weekend friends!

~

*Prayer guards hearts and minds and causes God to bring
peace out of chaos. ~Beth Moore*

A Sibling's Perspective: From Frick
Saturday, May 28, 2011 10:47 a.m.

This morning Dad and I discussed the problems with James's heart. We talked about the valves and the problem of getting blood and oxygen out of his lungs and into the rest of his body, especially his organs. I don't know what to think about James. I like the idea of having a brother. He looks like me. He holds my finger when I put it in his hand. He looks fine. It's kind of hard to understand that he's so sick. It makes me sad that he has problems. I hope he gets well. It will be better to have somebody else to play with in addition to Frack. We can play football, basketball, and ride bikes one day. I'll bet he will like going to the park. I'll bet he will like bacon. I'm worried about surgery. I don't know if he will survive. I just know that I hope he does. Mom looks good. She looks a lot better than she used to when she was pregnant. It makes me feel like she can do more things with us now. She has more energy and is more like her old self. I'm hoping she will be up to taking us to Monkey Joe's for lunch. We're trying to be on our good behavior so she will let us go, unlike yesterday. Mom and I had an argument. One step off the bed and Mom says, "back on the bed Frick." It was annoying. It wasn't like I was hurting anything. But Mom wants it quiet in the Ronald McDonald House so she gets aggravated with noise. Being quiet is not mine or Frack's strong suit, but we're having a better day today!

A Sibling's Perspective Part II: From Frack

I think James is cute. I like the fact he was born on my birthday. I love his black hair, his soft skin, and his cute little toes. James makes me feel good because he's getting better at this hospital and that makes me happy. I am not that worried about James. I'm only kind of worried about James. I really love him. When he gets home I'm going to take care of him. I plan on feeding him milk, holding him, loving him, and I don't know what else. I am NOT changing his diaper. I don't like the alarms that go off by his bed. They make us all nervous. When he gets home, I'm going to play with him, play with his baby toys and rock him to sleep. I think James will like his family, and his teddy bear, and his frog and bunny. He likes the fact that we're nice to him. I think he will like books, but I'm not going to read to him. Mom will read to him. I think he will like apples, grapes, bananas, everything. Most of all I just look forward to holding him. I think James will love me.

Steady ~Dad
Saturday, May 28, 2011 11:17 a.m.

No material changes over the last day. It's another day of stability. The numbers remain constant with very little change. Basically, we're hoping for slow and steady improvement in lung, kidney, and liver function. We would like to clear a little fluid off of James's lungs. The doctors want to allow him to mature over the next few days. The only plan for the day is to keep him nice and calm. The good news is that his lactic acid level have held constant. They have taken him off the paralytic and this time, he has performed well. Also, they have started him on breast milk and he has been able to maintain and tolerate the milk.

I know these sound like small things, but for James these are substantial gains. Keep praying. It's obviously worked a miracle for both James and us. Your support has been far greater than I could have ever envisioned. The creative ways and the lengths you all have gone in order to show God's love are nothing short of tremendous. I don't know how to show how thankful we are to our church, our coworkers, and our family for your support. Jacqueline is so excited about going to church tomorrow to worship God. It is because of His love, shown through you, that we are inspired to do His work. I don't know how to repay that. I don't know how to show my appreciation for this gift. All I can do is simply say thank you. Please keep leaving your comments in the guestbook. They are a huge lift for all of us.

James has a Pacifier ~Nurse Mom
Sunday, May 29, 2011 8:48 p.m.

Oh my goodness! I just left James's room and he has a pacifier! I am so excited. The wonderful nurse took a picture for me and I will post it when I get back to the room tonight. It's funny how the smallest things excite me. I am learning to cherish everything, even the smallest milestones such as a pacifier. I am thankful for the amazing nurses here at MUSC and their knowledge and care for James. You can tell they truly care about and love my son.

Today has been a great day friends. We worshipped at Palmetto Presbyterian this morning in Mount Pleasant, South Carolina. It was quite a drive from the Ronald McDonald House, but we drive thirty minutes from home to church each week. What a welcoming congregation they were. J. J. and I felt God's love from the minister as well as several members who greeted us and immediately asked to help. It was nice to be back in God's house and worship. Of course, we missed all of the Saints at St. Giles this morning, but while we are gone we will continue to praise God and worship him during this difficult time.

This morning we were all dragging and sleepy, of course, but we remembered how faithful God has been. It felt so peaceful to worship. The kids felt very comfortable this morning and it did my heart some good to see them look around and be a part of church.

We all took an afternoon nap today and slept for more than an hour. The past few days have been very long as we end the night with visiting James, reading books and saying prayers. Also, Saints from St. Giles sent a birthday cake for Frack today so we shared it with the house tonight. There are so many families with sick children at the Ronald McDonald House. It is sad. Tonight I found myself sitting at a table with another family listening to their story as we shared ice cream cake. I found myself thinking silently during the conversation, "I am so blessed. I am so blessed!" Not only did this other mom have one special needs child, she had another child in the hospital sick. Wow! Can you imagine having two sick children? I can't remember what condition her first daughter had, but it was very severe and she had been up and down the East coast trying to find help for her fifteen-year-old daughter in her arms. She only weighed thirty-five pounds. Can you imagine friends? So, as I listened to her and felt her pain I thanked God for my many blessings: two healthy children, an amazing husband, church friends and family.

Tonight there was a prayer vigil at St. Giles and we were able to Skype in and participate. It was so special! How amazing and comforting it was to see our friends in Greenville. The prayers uplifted and filled our hearts once again. Plus, the kids thought it was pretty cool to see friends over the computer. We are going to try to set up Skype so when the kids and J. J. leave tomorrow, I can see them and talk to them at night.

I am also excited to see my dad, "Pop Pop" tomorrow. He is coming down to stay a week with me since J. J. and the kids are heading home. Frick and Frack have three more days of school left and it is important for them, especially Frick, to be with one of us during this difficult time. It is going to be very hard for me when J. J. leaves; but guess what friends, I am going to be strong. I am going to be brave. I am going to continue to be faithful and pray throughout the day asking

God to continue to hold me in his hands as well as James. How about that for a girl who used to not like hospitals, much less being alone in one? But I do have my Dad. So get ready Pop Pop, I am going to turn you into a night owl.

I hope you have had a wonderful day. It's getting late and J. J. is still in the room with James hogging up all the time. I am here in the PCICU waiting room with the kids where we play and tinker on the Internet. The kids haven't had a bath yet so we are not letting them go inside the Unit to see James. Frack has dressed herself in typical fashion with a Duke Blue shirt and bright pink shorts. As I end my journal tonight I want to share with you what Frick's shirt says, although it is almost a size too small. I am going to save it for Frack and James. It says, "Have you hugged a Presbyterian today?" Love to you all.

CHAPTER 4

Out of Our Hands

The true test of character is not how much we know how to do, but
how we behave when we don't know what to do. ~ John Holt

Patience ~Dad
Monday, May 30, 2011 10:56 a.m.

There must be a reason they call people in the hospital patients. It's because they can't get well as fast as we want them to. It's hard to ask questions and talk to the nurse when every question is met with the answer, "no change!" James's numbers continue to remain constant. I have to remind myself that it's another, day he's still here and that's a good thing. I'm so analytical that I want his numbers to improve every day. When they don't, it feels like a step back. The nurse was quick to remind me today that James has a lot of obstacles in his way and sometimes he needs a day or two. It's hard for all of his organs to improve each day when there are so many obstacles.

These are hard conversations to have. I don't want to hear about his obstacles. I don't want to talk about his problems. I want to talk about James overcoming them as if the nurse could just wave a magic wand and make his lung function better or remove fluid from his lungs. I find myself questioning her tactics, but I have to remember she, not I, does this for a living. I do, however, have ten whole days of experience watching the doctors and nurses work. That should be enough to make me an expert, right?

It's frustrating to hear he's doing about the same. Call me greedy, but I want to hear the good stuff. I want to hear he's made dramatic improvement. Oh wait; he has made dramatic improvement, it just didn't happen yesterday. It happened over a two-week period. I have to remain patient.

James is lying on his side today and he's coughing, which looks uncomfortable. The nurse reminds me coughing is a good thing. It means he's getting some of the fluid to the top of his lungs. We need for that to happen. She also said his bilirubin levels have increased so they are going to run some tests to see if his duct is blocked or obstructed. It's something they can treat but they need to figure out how. It's another hurdle in a long line of obstacles that lie ahead.

I don't like hearing about more hurdles. I just want to kiss him (right on the lips), hold him close to my neck, and take him home. It's hard knowing I have to leave him here. Knowing I'm not going home with my child is difficult. It's hard knowing he needs to get better in order to have surgery, and another day passes and he's not better. It's frustrating knowing I'm not going to be here over the next few days. Unfortunately, it's just a hard day all around for me.

I know this update is not as positive as the last ones, but I think the purpose of sharing our daily journey is to take you on this ride with us. I think if you're going to share information, you have to share the lows as well as the highs. I think it has to be honest. And if I'm being honest, I'm having a tough time today.

That said, I do have a couple of tidbits of positive news. They now have James on 21 percent oxygen, which is the same air you and I breathe. They have also lowered his number of breaths per minute from twenty-six to twenty-four. His numbers look solid with, "no change," which in this instance is a good thing. If he holds steady, they plan to lower it again to twenty-two in a couple of hours. Also, my college roommate brought his family down here as a surprise for us. He has two girls similar in age to Frick and Frack. They took our two kids to the aquarium for the afternoon. It was good for them to do something fun—they deserve it.

Frack's party yesterday evening was a big hit. I don't think anybody turned down the ice cream cake. It was funny to watch the adults, even the employees of the Ronald McDonald House, say, "Do you want ice cream cake?" What kind of question is that? Heck yes, I want ice cream cake. Thank you Nutzman family for the wonderful gift. Thank you also for the prayer vigil last night. Thank you Becky for "almost" making me cry. Truly, all you guys at St. Giles are family to us. Thank you so much for all the incredible support you've given. Please continue to pray for all of us, and leaving comments on the guestbook. They are a huge lift for all of us, me especially. Thanks be to God for all of you.

Scare ~Nurse Mom
Monday, May 30, 2011 6:45 p.m.

Late this afternoon J. J. and I came into James's room to visit. The unit door was locked and we were asked to come back in fifteen to twenty minutes. I was thinking this would be a perfect time to pump breast milk and thought the Unit was closed as it sometimes is for procedures. Once we were allowed to come in to see James we discovered he had a very huge scare to the nurse and doctors. His heart rate jumped to 370 at its highest. It is normally beating around 170. The nurse and doctor were prepared to "shock" him to bring his heart rate back down to normal. Imagine walking into the room to see your precious son after an incident such as this happened? Thank God! Yes, thank God James was able to bring his own heart rate back down on his own. The nurse and doctor have no idea what happened and why this incident occurred. When we walked into the room and the nurse told us what happened, I stayed calm and listened to the information. I continued to think I needed to pay attention and hear what happened instead of doing what I wanted to do and just "shut down."

J. J. stood next to me as I held James's hands and sang him the lullaby I sing to him daily. I rubbed his head and continued to sing. I told James he scared us all and he had the Unit on their toes. Up until this point, James had been stable and relaxing. When people talk about this being a roller coaster, I reckon this incident was the part of the roller coaster ride when you reach the very top and you start to go down very fast. I continued to thank God for letting James pull out of this fast heart rate arrhythmia on his own and then sat down in the chair in his room and started to recite the Lord's Prayer as I cried silently in my hands.

I always tell Frick when he is scared recite the Lord's Prayer and it will provide comfort. I was taking my own advice tonight.

Awards ~Dad
Tuesday, May 31, 2011 9:40 p.m.

Today was Frick's "Awards Day" at school. It's the time when you've accomplished something and it receives recognition in front of the students and their parents. I was proud of Frick. He was recognized for being the top reader in his class. He was also recognized as the top male athlete in his class. This makes me extremely happy considering he's one of the smallest at school. He reminded me that although he is small, he is fierce and pretty darn smart. When you add the reading award to the top math award from last year, the PE award from last year, my boy is turning into a pretty well-rounded, gifted young man. I have to remind myself that he's one of the youngest of his peers and he has a learning disability (ADHD). Because of this he has had a whole ration of stuff to deal with; Jacqueline being sick, me being in school and working full time, youth group, and Frack's piano practice. It seems we never slow down long enough for them to catch their breath. Yet here he is: resilient, tough, smart, strong, ambitious, and kind. He's over-achieving even under tougher-than-normal conditions.

I see Frack with this attitude. She too has this unbelievably strong will. She does not care what anybody else thinks of her. She is completely secure in her own skin. Frack is tough, strong, smart and resilient. She has been bumped up to second grade for reading enrichment because she, too, is at an advanced reading level.

Both children endeavor to persevere. They could have made excuses. They could have under achieved. They didn't. No excuses. You get in there and you do the work and that work will be rewarded. That's the message: stay faithful, stay focused, be ambitious; endeavor to persevere, and you will be rewarded. Today Frick was rewarded four times with different awards. Along with that, he took $30 from his mother for earning all A's on his report card, again. Pay up Jacqueline!

I know it sounds silly but when I look at James, I see the same thing as I do in Frick and Frack. When we were going through this other people kept saying he's a fighter. I wasn't sure how to respond to that. The only thing I could think of was he better be a fighter because he's got a long way to go. I'm not sure I believed he was a fighter. I'm not sure I believe yet that he's a fighter. In the end, I don't think it's up to James. I think it's up to God. Nothing is more powerful than God's will. But I will tell you this. I don't care what the doctors say the odds are. I know that boy's brother. I know his sister. Most importantly, I know his mother. Don't bet against him. His Mom is the kind of person that checks herself out of the hospital, the day after major surgery, a c-section. She's the type of person that won't be denied. Once her mind is set, that's it. She's not going to change it. I'm hoping James has this in him. I'm hoping he has that will, that drive. I remember a line from the movie *Last of the Mohicans* when Daniel Day Lewis looks at Madelyn Stowe and yells at her with anger and determination, "You stay alive no matter what occurs!" I want to say this to James but Jacqueline won't let me yell at him with anger and determination. I just hope that he has that in him.

Today, I got back into my office. It was good to be in a familiar setting with familiar co-workers, talking to people about loans and interest rates instead of tricuspid valves and lactic acid levels. It's funny how work was my saving grace today. I think it was a combination of familiarity, friendship, and comfort from clients, friends, coworkers and bosses that made this day a real blessing. The bank I work for, The Palmetto Bank, has been an absolute blessing and friend. I don't know how many people can say that about their workplace but mine has been phenomenal. It was said by more than one person today that they were impressed with our family's strength. I received a couple of personal compliments along the way. People say, "I don't know how you're doing it." I happen to know the answer to this one.

~

"I can do all things through Christ who strengthens me." Philippians 4:13

Frick received a Bible at his milestone service at church a few weeks back. It was an award he had received along with the rest of the kids in his age group. St. Giles had each parent give their child the Bible. When I gave Frick his, I had taken out a golden rod prayer sheet from the back of the pew and wrote Philippians 4:13 on it. I gave it to him as a bookmark to look up when he returned to his seat. At the time, I had no idea what was about to happen in our lives. I've had a few friends put this same quote from the Bible on our guestbook and on my Facebook. I don't think that happened by accident. Then a friend brought me a little cross that I keep in my pocket. It has one word on it, "Strength." When praying or talking to James, or in times when it gets to be too much, I take it out and rub it. It works. This cross is my award for being strong for my family and I will be strong for my family. But it's not me being strong. It's faith. It's hope. It's love. It's God. I can do all things through Christ who strengthens me.

Day One ~Nurse Mom
Tuesday, May 31, 2011 11:55 p.m.

J. J. went back to work today so I am calling today "Day One." Today was the first day I didn't have J. J. with me at the hospital in two weeks. I told myself today I was going to be fine and learn how to talk to the doctors and get the answers J. J. would know to ask. I think I did pretty well as I learned the oxygen number went as low as 21 and James's respirator increased to twenty-eight breaths-per-minute. Yesterday it was set at twenty-four breaths and caused the gas levels to increase, so they adjusted it back up today.

I think tomorrow we are trying for twenty-six breaths. Plus, the x-rays of the bilirubin were read and there weren't any big concerns. James's bilirubin level is high that an x-ray was taken to make sure there was not blockage in the liver. The nurse said there was just a small bit of "gush" but no blockage. Hopefully, the bowel movements will help move the bilirubin and reduce the jaundice soon.

James started a new medicine yesterday to help his heart rate stay stable called a eurythmic medicine. It is being given to him through his left arm. I was a little sad to see he had another IV in his left hand. This is his favorite hand to put next to his face and James isn't able to do it right now with the new IV. High dosages were given today and the dosage will be reduced the next few days. His heart rate seemed consistent today, running around 170 beats per minute.

The physical therapist visited today and tried to work with James. He was sound asleep and would not wake up. She tries to visit six times a week and will hopefully be teaching J. J. and me soon what we need to do to work with James. I was quick to tell her he is a "pro" with a pacifier and can suck already. She stretched his arms and legs and the little fellow still didn't wake up.

The good news is I have my dad, Pop Pop, here with me in Charleston. It is good to spend time with him. He always knows what to do especially when someone in the family is sick. We ran a few errands today and enjoyed dinner together at the Ronald McDonald House. Dinner was ham, green beans, potato salad, and rolls and was very good. I found myself starving tonight around dinnertime, which is normally served at 6 p.m. There is at least one hot meal a day served at the Ronald McDonald House. They post a sheet everyday informing you about the meal and what will be served.

Tonight I spent a little bit longer at the hospital than Pop Pop and sent him home. He looked exhausted, plus it was around 10 p.m., which is way past his bedtime. As I walked downstairs to the hospital lobby to call the public transportation team to come and pick me up, I saw another lady from the Ronald McDonald House waiting on a ride. J. J. and I have been talking to her and her husband all week. Their baby is seven weeks old and is in the PCICU as well.

Our ride was a police officer in his patrol car. I sat in the back seat—what an experience! I didn't realize the back of a police officer's car was so small. Plus, there were bars on the windows. I informed the officer and driver of the car of how lucky he was to be riding with two beautiful women. The police officer teased me and told me I could get handcuffs if I liked. What a laugh we all had tonight during the five-minute ride back to the Ronald McDonald House.

This is the same police officer J. J. and I saw a week ago who told us he was getting off work and then going to his second job. He was working extra hours to help support his grandson. What a witness to us. This police officer is such a hard worker and still able to joke with me about riding in the back of his car like a criminal. I didn't get his name but next time I see him I will make sure to ask him his name. This is important.

I am off to bed as tomorrow will be a full day I am sure. Many of you have tried to call my cell phone and I am just not able to keep up with returning phone calls yet. Things are moving way too fast for me. Hopefully I will be able to return calls soon.

Help me Lord! "Tough" News ~Nurse Mom
Wednesday, June 1, 2011 11:29 a.m.

Doc Honesty told me this morning I will probably never be able to bring James home. Help me Lord! I can't describe to you what that felt like as I was listening to Doc Honesty talk. Wow! Tears were filling up in my eyes and streaming down like a hard rain. What do you think when you hear news such as this from a doctor? All I could think about after he told me this news was we need a miracle. Actually, we need another miracle.

The doctor wanted to be honest with me as he told me the tough news this morning. Doc Honesty said and informed me he was surprised James was alive. He was surprised he lived past two days. As I continued to listen to the tough news, I start to confirm what he says after hearing about the severe heart condition my precious sweet baby James has had since birth. The doctor tells me the tricuspid on the right side of James's heart needs to improve to think about any type of surgery; and it's a very high-risk surgery at that.

James was improving, but as of yesterday he has taken a step back with the respirator. It is still on a setting of twenty-eight. He continues to breathe on it due to an increase in his gas levels at 7.2 as of 4 a.m. They will take another gas level again in another 24 hours.

Although once improving, James is now just maintaining. The doctors tried to see how far they could take him, but he is resisting any more changes at this time. The medicines he is on are keeping him alive. With this news I swallow deeply, a lump forms in my throat.

So, what am I supposed to think? What am I supposed to do? Should I keep pumping breast milk? If I stop, will that mean I am giving up? Giving up on James getting better even if the doctor says, I will probably never bring him home.

I have talked many times before about my faith, but what is faith? Can you see it? All along we have watched these numbers on the monitors, watching them improve or so we think. All along it is the tricuspid valve; the heart we need to improve. We can't watch it improve. We can't see the heart. Well actually we can see it on an echo but we don't get to look at it when they take the test. We just have to patiently wait for the results. We must have faith and keep reminding ourselves even though we can't see the heart or watch the numbers improve; we have and must keep the faith. Help me Lord!

Today was very tough news. It was tough news to hear. James will probably not be coming home. Only God knows what James will be doing and where he is going. I hope, pray, and beg God multiple times during the day to give James a clean heart, heal him, and yes, please let me bring him home.

Apology ~Nurse Mom
Thursday, June 2, 2011 9:59 a.m.

I need to start off by saying I am sorry to scare so many of you yesterday with James's blog. I am okay and much better today. It was an extremely hard day as you all probably read. The stress of being away from home for over two weeks as well as finally talking to Doc Honesty hit me very hard yesterday. I was describing to a dear friend late last night on the phone that, "It hit me like a ton of bricks." Last night, as I was reading all of your comments on the guest book, I was

pulled toward the book of James again in the Bible to the verses that
state, "be careful with your tongue." Having left my Bible in my dorm-
like room at the Ronald McDonald House, I Googled the verse and
found two references that say:

~

"Because it will affect lives of individuals for a lifetime" James 3:6

"It makes our religion useless in the sight of God" James 1:26.

I hope you will be drawn to your Bible to look up these two versus
in their entirety. My point today is this; we need to be so careful with
what we say to others. We need to be careful what we speak and even
write in a journal. I scared so many people yesterday with my entry. I
wrote exactly what I felt and then, after realizing last night how scary
it sounded, I felt ashamed. I had upset so many of you.

After thinking back to what Doc Honesty said to me yesterday,
I know he was being completely honest with me, even with his
compassionate tone. But then I think about how the news affected
me and how much I scared others with his news and my journal entry.
Does that make you think twice about how you use your "tongue"
when talking to others? This certainly resonates with me, especially
since I think honesty is always the best policy. Well boy, did I get a
dose of pure hard cold honesty yesterday! J. J. reminds me all the time
that honesty is good but sometimes it needs to be scaled back a little,
especially when it spits fire or venom.

The good news today is that James is stable. He had a stable
night and is resting peacefully. He has a new IV in his right arm
so now his left hand is free again to put against his face. James
is a fighter. I am sitting in his room watching him sleep with his
bunny, frog, and new Panda friend, Jiles. Jiles is handmade by a
previous youth at St. Giles who is now a college student at Clemson
University. Frack is much more interested in Jiles most of the time
when I talk to her at night via Skype. Thankfully through Skype,
the kids and I can see and talk to one another through a video feed

over the Internet. I show them the baby every night and let them talk to him since they cannot be here.

Tonight, however, the kids are coming, which is a pleasant surprise for me. Our family has been asked to participate in a live remote radio show in the morning for the Ronald McDonald House. We will be sharing James's story over the air as well as talking about how wonderful the Ronald McDonald House is for families experiencing a difficult time such as our family. What a fantastic opportunity for us to witness to the listening area tomorrow morning. Frick is very excited about being on "air." Frack told me last night that this still wasn't going to make us famous. I replied with, "who wants to be famous?" Hope you have a great day!

Open My Mouth Oh Lord ~Dad
Thursday, June 2, 2011 11:19 p.m.

~

Open my mouth oh Lord and my lips shall proclaim your praise.
Psalm 51:15

Talking to a cardiology doctor is a lot like taking a cold shower. If you're not careful, it will shock you, wake you up, and hurt a little. Two days ago I was given a "cold shower." Perhaps the important thing for me was that I wasn't alone when this news was broken. Did you notice who was there? I had family with me: my St. Giles family. It was Doc Mission, Partner in Crime No. 1, and Partner in Crime No. 2 that were in the room with Jacqueline and me when I left Greenville. It was the Schillizzi Family that was waiting on me when I touched down in Charleston. Imagine that friends. We had a personal friend, family member and doctor helping us when we left. We had a friend, family member and doctor helping us when we arrived. Nobody can do God's work like God.

You wouldn't believe the series of events that transpired to put these people in just the right place at just the right time. And no one will ever tell me that it was just a mere coincidence.

~

"Though I walk through the valley of the shadow of death, I will fear no evil for thou art with me." Psalm 23:4

You had better believe God was letting me know beyond a shadow of a doubt that He was with me every step of the way. He let me know my family had not expanded by not just one when James was born. There are many people surrounding us who have become a lot more to us than friends. I don't know how to express my gratitude to those who have fixed dinners, kept our children, come by work to hug my neck, talked with us and our doctors, and smuggled Jacqueline and a bunch of stolen hospital items to Charleston. You're not friends any more, you're family.

To switch gears a little bit, I do want to give my two cents regarding Jacqueline's recent update. James is in rough shape. He needs a miracle. Long story short, he needs his tricuspid valve to get a lot better for him to have a shot. A dear friend brought me two mustard seeds in clear cases. I gave them to Frick and Frack to hold tonight and explained to them as best I could the parable of the mustard seed.

Basically, though it's one of the smallest seeds in nature, it grows into one of the largest trees. James is our little mustard seed. He is this little guy, the smallest of us all. He's so fragile. His life is precious and hanging on a limb. Yet, our family tree continues to strengthen and continues to grow. Our church has rallied around us like Jesus commanded.

~

"Love your neighbor as you love yourself." Mark 12:31

You've done that. We've felt it. We've been lifted by God through you every step of this journey. This is miracle number two. There is only one commandment left:

~

"Love the Lord your God with all your heart, soul, mind, and spirit." Luke 10:27

I'm not exactly sure how to do this but I'm pretty sure it requires a lot of prayer. Paul says,

~

"Pray without ceasing." Romans 12:12

So that's what I'm going to try to do. It's my understanding that we need three miracles to be a saint. One of the prayers that Jews say during Hanukah goes like this.

~

"Blessed art thou, Lord our God, King of the Universe, who has performed miracles for our forefathers in those days, at this time."

It's important to remember God has been in the miracle business for a long time. So we'll wait patiently to see if James's tricuspid valve performs its own little miracle. In the meantime, we're seeing other miracles take place before our very eyes. Thanks be to God and to all of you for being here with us, for us.

CHAPTER 5

Promise of a Rainbow

Painting By: Frack (Julia Martin at MUSC)

So after the rainstorms, dear child of mine,
Whenever you see it, that rainbow's a sign
That God is with you; and God is kind:
He'll never let you go. ~ Gerardo Suzan, artist

Just Breathe ~Dad
Friday, June 3, 2011 3:24 p.m.

I came in to see James this morning and afternoon and not much had changed. All the numbers looked pretty much the same. I noticed they increased his ventilator again from twenty-eight breaths to thirty breaths. That's no big deal, but I thought it was moving the wrong direction. I always get my thoughts together for the questions I want to ask the nurse and the doctor in those first few minutes when I walk in the door.

My first question this morning was, "Why did they go up on the ventilator?" Her response surprised me. In fact, her response pleasantly surprised me. She said they had not gone up on the ventilator, but the extra breaths were coming directly from James! When he initiates a breath it shows up in purple. The ventilator automatically pumps to insure a full breath. I then asked, "Is this a good thing?" She replied, "It's a very good thing." This is a small sign of a step in the right direction.

At the same time James's lungs, though still wet, appear to have slightly improved. His coughs seem to be slightly more productive. One of the numbers that measures his breathing is also better than it has been. The doctors and nurses appear to be making a little progress with this fluid on his lungs. At the same time, James's liver function appears to be improving and his bilirubin appears to be getting better. It was at fourteen. Now it's at twelve. It's another step in the right direction.

I had been holding off on updating this journal until I could talk to one of the doctors. Unfortunately he hasn't had time to update me yet and I wanted to go ahead and update everyone before the weekend begins. Things look stable. James looks as handsome as I've ever seen him. Jacqueline and Frack went and bought him some clothes today. Frack was very excited about the outfit she picked for him. She was also pretty crazy about his shoes. What am I going to do when that child turns thirteen? Frick and Frack are with the Hamann Family this afternoon swimming in the pool. We had lunch with them today and it was a great meal!

I have not been able to confirm what the doctors have decided about James in their conference yesterday afternoon. All I have heard is they plan to continue to wait and see if James takes a step forward or a step back. They plan to continue to try small things to help him along and see what he is able to tolerate. According to his nurse, they don't have any major changes scheduled for James as far as she knows. I'm guessing this to be fairly accurate. I'm thinking they will want his heart, more particularly, his tricuspid valve to grow stronger before they make any major decisions or changes. In her words, the future is up to James right now. He will be the one to dictate what happens next. Deep down, we know that ultimately, his heart is where the improvement will need to come.

In the meantime we will take these small changes in respiratory functions as positives. The better these other organs work, the stronger James will become. The stronger he becomes, the more he begins to look like a candidate for surgery. In the meantime, I will rub his head and tell him stories about John Elway and Peyton Manning. Jacqueline can rub his head and read to him about kissing hands and rabbits. I'm a little worried that he continues to respond better to the kissing hands and rabbits. We will have to work on that.

Day to Day ~Dad
Friday, June 3, 2011 6:20 p.m.

I finally met with Doc Hope tonight for about ten minutes. He thinks James has plateaued a little bit. The first week, James made a lot of progress. He made far greater progress than any of the doctors could envision. This second week has been a week of progress but very small progress in different areas. When James first arrived at MUSC he was not a candidate for surgery. The thought of surgery wasn't even on the table. Now, surgery is on the table on a day-to-day basis. The doctors meet and talk about James every day. They aren't sure what to do because his case is so unusual and interesting. The doctors are still getting in touch with other pediatric cardiology units looking for possible options and ideas for what to do next. They are confident, however, they are doing all they can.

James's physicians have a pretty good "medicine cocktail" that seems to work well for him. They are starting to wonder how much benefit he can receive from his current treatment because his progress has certainly slowed. On the other hand, he's still making progress, and he's still five weeks premature even now. As he matures, it's possible to see some increased function in both his organs and his heart.

So what do we do now? That's the million-dollar-question. The plans as of now are to wait and see. Just when we think James has "plateaued," his respiratory system has started to function a little better. I was able to confirm with the doctor the numbers I wrote about in my earlier journal entry were definitely a step forward.

James is starting to put forth an effort to breathe on his own. His numbers indicate he may get another try to reduce the support on the ventilator. Getting him breathing independently and reducing the amount of ventilator support is a huge step forward and benefit for James.

We have also seen his liver function improve. Last, we have seen some kidney improvement. According to Doc Hope, he would like to see James's kidneys accept bicarbs better. They need to mature and get a little smarter. These are his words. I'm not sure what they mean, but we are continuing to see improvement in these areas. So we wait. We let James tell us what to do and when.

All this boils down to a pretty simple idea. As long as James continues to improve and respond to the medications and treatments being given, we have to leave him alone and let him improve. When this progress stops, or when he's reached a level where he's strong enough to give it a try, then we pull the trigger and go for the hybrid surgery. Long-term, this is his only shot. In James's case, this is extremely high-risk. His chances aren't good, but we have to go for it. The doctors are going to let him improve as much as he can before they move. I asked Doc Hope, if I should plan to be at work on Monday or plan to stay in Charleston? He told me to be at work on Monday. I then asked about Wednesday? He told me that he didn't know about Wednesday. They would have to wait and see.

I asked Doc Hope if he thought he would survive the surgery. His response was interesting. He said, "I don't know. To be honest with you, I didn't think he would make it this far. At this point I don't know what to make of James. Based on how he was when he first got here, he shouldn't be here right now. It's a miracle he's still here." I responded by telling him how pleased I was with the doctors, nurses, and the hospital and how grateful we were for all they have done to keep him alive. He then said, "I don't think it's us that have kept him alive. We're just tools."

Saturday ~Nurse Mom
Saturday, June 4, 2011 11:12 a.m.

Today is Saturday. I am having a hard time keeping up with the day of week and date, as each day seems to run together. It will be three weeks this Tuesday since James was born, and if he was still in my belly he would be thirty-five weeks tomorrow, Sunday. Maybe I should start looking at my planner again every morning like I use to do when I was in Greenville in order to keep up with the date and day?

I don't have much to say today in the journal about an update. All I have to report are just feelings again. We met with the doctors again this morning and not much has changed. They will keep all settings the same over the weekend and give James a little blood. The doctors will do another echo (heart x-ray) on Monday and have a doctors' conference Monday night.

I have to be honest with you. When the doctor started talking this morning I kind of tuned him out. I went to my place in my mind that is safe and blocked out the pain and hurt. It worked for a while during the doctors' (yes there was probably four or five in the room) visit, but after they left, my safe place left me. I tried to recite the Lord's Prayer in my head again. This is what I do when I get scared. But for some reason I couldn't remember the words to the Lord's Prayer and got stuck.

Frick and Frack were sitting in the chairs next to me as I went to sit down and put my head in my hands once again to cry. I thought I was all out of tears? Not today. Some of you may think it is weak to cry in front of others. I used to be able to control it much more before this journey with James, but as for now I have no care about who sees me cry or where I decide to do it. It's funny how things like this change you and take away all control.

J. J. continued to stand next to James, looking so strong and telling me to stay strong. Then he brought me a folded piece of paper. I opened it and read, "It is all in God's Hands. Stay Strong." Although it was very touching, I must tell you the most touching thing today yet. As I was crying Frick came over to me, wrapped his arms around my neck, and gave me the best hug. He held on to me and rubbed my hair while I continued to cry. What an amazing thing for an eight year old to do while he is watching over his sick baby brother in the hospital and his very upset mom. What strength! Then Frick got up and went over to James and started talking to him. He turned around and said to me, "It will be up to God and His will, mom." Wow! As a parent, you drag your kids to church, fight with them during worship to "pay attention," and try your best to show them a Christian home. As Frick comforted me and talked about God's will, I realized J. J. and I are trying to do right.

I know Frack feels the same but she was the one grabbing the nurse's flashlight and asking me over and over for a piece of paper so she could draw a picture. She is my little art student. We all handle things differently, the PCICU waiting room attendant told me a few weeks ago. Maybe one day I will tell you the story about how I was judging others and I was quickly corrected by the waiting room attendant. I hope your Saturday is fun and relaxing. Yes, today is Saturday.

What Do You Say? ~Dad
Saturday, June 4, 2011 4:52 p.m.

Jacqueline has been extremely tired today so she slept a good bit this afternoon. I stayed in that little room about as long as I could but then came back to the hospital. The whole walk over to MUSC I thought to myself: I need to spend every second I can with James. I only have today. I have a little bit of time tomorrow afternoon and then back to Greenville for work on Monday.

I wondered, how many days? How many hours will I get to spend with James? In the back of my mind I thought, not near enough. There are so many things I want to teach him: how to shave, and how to drive a car. Before that, I need to teach him how to ride a bike, how to read, how to do math, how to pray. All of this stuff was going through my head with regard to time—not enough time and how much time?

Then I arrived at the hospital. I went straight to James's room and started to talk to him and quickly ran out of things to say. After sitting there just staring at him for a few minutes with absolutely nothing worthwhile to share with him, I bent on my knees and began praying to God. I found myself trying to make sure I did it like I was taught. I must first be humble and praise God for my many blessings. Then, I must sincerely ask for forgiveness from my sins. The sins I know about and the ones that never even occur to me. I asked God for the wisdom to learn from my mistakes and see them so I don't make them again. Then I began to ask for those personal things pertaining to James, Jacqueline, and me.

I found I had a lot to say. Shortly after the nurse walked in and began going about her normal business of checking medicines, tubes, syringes, IVs, etc., she asked me if everything was okay? I guess she could tell I was having a little bit of a rough afternoon. I asked her about the valves in James's heart and if parents had compatible tissue. It occurred to me that as small as his heart is, it wouldn't take much in the way of tissue to repair it. She told me they have done that before in larger kids with bovine hearts, pig hearts, and even tissue from a cadaver. Unfortunately, James is not a candidate because he is so small and fragile.

Plus, those types of things begin to call into question James's quality of life. Once you start down that road, it becomes one surgery after another. So what am I supposed to think about that? What am I supposed to say? I quickly shut up because I'm not ready to talk about such things. She continues to pile it on about the difficult road ahead. I began to look around the room for a gag or some duct tape but couldn't find any. I began to focus my attention back on James. After all, he is what we're here for. This is about him.

I may have precious hours left to spend with my son. So what important things do I have to tell him? This is that time where you have that heart-to-heart conversation. We're by ourselves, and it's time for me to say these important things and I have nothing. I feel a little ashamed. Here we are, in the midst of crunch time, and I have nothing to say. But what can I say?

When it all boils down to the most important things in life, what do you say? I told him I loved him. I told him he was in God's hands. I told him I wished there was something I could do.

Maybe that's one of the hardest things about this whole situation. I have had so many people ask me to give them something to do. They've asked me to call them. They've told me numerous times they want an opportunity to show their love and support of our family. Sometimes, I find something I need help with and without fail everyone has told me "yes." No one has told me "no" to any request or need that we've had. The problem is that there's not that much we can do. There's not much to be done. In the end, we're all in God's hands. I found, in my deepest time of need, that I ran out of words for my family. I don't want to hear the words from the nurse and then run out of things I need to say to God.

So my prayer goes on. The only thing I really need can come from God and that's hard. That's the moment where you better have faith.

Thirty-five Weeks Today ~Nurse Mom
Sunday, June 5, 2011 11:52 p.m.

Today marks thirty-five weeks for James. It's interesting to try to explain that to an eight year old who thinks his brother is almost three weeks old and trying to figure out why Mom is saying thirty-five weeks today. "How do you know what week was week one?" wondered Frick. I figured that will be a conversation I will have later and not today. Sex education is not going to be discussed now, even if the time may be right with Frick asking.

If James was still in my tummy he would be thirty-five weeks today. I know this is a strange thought process but I have a dream that once forty weeks hits, James will be a healthy baby and we will be able to bring him home like all the moms, dads, brothers, sisters, grandparents, and church families I see exiting the hospital with their healthy, happy babies swaddled in hospital blankets. A girl can dream, right?

Today is also one of my favorite days of the week: Sunday. I am reminded today how much I look forward to going to church on Sundays and feel at peace as I listen to a great sermon. Once again we enjoyed an inspiring morning at Palmetto Presbyterian worshipping and then lunch with "saints" from church. The sermon was absolutely perfect for today and the minister preached on the topic of suffering as well as anxiety and worry. Boy did I feel right at home. Frack enjoyed the children's church with all the other kids and Frick looked at me during the middle of the sermon and said, "This is the best sermon I have ever heard."

The minister and his wife at Palmetto Presbyterian as well as the members of the church are truly offering hospitality and showing God's love after meeting us just once. I only hope and pray that next time I am in church and a new family visits I am able to offer the same help and support to them as we are receiving here in Charleston. Plus, lots of our church friends from Greenville are visiting, calling, sending cards as well as care packages. We are blessed. This helps comfort us and keep our minds off James's condition. It helps us stay normal. Our families as well have visited many times and continue to support us during this difficult time. Thanks be to God for you all.

James had a pretty tough night last night but had a "comeback" fairly quickly. J. J.'s phone rang at 5:45 a.m. this morning and as I grabbed the phone, I saw "MUSC" on the phone. My heart raced but I didn't have time to sink as I grabbed the phone quickly to answer the call. It was James's night-shift nurse and she was calling to tell me he had an incident but was ok. She wanted us to hear it from her first. I appreciate her saying he was okay first. James enjoyed being on his belly yesterday and when they went to turn him over as they often do, his breathing tube fell out. He is very dependent on this tube. They had to reinsert another breathing tube into James, which was evidently a very scary thing. James is such a fighter. He doesn't give up even when his breathing tube comes out.

At the hospital this morning, I didn't have a clue what we were walking into but was quick to smile when the doctor mentioned James's incident. You are probably wondering why I was smiling? The doctor mentioned how surprised he was with James's quick comeback and said, "James is stronger than I thought." I quickly reminded him yes, he was right, because James is a fighter and isn't going to give up. *We* are not giving up. I wanted to let him know how many people were praying for him but tried to remain very kind and thankful for his expertise and help for my sick son.

Thanks be to God for James's ability to handle this experience and hang on yet another day. James's Guardian Angel and cross hanging on his hospital "crib" continue to protect and watch over him with God's help while we are away.

James's nurse told me tonight he will be getting a Peripherally Inserted Central Catheter (PICC) line insert within the next few days. It is important to remove the lines from his belly button now so they won't get infected. The PICC line will replace the wires inserted when he was born. It will be inserted in his vein and can be used for a long time. I thought back to when my Mom had a PICC line inserted during her Chemo treatments. I will keep you updated when James successfully has his line inserted, as he will have to visit the cauterization lab for this procedure. I feel so sorry for this poor little baby going through so much at such a small age. He is being stuck and poked just like me during the pregnancy. Have I mentioned to you how strong he is and what a fighter he is?

As I visited with friends today I was told that several people are worried about me and want to know how I am doing. I did have my staples removed in the Emergency Room the Sunday after James was delivered and also had my blood pressure checked. J. J. checks my incision frequently and says it looks good and is healing. My blood pressure is slightly elevated, but I continue to take my medicine twice a day and a vitamin each night. I think the blood pressure is elevated from the stress not the pregnancy. I am walking back and forth to the hospital and making sure I eat three meals a day and drink, drink, drink lots of fluids as well as nap occasionally when I am tired. I try to visit James several times a day and talk to him and let him know what is going on. I rub his head and pat his bottom when he is on his tummy. I continue to pump breast milk several times during the day. This all is my new "normal" as a mom with a sick child in the PCICU.

I am also washing clothes daily, which is a surprise as J. J. normally takes care of all the laundry. I told him today that once we all come home he is back on duty. He will have no excuse and can't get used to me washing clothes. Mama Peacock thinks it is our "fancy" washing machine at home, but it is the fact that I hate to do laundry. Washing clothes in Charleston is not as bad because the family only has a few outfits here due to the small, living space. We don't have much room and are living out of suitcases. Imagine four of us living in a dorm-size room with two twin beds and a blow-up mattress for the kids. My house in Easley seems like a castle now to me having more than one room for all four of us to live.

I don't make many decisions during the day. At times I feel like I am floating through the hours of the day. I stick to the aforementioned basics as well as hold Frick and Frack, kiss on them and try to stay strong. J. J. even gets a few hugs. I am working my way back up to cutting my cell phone on as well. I think this is probably normal for any mom experiencing the challenges I have now with a sick baby.

There is a social worker here at the hospital and I may consider meeting with her this week to find out what my "normal" needs to be now. No promises yet. Please do not worry about me. I am strong and will make it through this difficult time. I just need time to figure out what I am supposed to do now, as things have not turned out like we planned.

I am not complaining by any means, as I am thankful to have a bed and shelter over my head so close to the hospital. I reminded myself tonight to stop by the office here at the Ronald McDonald House and thank the director for such a wonderful program and shelter. I am reminded all the time of our program at St. Giles called GAIHN (Greenville Area Interfaith Hospitality Network). Every quarter our church opens its doors to homeless families trying to get back on their feet. GAIHN offers and provides food, shelter, and comfort to these homeless families. This program takes tons of volunteers to pull this off each quarter.

I found myself telling the director how humbling this experience was becoming as I am used to being the one who helps charities and not the one on the receiving end. Receiving is much harder for me than giving. Thank you to all of you who help charities like the Ronald McDonald House and GAIHN serve families in need like my family. Keep up the good work.

I hope you find this update peaceful. Tonight I feel peace. Everybody is sound asleep here in Charleston. Guess what? My mind is telling me it is time to sleep. I am signing off. Blessings to you all and please do not stop praying for James's heart and body to heal. It is with your prayers and support that continue to keep him alive. God has to be listening to all of your prayers, pleads, and confessions. In just a few days, James will be three weeks old and yes, he is thirty-five weeks old today.

Part 2

HOPE

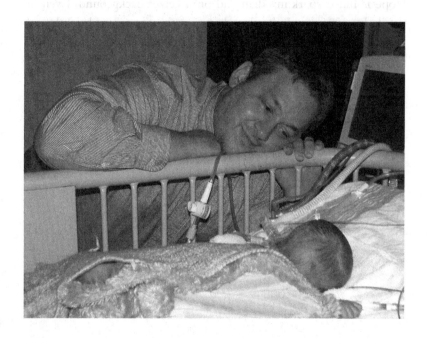

Where hope grows, miracles blossom. ~ Elna Rae

Hope is to have a wish to get or do something or for something to happen or be true, especially something that seems possible or likely. I hold on to hope daily James will recover and come home soon. I hold on to the thought of holding James in our church sanctuary and talking about the miracle of his life. Holding onto hope during dark and trying times proves to be difficult even for the most faithful Christians. Experiencing trials and tribulations in life can slowly chip away at a person's hope or wish for a different outcome or truth. The negative and dark thoughts can slowly begin to overtake positive attitudes if a person allows their hope for a better outcome to disappear.

Remember to never give up hope in situations that seem impossible. Miracles do happen with the help of God. Wishes of hope can help us continue seeing through the darkness while searching for the light. Hope is like a sparkling diamond on a velvet background. Even in the darkness of the black velvet, hope continues to shine brightly and provide a glimpse of the bright light, small treasures, and unthinkable miracles God provides.

CHAPTER 6

Discover Small Treasures

*Miracles-whether prophetically or of other sorts—always occur in
connection with some message from heaven, and are intended by
God as a seal, or endorsement of the messenger and his word.*
Aloysius McDonough

Changing What is Possible ~Nurse Mom
Monday, June 6, 2011 11:47 p.m.

"Changing What is Possible" is the motto at MUSC. I
was reminded tonight again of this motto on the
television tonight during a commercial for MUSC. Plus,
it is printed on the public transportation buses around the hospital.
"Changing What is Possible." God can change and help heal James's
heart. It is possible. God can use tools such as doctors, nurses, friends,
family, medicine, and even machines to "Change What is Possible."

One of the doctors, Doc Hope, mentioned last week he was a
"tool" and reminded us God was in charge. How true. I saw Doc Hope
late this afternoon as I was waiting to meet with the head cardiologist
to get a report on James. Doc Hope was not on call but just wanted
to stop by to say hello and see James. Isn't that nice? By this point you
probably can tell Doc Hope is one of our favorite doctors. He was
quick to let me know he didn't know anything new as he was not back
on call until Wednesday again and would see us again in a few days. I
told him he was one of our favorite doctors. He laughed humbly and
reminded me there was a chain of command and he was low on the
chain. Doc. Hope is not low to us. He is very high up on the chain and
I hope he realizes it.

Doc Hope assured me and my wondering mind that James's bilirubin level was very low on the worry list right now. I felt at ease to drop one less worry. James's bilirubin level went back up to fifteen yesterday and looks like he has a very dark suntan. This doesn't worry me anymore. Suntans in Charleston are common, right?

I was able to meet with a new doctor ("Doc Optimistic") this evening after I saw Doctor Hope and the team of doctors made their rounds. This was the first time I had met him or heard his name. I really like him as well and he took lots of time talking to me tonight and answering all of my questions as I rambled on and on.

My first concern was James looked very swollen to me. Doctor Optimistic stopped what he was doing and walked over to look at James. He told me that I was mom (Nurse Mom as I like to call myself) and I would know how he looked more than he did. What a nice thing to say to a mom who has zero previous medical knowledge concerning pediatric heart patients. Doctor Optimistic told me that James looked good to him by just looking at him so I was reassured once again. I might need to drop another one of my little uneducated worries. How many "uneducated" worries do we have every day that we should drop completely? Think about it friends.

Ok, back to the facts. Since birth, James's fluid has reduced around his lungs, his liver looks okay with a little bit of "gush" on it, and he is holding steady. He is swollen as the nurse confirmed my suspicion, but this seems to be common with heart patients. Also, James will not be getting a PICC line after all, as they want to do surgery and a PICC line will not be inserted if surgery is being considered. They want to save the veins if needed but are having trouble with James's IV. Today he showed signs of blood clots, which are common I think as well. Here's another small worry I am dropping.

During my conversation with Doc Optimistic the nurse called him over to look and indicated the blood clot medicine was already starting to work. I smiled inside thinking God was still giving me signs to proceed, fight, and hang on. I truly believe God gives us signs along our journey. The hard part is paying attention to them and listening. I took this as a sign to continue to be James's main advocate for healing and reassure the doctors, even Doc Honesty, God is hearing our prayers, pleads, and even "deals" as a youth told me tonight.

I'll stop rambling and get to the facts. The facts of our conversation are as follows: James will probably have the hybrid surgery (surgery No. 1) this week to attempt to start fixing his heart. His surgery is not scheduled yet but the doctors are ready to take the next step as James's condition has hit a plateau. He has not taken a step back yet but has not improved either. The good news is James is still alive. Thanks be to God. James's heart is the size of his fist. It is very, very, sick and extremely small. The two bleeding valves need to be repaired and were compared to soft and fragile tissue paper. Surgery No. 1 will be extremely high risk but James has shown us he is a fighter. Even Doctor Optimistic agreed and said, "babies are unpredictable. We don't know what they will do."

Even though James's heart is very sick, they want to try the surgery and give him a shot. The heart is a muscle; it can be patched, but hard to repair itself. The decision to proceed is all up to J. J. and me, and we can decide against the surgery. J. J. and I both agree, though, we want to try to give James another chance as well as allow God's will to shine. It is completely up to God. How can we quit at this point? There are so many prayers, so much love for this small little baby, James. He is created in God's eyes for us all.

There are already two other surgeries scheduled so we do not know yet when to expect surgery No. 1 to happen. I was promised that I would get a chance to hold James before the surgery. As a mother this means the world to me. I took this for granted with Frick and Frack. I asked J. J. if he wanted to hold James before the surgery. If the doctors decide to do surgery, I want to make sure J. J. has a chance to hold him as well and can get here in time.

Doctor Optimistic is on call this week as well as this weekend so things will hopefully stay relatively consistent. There was lots of information to report tonight but I left so many things out. Hopefully you are able to keep up with me rambling on and on yet still feel connected to us in Charleston.

"Changing What is Possible." Yes, we are going to change what is possible with your help as well as with God's help. God will be using his tools here on Earth. Who knows what is possible at this point but hopefully soon surgery No. 1 will get us one step closer. Blessings to you all!

P. S. Continue to hang in there James. I love you!

Quick Update ~Nurse Mom
Tuesday, June 7, 2011 1:36 p.m.

About one hour ago the doctors came in to do another ECHO on James. I was able to watch the heart ultrasound and see the blood flow the doctors have been talking about. The tricuspid is still leaking moderate to severe. The surgeon ("Doc Heart") wanted to take a look one more time before a decision is made on surgery. I was told a decision would be made by tonight. Please take time today to pray for James and the right decision to be made for his little body.

I cherished the time this morning with James, giving him his pacifier, and watching him suck on it like he was a professional. When I took it out of his mouth his little tongue would come out as he was saying he wanted it again.

God continue to give me the strength to be strong, love on James as well as his family, and watch over him during this difficult and fragile time.

St. Giles at Noon ~Becky
Tuesday, June 7, 2011 8:12 p.m.

St. Giles sanctuary will be open at noon tomorrow for anyone who desires to come and pray with others while James is in surgery. If you are unable to come to the sanctuary, please stop wherever you are at noon and pray for James, his doctors and nurses, and his family.

Surgery No. 1 Tomorrow ~Nurse Mom
Tuesday, June 7, 2011 10:31 p.m.

Late this afternoon I was able to meet with Doc Optimistic and then Doc Heart to talk about James potential for surgery. Tomorrow around noon, James will have a surgery (surgery No. 1) called the hybrid. Doctor Heart will place bands around the pulmonary arteries attached to the left and right lungs. He will also place a stint in the ductus to keep it open. Currently, medicine is being used to keep the ductus open.

The hopes for the surgery are to help clear up the lungs as well as help James's gut be able to handle more food, aka breast milk. We will not do valve repair tomorrow. J. J. and I will be arriving at the hospital in the morning by 9 a.m. I will finally get a chance to hold James like a baby. I am so excited since I have only been able to lift him straight up when his bed linens are changed. The thought of holding James is warming my heart already.

This surgery is high risk. I have to tell you all there is a risk and chance James may not make it. This is hard for me to report but I want you to know the risks and be honest. I feel good about the surgery and am very optimistic my fighter will once again amaze us. Doc Heart was very helpful and kind to talk to me this afternoon and let me know exactly what is going to happen. I was able to stay extremely strong and hear everything he said and make notes in my head so I could report back to J. J. I signed the consent form and am hopeful we are one step closer to healing James. This is very important so please read the following twice:

Doc Heart wanted me to know we will need another "intervention" as well for James. We need God's hands to help. He didn't say these exact words but I told him I knew what he meant. I told him I felt like God was intervening already as James was here three weeks today. An abundance of prayers are going up for James and I truly feel these prayers are keeping him strong. I know they are keeping us going.

Many of you have asked what you can do to help us. I am going to ask everyone to please pray, and pray hard the next 24 hours for James.

Please ask for God's healing on James and help him get through this tough time.

I am logging off now because my heart is breaking. A Ronald McDonald House neighbor knocked on my door and told me the other lady here just lost her baby boy. I am sad for this mom, as she was very young. Hearing others stories is so heartbreaking as well, so I have tried to not get too involved for this reason. My heart breaks for her, knowing her son was in the room next to James. I will pray for her healing. All children are creations of God even if they are not ours by birth.

Hold On ~Dad
Wednesday, June 8, 2011 6:01 a.m.

~

"Lord prepare me to be a sanctuary, pure and holy, tried and true.
With Thanksgiving, I'll be a living sanctuary for you." (From the song
"Sanctuary" by John W. Thompson and Randy Scruggs) Amen.

I woke up this morning and this was the first thought that hit my brain. I need to be a sanctuary for Jacqueline and the kids today. I need to be their safe place. I looked outside and saw that the sun was shining. I almost laughed because I slept pretty decent given the circumstances. In fact, I slept like a baby.

It occurred to me the Mavericks beat the Heat last night. My team at work is meeting their goals. My extended family is either on their way to be with us in Charleston or planning to send up prayers at noon. I'm reminded of Donald Sutherland's character Oddball from the movie, *Kelly's Heroes*. He said, "With so many positive waves man, we can't go wrong." It's important for us to have peace and think positively. And for some reason, I think we are. Jacqueline is smiling, the kids are sleeping, and I'm quoting old movies. I can only attribute this to the many prayers going up on our behalf. Otherwise we would be absolutely stressed to the gills and losing our minds. But we're not. Thanks be to God.

It's a fairly normal morning. We're excited about holding James for the first time. We're looking forward to seeing friends and family in a short while. I'm looking forward to seeing my sister and my niece and their children. I've never met their youngest baby. I don't get to see my sister very often, so I'm glad she's here. I feel strange. Normally I would be the most anxious, nervous person, but I'm not. I've got peace like a river in my soul.

What a testament to God this would be if James could make it through this. What a testament to God this experience has already been! I look around at how James has brought my family, church family, friends, coworkers, clients, and everybody surrounding us together in prayer. James's life has already been a witness for God. What we have witnessed has been nothing short of amazing grace.

I titled this entry "Hold On" for a few reasons. First, we finally get to hold James today. This has been the payoff for months of agony for Jacqueline. She was so sick for several weeks prior to delivery and her payoff was supposed to be when she held James for the first time. When this didn't happen, she bowed her head in her hands and cried. So today, the payoff comes and it will be a moment that I plan to soak up. Jacqueline will finally hold James today. As Kenny Chesney says, "That's the good stuff."

The second reason for the title "Hold On" is for you. I need you guys today. I need you to hold us up in prayer. Today is going to be hard. Whether James lives or dies, this is a tough day. The surgery is scheduled for noon and is supposed to last three or four hours. We will be sending updates via our designated points of contact throughout the day. If you don't see an update on our website or hear about it via email, hold on. As soon as we have anything to report, we will.

The last reason I chose "Hold On" is this: I encourage all us to hold on and remain faithful to God no matter what occurs. I know this sounds a little preachy, but God is good all the time. That's easy to say in the good times. But God is the only thing that gets you through the tough times. I have no idea what this day will bring for James, but I will praise God in the storm. I will remain faithful. I will hold on to my faith in Him because regardless what happens, it is God who will restore my soul. It's important that we all hold on to our faith, our hope, and our love that is Christ.

Painting By: Frack (Julia Martin)
Julia's Interpretation of James' Surgery

In Surgery ~Dad
Wednesday, June 8, 2011 12:47 p.m.

It begins at 12:40 p.m. The doctors began transporting James out of his room in the PCICU and into the great unknown! Jacqueline and I are going to have some lunch along with family and friends. It has already been a wonderful morning. We held James for about an hour. I think Jacqueline edged me out by a few minutes. Tears of love flowed like a stream, but she finally got her payoff after months of difficulty. It's those simple things, like holding a baby, that are the most wonderful moments we often take for granted.

Anyway, keep us, James, the doctors and nurses all in your prayers. May God's will be done! Thanks to all for your love, care, prayers, and effort in helping us through this. Without you we would have fallen apart a long time ago. So come on James, be strong. And come on Doc Heart, do your best! Let's make a miracle happen today!

Wednesday, June 8, 2011 2:26 p.m. ~Dad

Doc Heart has completed the banding of the pulmonary arteries. Next comes the stint in the ductus. We are about halfway through the surgery and so far, so good. James remains stable and the surgery is going according to plan.

Wednesday, June 8, 2011 4:49 p.m. ~Dad

James is doing well. He is still stable. The surgery is almost complete. They have successfully put in the stint, banded the pulmonary arteries, and are closing up the chest with stitches. They did not have to give James any additional medications. Everything has gone according to plan. Doc Heart is closing James's chest as we speak. They are also in the process of putting in James's PICC line. A PICC line means less sticking and moving of various IVs and ultimately less risk of infections to James.

James will remain in surgery for approximately another hour. Doc Heart will be coming to see us in a short while. They will need to monitor him closely to make sure his condition remains stable and see how he responds to these changes. Once again we are amazed by God's grace and the miracles He has provided. We send you a big thank you to you, our friends, for praying without ceasing and the many loving comments on the CaringBridge blog. More updates to come later. Peace to you all.

Exhausted ~Nurse Mom
Wednesday, June 8, 2011 10:09 p.m.

Today was a very long, exhausting day, as you all know. Thank you all for your support, prayers and comfort today during James's surgery. Our day began at 8:30 this morning at the hospital and I am finally settling in at the Ronald McDonald House for a restful night's sleep at 10 p.m.

J. J. and I were able to hold James this morning for almost one hour. The nurse was fantastic and very patient with us. Also, James was terrific while we held him. He felt very light, and my guess is he is probably still close to his birth weight and just a tad bit longer. We took lots of pictures and I added the pictures to my Facebook page at *https://www.facebook.com/jacqueline.m.martins*

Right before they took James to surgery he was so attentive to J. J. I was amazed. J. J. was bent over, talking to him and James's eyes were wide open. Then James started moving his mouth like he was trying to talk to J. J. and tell him something. I have never seen this happen. It went on for nearly five minutes. Everything is stable now and J. J. will be going back to the hospital in a little bit to check in on James and spend time, read books, and say prayers. As for me, I am going to bed. I am exhausted. I'll send more details tomorrow when I am caught up on sleep!

CHAPTER 7

Hades on Earth

*Do not remember the former things, or consider the things of old. I
am about to do a new thing; now it springs forth, do you not perceive
it? I will make a way in the wilderness and rivers in the desert.*
Isaiah 43:18-20

I Don't Have the Words ~Dad
Thursday, June 9, 2011 6:30 a.m.

We just received a call from James's nurse that his condition
has taken a turn for the worse. Within the last two hours,
James's condition began to deteriorate and his acid levels
have begun to climb. We are on our way to the hospital. Pray for us!

Thursday, June 9, 2011 1:01 p.m. ~Dad

When James was two days old, we arrived in Charleston. His lactic
acid level were 13.7 and rising. The doctors were able to put him on a
series of medications and lower the levels back down under two. That is
where we need them to be. The lactic acid build-up in his blood affects
the function of his organs and damages the kidneys and liver in particular.

James's lactic acid level started rising this morning about 5 a.m.
His lactic acid level continued to rise, and by 10 a.m., they had peaked
to 20.0. There was another test at noon and the gases are at 19.9. The
physicians have increased the amount of support and medicine and
are nearly maxed out on everything possible. The outlook right now
is pretty grim, but we still have our hope, our prayers, our faith, and
our love. We have a heartbeat and a stable blood pressure. I wish I
had better news to report. They will do lactic acid level tests every

two hours but it may be a while before I update again. Please keep us in your prayers. Thank you for all you have done and continue to do.

Visit to "Hades" This Morning ~Nurse Mom
Thursday, June 9, 2011 2:12 p.m.

What a morning. After receiving such wonderful news yesterday with the surgery going well and James being stable, I thought we might have a good day today and I would get to visit the beach for the first time. This would be heaven on earth to me.

Actually, the opposite happened today. I still haven't visited the beach. In fact, I feel like I visited the dark under world, Hades, this morning. I sat by James's bedside this morning in my "endurance outfit" holding James's tiny swollen hand. Once again, I was crying and full of anxiety and worry. It was like Hades on Earth. I say, "was" because I was in a very dark place this morning.

I watched my precious baby's health deteriorate, watched the nurse work five times harder than she needed to, and watched James's blood pressure drop. I heard Doc Hope say the outlook was "grim." Doc Hope doesn't say grim; he is supposed to talk about lightness.

I didn't want anybody to touch me or even talk to me. I needed to find my safe place out of this visit to Hades on Earth I was experiencing. I felt completely numb, sad, and even mad.

Why do I have to continue to suffer? Isn't this enough God? What do you want me to do? What do I need to give up in order for you to take this hurt and suffer away from me, God? I asked God these questions as I watched James lying down on his bed changing all sorts of colors by the minute. His body continued to swell. How horrific is this for a mom to watch, especially since I struggled with sickness at the end of the pregnancy during the last two months? Isn't the payoff supposed to be when the baby is born and a mom gets to hold him? My payoff came three weeks late this time as I held James yesterday. We took pictures but I was too exhausted yesterday to post. I suppose that is why I wore my "endurance outfit" today instead of yesterday. Today truly needs the endurance. I call it my endurance outfit because

I can slip on the outfit and quickly head out the door. Can you all put your endurance outfits on for me as well?

After thinking about my visit to Hades today, I realized one important thing. Visiting Hades on Earth is partly our fault. First, we allow ourselves to take the trip. We choose the right or left turn that drives us there. We allow our minds to wonder and forget to be faithful. As James's condition was continuing to get worse, I started to experience a range of negative emotions. I started to give up on hope and faith as well as God. I allowed myself to take the dreaded attitude that I talk to the youth at Church about all the time. This attitude that leads a person nowhere is what I call a wrong turn.

So, how do you get out, find your way when you are in the "wrong place" and have taken the wrong turn? Anxiety isn't the answer. Worry is definitely not correct as you then start to get a headache. Going hungry doesn't help as your stomach feels sick and may make you vomit.

The answer is to stop what you are doing and ask for directions of course! I finally looked up from James's bedside and asked God for directions. Where do I go with this God? What do I do now? I have already read James every book in his room at least twice, trying to let him know I am close by. I am listening, so which way do I go? Everybody is still praying, praying, and praying for this disciple.

I am still sitting at a roadblock. The good news is I am out of Hades. I have eaten lunch, my headache is gone, and I am back talking to God and telling him I am faithful. I am faithful. The anxiety is gone and my eyes are dry. I actually caught myself smiling a minute ago. I am trusting God with James. I know God is and will use James to witness to everyone. I also know I plan on helping God as well as James every step of the way, along with many of you I know as well. God hear our prayers. Heal James's sick heart!

Peace and Quiet ~Dad
Thursday, June 9, 2011 6:37 p.m.

It seems the best medicine for James right now is peace and quiet. We concentrated the last two hours on keeping the room quiet and calm. As a consequence, James's lactic acid numbers dropped from twenty to seventeen. This is our first positive sign for today. Seventeen is still way too high but it's better than twenty. Sometimes, the first twenty-four hours is very difficult. James certainly falls into that category.

In looking at it from the doctor's perspective, our hope is that James's heart reacclimatizes to the new blood flow route created by the hybrid. In other words it's in God's hands. The hybrid is working just like it's supposed to. The problem is the heart is not getting a good pump of oxygenated blood. They have him on the highest dosage of dopamine to get the maximum out of it. He may have just enough left to get through this.

We have a long way to go and certainly odds are still stacked against us. But we take it one minute at a time, one hour at a time. The next lactic acid level test is at 8 p.m. Maybe James's lactic acid level will drop some more. The more the lactic acid level drops, the better James will be. Your prayers are appreciated.

Return of the Jedi ~Dad
Friday, June 10, 2011 10:14 a.m.

Yoda would say, "Strong with this one, the force is." What an unbelievable roller coaster of a day. Even after a good night's sleep I'm still exhausted. James has started to recover. Throughout this morning his lactic acid numbers have continued to drop. The goal is two. Yesterday at his peak we were at 20. This number has continued to drop over the last sixteen hours and is now down to under five.

What has us in awe is the series of events that took place yesterday. Yesterday around 3 p.m., the doctors had seen enough. James's lactic acid numbers were at 20 for eight hours, which was way too long. His organs were damaged and time was running out. They had to act. They had to figure out what was wrong or we were going to lose him.

The first thing they did was call in ECHO ultrasound equipment to look at the stint and monitor the blood flow. They found nothing. Then, they began to look at James's valves, at his arteries, his aorta, to see if there was another obstruction they had missed. They found nothing. The doctors began measuring the blood pressure on his limbs to see if there were any discrepancies. One leg read a different blood pressure than the other. They looked at his main artery up and down his legs to see if there was something, anything. They found nothing. They called in an x-ray technician to photograph his chest and other internal organs. There was still no answer as to the problem.

In tears, I looked at Doc Optimistic and asked if it was time? Was it time to let him go of James? He looked at both Jacqueline and me and said, "No. It's not time. When I look at James, I see some fight in him. There's still a chance." Doc Optimistic went on to say that sometimes children have a difficult time in the hours following surgery. He said, "The 12-24 hour period was most critical and sometimes the heart acclimates to the new blood flow." He assured me they were already doing everything they could but we just had to wait and see how James would respond.

I said, "So you're telling me that it's in God's hands?" Doc Optimistic said, "Yes, it has always been in God's hands. So we wait. We give James every opportunity to make it. This isn't over. I will tell you when it's over. It's not over."

We didn't end the conversation there. We began talking about CPR and DNRs and all sorts of topics that I hope you never have to have regarding your child. It was heartbreaking but necessary stuff. With help from a dear and trusted friend from our church, Doc Mission, we went into a private room and made some difficult decisions. I'm keeping those private. I only hope that you never have to have that conversation. It's gut-wrenching, literally!

But then, once the doctors had had their opportunity to get it turned around and couldn't find anything, God said, "My turn!" Amazingly, inexplicably, without doctors doing anything differently from the last four hours, James's acid numbers began to decrease. The only variable was the absence of doctors, nurses, the respiratory therapist, computer techs, the ultrasound technician and x-ray technician. They were all gone. The only people in the room were James, Jacqueline, me, and Nurse Awesome who was charged with his care.

It was quiet. We had nothing to say. We were emotionally spent. Jacqueline sat down in a chair, put her legs up in another chair, wrapped up in a blanket, closed her eyes, and rested. I sat in the nurse's chair and quietly drank a cup of coffee while we waited out what we thought could be James's remaining hours.

The first numbers came fell from twenty to seventeen. We made the decision to keep everything in the room quiet and have no more visitations. Two hours later, the numbers dropped to 13.4. Nurse Soft-Spoken came in at 7 p.m., two hours later, and James's numbers fell to 10.5. After another two hours the numbers were down to 7.2. Nurse Soft-Spoken looked at me and said, "Now go home. You've been here all day. You need to rest. He's in good hands. Go home." I did go home to my "home-away-from-home," the Ronald McDonald House, knowing we had a trend going and the quiet was good for James.

I'm sure the doctors are doing all they can. Jacqueline and I have had conversations about how we think certain conversations between the doctors have occurred. It's important to note that Doc Heart is the main surgeon and doctor in charge. He's the five-star general of the operation. You can tell by the way the other doctors and nurses are in awe of him when he enters the room. After "Doc Delicate" and "Doc Curiosity" came down and could find nothing wrong, Doc Heart came in to look for himself. He couldn't find anything. He looked at our nurse, "Nurse Awesome," with such intensity I can't express and said, "I need you to get that number down." He was referring to James's lactic acid number. He said it calmly and sincerely, looking Nurse Awesome dead in the eye. It was one of those stares where your mom looks at you and tells you her expectations. You want to look away, but you know better. You know you have to keep looking into her eyes because she's still speaking to you through her eyes instead of her lips. The look lasted several seconds. Doc Heart turned around and walked to the group of other doctors standing a few feet away.

Nurse Awesome turned around and looked at me. I was staring at them talking so she knew I had seen what transpired. She's normally cheerful and wonderful. I could tell by her look that she felt nervous and unsure of what else to do. She jokingly said to me, "No pressure!"

The head cardiology surgeon was demanding something of her that was completely out of her control. He wanted to "will" this number down. Well, by God's grace the number was willed down.

Doc Mission told me last night that anybody who believes lightning hit some swamp gas that created a big bang, which created life, has never seen what we have witnessed. Those were his words not mine.

Long story short, our Little Jedi has returned and the force is strong with this one. James's lactic acid number is below five. His urine output has increased and his kidneys are functioning better. James's blood pressure is stable while his heart rate is back down from 207 to 189. All of this is positive news.

Does he have a long way to go? Yes. Is he out of the woods? No, but he's scrappy. He won't quit. He's still here. He's had his chest cracked open at three weeks old after being born eight weeks premature with three of the four valves in his heart not working properly. His liver is still struggling, but he's still here. Now, I'm not saying he's Chuck Norris, but the kid is pretty tough and he makes his daddy some kind of proud! Thanks be to God!

Between Rounds ~Dad
Saturday, June 11, 2011 12:36 p.m.

My sister wrote today on the guestbook and talked about how hard it is to wait for news. She talked about the need to be patient and how hard it must be for us all to wait for news. She talked about how "she couldn't imagine being in our shoes waiting on the doctors between rounds."

She was right on target. Sometimes, the hardest thing is waiting on doctors to make rounds. One of the most difficult times is when they gather in mass right outside James's room. They pick up his little folder and begin to discuss his case, his numbers, and his progress or regress depending on the day. They talk about a lot of different things. Some of it I can hear. Some of it I can't hear. Some of it I understand. Some of it is in code that I can't begin to interpret. It's hard.

We learn what we can. We try our best to interpret the numbers for ourselves but too often we are wrong in our assumptions because we don't understand what it all means. For example, today I asked about the lactic acid numbers and it was back up from 2.2 to 2.9. I started to interpret this as a bad sign until Doc Optimistic corrected me.

Right now, they are giving James an increase in treatment on his lungs and respiratory. He's breathing more on his own. They've reduced the support on the ventilator. His kidneys are healing and functioning better on their own. His oxygen saturation levels are good and he couldn't be happier with how he has progressed over the last two days. The fact the lactic acid number has increased from 2.2 to 2.9 is a result of them asking James's body to do more. Doc Optimistic is very happy with that number. He's happy with what he's seeing out of James.

So I listen and learn. Every time they make rounds I try to learn. "Between rounds" we heal up. We process what we've learned. We attempt to learn how to apply these numbers and what they all mean. We try to monitor what we do that helps or hurts James. For example, when we first got here, we found that talking to James, rubbing his head, and reading to him kept his blood pressure up, his heart rate up and that was good. Two days ago, we found we needed to leave him alone. He needed peace and quiet and time to recover.

It reminds me of a fifteen-round fight. Sometimes a boxer goes to his corner between rounds and his coach or corner man is in his ear letting him have it telling him what he needs to do differently, how to attack his opponent, encouraging him. Sometimes the corner man simply wrings cold water over his face, rinses out his mouth piece, rubs the back of his neck, and offers a whisper of encouragement. Today, as one of James's "corner men", this is what I'm attempting to do.

Today is a day where we praise God that he is healing and recovering between rounds. We know the fight is a long way from over. We pray he can rest up for the next round. Boxers are given a couple of minutes between rounds to recover and learn. James and I have two to three weeks. We have a little time to heal up between rounds.

When I walked in this morning, James and Jacqueline were sitting in his room and for the first time they had music playing. It was really soft music made with either hand bells or chimes or some kind of very soft instrument. As I looked at Jacqueline and listened I started to make out the song. It was a chimed version of the Eagles song, *Witchy Woman*. As I looked at Jacqueline and listened to *Witchy Woman*, a little joke popped in my head. It was too easy. I almost went for that ball that was up on a tee waiting for me to swing. *Witchy Woman*, that's funny. Then I did the smart thing for once; I kept my mouth shut. Yes it's true, she hasn't been in the best of moods during this process but I'm glad she has moxie. A mother in her position better be tough. She better be a fighter. Fortunately for me, I have a wife that when the going gets tough, she gets going. I have to give her an A+ for being strong. In a time like this you thank God that she is the way she is. She is tough as nails.

So we rest and recover today. We spend time between rounds healing up, waiting to hear the latest recovery updates and saying a little prayer before each update for good news. My sister was right, that time between updates is hard on everybody. This time is hard when you're anxiously waiting for answers to real questions that matter. We become anxious. It's the same for you guys today. We're going to take a breath and thank God that we're all still here. We're still in the fight. We're "between rounds" knowing that more rounds wait. Please remember that we have to be patient some times. We have to use this time wisely to recover.

James is recovering as well as the doctors could have hoped. Maybe even a little better. His tricuspid valve appears to have miraculously begun to function better. The hybrid surgery is not designed to fix this aspect. It's only designed to help blood flow to get oxygen to the other organs and body tissue. However, the heart has acclimated to the new blood flow and appears to have had a positive impact on the functionality of the tricuspid valve. That said, we lost some power in his heart's pumping ability. James is still on the maximum amount of dopamine to help his heart squeeze. Because of this, his doctors have lowered his Epinephrine dosage and have started to wean down some of his other medicines.

His urine output was 20 ccs last hour, which is fantastic. It's a sign his kidneys are functioning better. The liver has started to show a few signs of recovery with regard to enzymes, though we have a long way to go. The lungs also seem to be doing pretty well despite James's partially collapsed right lung. This is pretty common in children his size and the respiratory therapist is working to inflate his lung again. Like a balloon, inflating the lung is the hardest in the very beginning. Once the balloon begins to inflate, it becomes easier.

James's numbers continue to reflect very positive signs—as well as Doc Optimistic could possibly ask for given where James was two days ago. Doc Optimistic's smile was almost as big as mine. So the order for the day is rest, relax, and recover. We're "between rounds!"

CHAPTER 8

May the Force Be With Us

God has given us two hands—
one to receive with and the other to give with.
Reverend Billy Graham

"Talk the Talk" and "Walk the Walk" ~Nurse Mom
Saturday, June 11, 2011 5:27 p.m.

It has been three-and-a-half weeks since James was born. Tomorrow he will be thirty-six weeks old. Here I go again counting in utero (in the uterus) weeks for James. The numbness I feel is starting to finally wear off. Although the numbness is not completely dissolved, I do feel periods of time when I remember myself again. Having a sick child in the PCICU makes me feel very numb and lifeless at times.

I catch myself sitting and just staring in space without feeling. Family members and friends have been trying to share other sick families' stories with me. I had zero interest in hearing another stranger's story about how sick their child was or how much suffering they were currently experiencing. This is very different from the Jacqueline you all know before James was born. Before James's birth I would actively ask about others' suffering, their stories and try to find a way to help or counsel those in need.

Thankfully, during the past few days the numbness is beginning to disappear. Yesterday, as I was visiting with dear church friends who came to Charleston to visit, I noticed a young, beautiful mother come into the PCICU waiting room in a wheelchair pushed by her husband. Oh, how the shock of memories hit me instantly. I started to have an out-of-body experience. I was sitting across the waiting room talking with friends in conversation while my heart immediately jumped to the new mom.

I remember coming to Charleston less than two days after delivering James by C-section and entering the hospital in a wheelchair as well. The new mom was crying and then slowly stood up out of her wheelchair. She was hunched over, walking toward the bathroom. "Oh no," I thought. She has just had a C-section as well. My conversation with friends continued. I was still there in body as I continued to nod my head, but my heart and body were not there. They were with the new mom. I kept telling myself to go over there and talk to this new family and hear their story even though I had no interest before hearing stories of other suffering people. Why should I care? I had enough suffering of my own to handle.

The bathroom was directly next to where the couple was sitting. It was just the two of them. How lonely and sad. Where was their support? Finally, I didn't feel numb anymore. Where did my numbness go that I had been carrying for over three-and-a-half weeks? My heart was actually starting to hurt again for others. I stood up and went to the bathroom and thought, "I have to do something. What do I do?" As I walked out of the bathroom I stopped and kneeled down next to the mom and put my hand on her shoulder. She was crying. I told them I was sorry and asked about their baby. He was three days old. I had no clue what to say. She told me she was so tired, emotional and shocked to be here with a sick baby who they thought was healthy and just had a heart murmur. Boy, did I understand.

I listened to her story and watched her cry. My numbness had completely worn off and I could feel my heart again. It was aching for this new mom and her first baby as well as the father. All I could think to say to her was, "No matter how bad the doctors say it is, do not give up. We are still here. I know it may sound bad but continue to have faith but do not give up. My son was not expected to still be here but he is alive." I asked the name of her baby and told them I was going to pray for their son.

Thank you God for allowing me to feel again even if it was for a small time. Thank you God for giving me the courage, strength, and heart to share your love with other "suffering" new parents I didn't know. This experience reminded me of who I am and the person I want to be. I want to comfort others in times of suffering. I want to "talk the talk" as well as "walk the walk" for God's glory. What would my family do without others "walking the walk" and "talking the talk" to help us during this difficult time?

The Book of James is a good description of the relationship between faith and good works. The Book of James challenges us to continue to be faithful followers and not just "talk the talk" but "walk the walk." My first walk was from the corner of the waiting room, to the bathroom, to the new mom sitting in her wheelchair. Even though I am going through a tremendous amount of numbness, pain, and suffering, I reminded myself I still need to continue to walk and help others through good works.

I continuously thought about this couple last night and actively looked for them today. I saw them in the waiting room earlier around lunchtime and asked the dad how things were going. To my pleasant surprise things had improved. Doc Optimistic told them things were serious but not as serious as others in the pediatric heart unit. Their son's condition can be fixed. Once again I felt warmth in my heart for their victory and news. Also, I saw the dad holding his son today as I was walking out of the Unit and found myself counting the medicine pumps next to their bed. They only had a few pumps, which to me was a good sign. James has probably ten to twelve medicine pumps and they are lined up distributing medication continuously.

Why do I share this story with you? I share this story because I truly feel in my heart, even if it becomes numb at times; we all need to walk the walk. I hope and pray I will continue to feel again and be able to help others in need. I plan to continue to talk to these new parents and try to do something nice for them to glorify God. I have no idea what J. J. and I would do without all the "walking" you all have done for us. Your support, love, kindness as well as generosity to us have been nothing but amazing and a testament to Gods love for others. As always, blessings to you and all for an amazing "Talk and Walk."

Recovery for All ~Nurse Mom
Sunday, June 12, 2011 10:11 p.m.

James had a good day today. He continues to rest and sleep. His little body must be exhausted. J. J. and I just came back from the hospital for the nighttime visit and routine. At 9 p.m. his lactic acid levels were 1.6 and they are reducing his blood pressure medicine as well as Lasix medication, which increase his urine output. He still looks swollen, but I do think the swelling is reducing little by little as his eyes didn't look as "puffy" tonight as they did last night. James is relaxing with Jiles, Senior Frog, Mr. Lamb, and Hoppity. The Nurses prop his arms and legs up on his animals to help reduce the swelling as well as put little socks on his feet to help him control his temperature.

Tonight, on the top of James head his hair looks like it is coming in blonde. Who knows? J. J. doesn't want to hear that his hair is looking blonde, as he still has hopes it stays black like the back of his head. James still looks like Frick did when he was a baby. Frick gets a kick out of knowing James looks like him.

Today, James was enjoying lullaby music. The nurse put on Bible Songs late this afternoon as she told me that we were going to bring Vacation Bible School (VBS) to Charleston for James since he couldn't go with Frick and Frack to VBS tonight in Greenville. I thought that was very sweet. I recognized several of the songs as they played on the CD player. The nurse says listening to the sounds of all the medication machines, respirator and warmer start to get old and boring for James. His nurse wants James to be able to hear other music. I enjoy sitting in his room (room No.8) in the PCICU and listening to music as well. It is very peaceful. James is in a room all by himself toward the back of the unit.

There is not much to report today. Today has been an uneventful day for James, which is good, and a day full of rest, rest, for me. Today was a day of recovery for all. I think I am finally able to recover as well and catch up on much needed missed rest. I slept almost ten straight hours last night and woke up around 10 p.m. this morning to Frick in the room patiently waiting for me to wake up and get breakfast. J. J. had already headed to the hospital to make our "morning rounds" to visit, talk, and love on James. Plus, I took a very long nap today and enjoyed lying around in the bed. I have started my list already for this week of things I need to do: visit the social worker, call doctor's office, contact insurance, and visit friends on Wednesday night in Greenville. If James continues to be a "good little boy," I am planning on coming home Wednesday and spending the night at home. I am going to try to finally get a doctor's appointment either Wednesday or Thursday with my OB-GYN and have a follow up from delivery. Frack has already asked if she could sleep with me in my bed when I come home. Sleeping in a king-size bed again will be amazing as I have been in a twin-size bed for almost four weeks this Tuesday.

Thank you for all of your continued prayers. I know in my heart God is hearing all of your prayers and is holding James up in his arms as well as my family. I do not have a clue what the future brings but I do know we are hanging on tight and continue to be faithful and fight for James survival. James will continue to recover from surgery this week as well as myself. Thanks be to God for miracles and healing. Blessings!

Enough is Enough ~Nurse Mom
Monday, June 13, 2011 8:33 p.m.

Have you ever reached your max when you felt like enough is enough? You just can't take much more? I spent this afternoon in the Emergency Room. This morning I woke up covered in sweat and thought I must have broken a fever during the night. Do you remember how I told you all yesterday I was very tired? Today was the same but I started to feel like I had the flu as my body started to ache and my head hurt. My head hurt all morning and I felt like I had a fever. After talking to my doctor in Greenville and J. J., I decided to go to the emergency room here at MUSC and get checked out. I discovered I had a 102 fever when my vitals were taken. After receiving two bags of fluid through an IV the doctor told me I had a urinary tract infection as well as an infection called mastitis. Mastitis is a very painful infection in your breast that causes fever, soreness, and aches.

"Enough is enough God," I thought as I lay on the bed in the emergency room and the Physicians Assistant "dug" around in my veins trying to get the IV inserted. After failing the first time he was trying again a tad bit higher for another vein. This was very painful.

I lay there thinking about James while the tech was "digging." I thought about how much James has gone through so far especially getting his chest cut open. I decided I wasn't going to complain and just take it while the digging continued. At one point, I remember saying out loud, "Oh God" while he was searching for a vein. Enough is enough. How much can one person take?

Actually, a person can take a lot. I tell you from personal experience. Just when you think you have reached your breaking point, you find the strength to continue. I find my strength to continue knowing you are praying for us. I know I can't quit. I know I have to continue even when I feel like "enough is enough."

James had a great day. His nurse was excited to tell me he is completely off of the blood pressure medicine and tonight they will start to reduce another medicine for the blood flow. His bilirubin number came down to sixteen last night from twenty-four/twenty-five. He is still resting and lying with all of his animal friends. I went to see him after I left the emergency room to tell him good night and read him a story. I am now in my room getting ready to go to bed early, as I still feel sick with headache and fever.

Let's hope tomorrow brings sunshine and good news. Today I had enough.

A Site for Sore Eyes ~Dad
Monday, June 13, 2011 10:15 p.m.

I remember a time a long time ago in a galaxy far, far away when work, yes work, was the hard part of my day. I had to drive 40 minutes each way fighting traffic, usually spilled one spot of coffee in the same place on my dress shirt every day to arrive at work to begin the "hard part" of my day around 8 a.m. At 6 or 7 p.m., I arrived home wondering what we were doing for dinner. I would take time to play on Facebook, watch TV, wrestle with the kids, spank Frick, argue with Frack, and go to bed. Oh yeah, and talk to Jacqueline about how tough my day was.

It's moments like this that bring that expression to mind: "You don't know how good you had it." It's true. I have a loving wife with a spitfire personality. I have a son who is athletic and tough yet tenderhearted all at the same time. And I have a daughter who's an even bigger spitfire than her mother. When it boils down to it, "my cup runneth over." I am one of the luckiest people on the planet.

The fact that I'm going through a tremendously difficult time doesn't change any of that. God has surrounded me with good fortune. But I'm not just talking about my wife and two kids. I'm talking about family, extended family, people who love you in spite of your flaws.

Today, I arrived back at work and had several conversations with co-workers. They all sincerely care about my family and me. As I read the online Guestbook tonight, I noticed a message left by a previous boss. He was my boss at Blue Ridge Bank. It was a reminder to me that although we don't work together anymore, we don't stop caring about each other. We go through this world and develop relationships with everyone we spend time with. When those relationships are good, and most all of mine have been, you never stop caring about those people and they never stop caring about you.

I have noticed out of the three most active people I communicate with from work, one of them reports to me, one of them works beside me, and the other I report directly to. Our standing in the corporate world doesn't matter at this moment. To those people, it's more about being there for the family member that needs you. At this moment in time, that family member in need is me. I didn't really think about it during the course of the day. All in all it was a pretty typical day. We laughed and we worked hard. And we got caught up on a lot of things. But it didn't really occur to me until tonight.

Tonight I went to Vacation Bible School at my church. Everyone was excited to see me. The younger girls at church are going to have to pick up the pace in their efforts to get to me for hugs. It's noted Laura Burrows, at the tender age of 92, was second in line to give me a hug.

She is "the bomb." I love her! She trailed only Freda, who gets a big shout-out, for being first in line! I can't begin to tell all of you what a wonderful feeling it is to enter a place, any place, and see people's faces light up with joy when they see you. It's amazing to see people make their way over too you because they love and care about you and just want to give you a hug and let you know! There's a feeling that is hard to describe. Some people might call it a comfort zone. That church is my comfort zone. The people that go there are my family. I feel looked out for, protected, watched over. There are too many people to bring up by name to acknowledge all the wonderful things you've done for us. I would be too afraid to make a list because I would forget somebody and accidentally hurt their feelings and that is the absolute last thing I want to do. You guys know who you are out there. You know the many great things you've done for my family and me. I just want you to know that they are appreciated.

There's a line in the movie *As Good as It Gets* where Jack Nicolson looks at Helen Hunt. He suffers from Obsessive Compulsive Disorder and he's enough to drive anybody crazy. The two characters are out to dinner and Helen Hunt wants him to say something nice . . . give her a compliment. Jack Nicolson tells her a story and ends it with the line, "You make me want to be a better man." This line sticks out to me. Whenever people around you show you God's love, through any actions, it inspires you to pay it forward. It makes you want to do something positive for others. I feel so blessed; I want to be a better man.

I'm not sure, but I think this may be the great calling. This is how you witness God's love. Pastor Matt often says, "Preach often, if necessary use words." How many sermons have we learned on this journey? How many lessons have we learned? It's through you, from you, that I've learned about God's incredible grace and love. I can't wait for Jacqueline to get up here on Wednesday. She's feeling down today, and sick, so I'm hoping she's well enough to travel. I think seeing our friends would give her a tremendous lift. I know it did me.

Short Report ~Dad
Tuesday, June 14, 2011 10:43 p.m.

The doctors and nurses seem to be pleased with how James is doing, but based on the numbers it seems like we're kind of holding our own at best. He did have to go back up on the ventilator from sixteen to twenty. They tried to reduce dopamine but had to go back up as well. Also, his fluid levels are pretty high. The liver and kidneys seem to be functioning better, but James is still getting more fluids into him than he is able to get rid of via his urine. Perfusion to the kidneys seems to be better, but we need more work out of those kidneys to remove those plural fluids. The fluids put additional pressure on his lungs making it more difficult for him to breathe.

Priority number one for James is respiratory therapy to keep his lungs as inflated as possible. Priority number two is reducing the fluid from his tissues and out of his body. These two goals work hand-in-hand to help the body function better. The hope is this will allow the organs to eventually rest more, heal, and increase blood flow through the kidneys and liver. We hope he will be able to send more oxygen from the lungs to the organ tissues and speed up recovery. I'm an analytic, so I like seeing the numbers go down. Unfortunately, they went up today which tells me we took a step back. The doctors say that James is doing fine and that it's not a step back. They say his organs are recovering and doing what we need them to do. Again, the word patience creeps into the conversation. We have to be patient and let the boy heal slowly.

At VBS tonight, we have a prayer wall. The kids wrote on the prayer wall one thing they are thankful for. Frack wrote that she was thankful for memories. Frick wrote he was thankful for James living another day. I'll give you a minute to recover from that one. It got me too. What a precious gift today was. James lived another day.

I keep reminding myself of those precious hours when we first arrived in Charleston and the doctor told me he may not live long enough for Jacqueline to make it from Greenville. Yet here we are, precisely four weeks later, and we're still here. Happy birthday sweet baby James. You're four weeks old today. What surprises do you have for us tomorrow?

CHAPTER 9

A Mother's Fight

No language can express the power and beauty and heroism of a mother's love.
Edwin H. Chapin

Back to Charleston. Need your help ~Nurse Mom
Thursday, June 16, 2011 6:52 p.m.

I am back in Charleston. What a quick trip to Greenville/Easley.
Frick and Frack came back with me today as well. I am feeling
much better from being sick earlier this week. The antibiotics
are working and my doctor in Greenville gave me the "green light"

this morning at my visit. As soon as we arrived in Charleston we went straight to the hospital to see James. He is now sleeping on a "waterbed." Wow, he is almost a month old and already has a waterbed. We all are going to be in trouble when he comes home—spoiled rotten!

James has had a stable day. His gas numbers stayed under two, his ventilator is still set to twenty with oxygen saturation at twenty-five, his blood pressure is in the 60/30s and heart rate was 158. The great news is the nurse was able to decrease James's dopamine medicine today from 1.0 to .75. We had to add a little bit of blood pressure medicine back, Epinephrine, because James's blood pressure slipped back to the mid 50s. Thankfully that is okay. James was peacefully sleeping when I arrived to visit.

Now, you are probably wondering why I labeled this post "Need your help." Yes, I do need all of your help. I need your help, your family's help, as well as your friend's help. Even people you don't know, I need their help and I am finally going to ask you all. Many of you ask me what you can do to help. We need you to pray, pray, and pray very hard tonight and tomorrow for James to pee. Pray for pee. James's fluid is starting to settle around his middle area and we really need for him to get rid of this extra fluid. We cannot do much more until Mr. James starts expelling the extra fluid he is retaining. I know this is a strange request, but I realize God is hearing your prayers. Oh the power of your prayers. I truly believe James is still alive because so many of you have helped us through this difficult time and have been asking God through prayer, along with us, to heal James. It is very hard for me to ask for help. As many of you know I am extremely stubborn. Yes, I am admitting this in print. Half the battle is admitting our faults and asking for forgiveness, right? I was extremely stubborn about driving myself home to Greenville. I didn't want to put out anyone and especially have a dear friend who is a saint drive all the way back to Charleston a day later only to have to drive straight back to Greenville in the same day. Thank goodness he has forgiven me and is speaking to me again.

James's wonderful nurse told me tonight that his fluid output should be more than his fluid input. This will help him release the puffiness around his belly and his boy parts, as the nurse named them. You can see where the fluid is settling around James's sides and waist. It is starting to look bruised to me, but you know how sensitive I am to any color change on James body.

Hopefully one day we will all sit around and laugh and joke about James's "Crazy Mom" asking for help from you all for James to urinate. I have found myself recently telling anybody and everybody I know about James and how we need him to flush out these fluids. I realize I am witnessing to others about the power of prayer and God's ability to answer prayers. James's urine output today was around seven-twelve units per hour.

It's time for me to run and go feed the children dinner. Remember: PRAY FOR PEE. Blessings to you all and I hope I am able to report to you tomorrow success of fluid output.

God Sends "Dinner Blessings" ~Nurse Mom
Thursday, June 16, 2011 10:06 p.m.

Just as I was sending you all tonight's first update titled, "Back in Charleston need your help," the phone in my room rang and the Ronald McDonald attendant lets me know we had visitors. What a wonderful surprise to see two dear friends from Greenville. It was nice to sit down with them and chat, even if Miss Frack was having a meltdown over her new scrape on her leg. (By the way, she is fine. As soon as I told her she was brave—braver than James, she perked up and decided to clean it and change her tune.

After our friends left we went into the kitchen area and sat down to have dinner that was provided by volunteers. How wonderful it was to have baked ham, green beans, homemade macaroni and cheese, and homemade potato salad. The Ronald McDonald House provides one hot meal for free per day for the families and guests staying in the house. I asked Frack to say tonight's dinner blessing and she refused. Actually, she told me she didn't know any blessings. She sat silently and then told me she needed to think. So, as I always do, I gave her a minute to think. This is a control game she likes to play with me. You have to love it! After waiting without a response or sound from Miss Frack, I finally reached over and grabbed her daily treat—a 25-cent cherry soda from the drink machine. Everyday Frick and Frack get to go to the soda machine and buy a drink. Coca-Cola® donates the drinks and all proceeds help pay the utility bills for the house. Knowing the proceeds help pay utility bills makes me feel better about letting the kids have soda daily. As soon as I pulled the soda away and told Frack, "Maybe you can think of a dinner blessing if you do not have this soda in your way distracting you," she immediately remembered her standard, "God is good, God is great," traditional blessing. How quickly she remembered a dinner blessing once her mom took away the soda. Frick just gave her the stare with the silent thought, "Frack you will never learn. Do not mess with Mom, especially concerning a blessing or prayer."

We were sitting down enjoying a quiet dinner together with the kids when a lady came and sat her baby down with us in a high chair at the same table. There are four or five total tables in the dinner area, yet she sat down with us. Typical me started to think, "Why in the world didn't she sit at a different table?" There are three other empty tables. The little baby, a girl, is very talkative and friendly. She waved constantly at us and said, "hello." The woman fixed her baby girl a plate of food and then asked me to watch her, as she needed to get a juice box from her room. I am confused for a second. I agree, of course, but think why didn't she sit at a different table?

Finally, once the mystery lady returned, she left the table again to go into the kitchen. I asked her the age of her daughter. She is almost two years old and a perfectly normal looking little baby girl. She has a slight speech delay to be almost two, but I have always looked at children's milestones as I expect a lot out of Frick and Frack and now James. I finally asked the dreaded question, "Who are you here with that is sick?" I hate it when people ask me this question because I have to engage into conversation that hurts my heart, but I was now asking this question. The lady pointed to the little girl. I know my mouth dropped wide open, full of food of course, because this little girl looked "normal." I use the word normal because now that James is sick,

I wonder what normal is going to look like for him. The mother then pointed to the little baby girl and said, "her." Of course I argued with the lady and started to say "no, not her." I wonder where Miss Frack gets the arguing from? Hmmm? J. J. of course! I was quickly informed that this precious little baby girl had a heart transplant three weeks ago. Yes, three weeks ago. Ok, get your mouths up off the floor. I know this is shocking. I argued again with the lady whom I discovered was the grandmother. God sends dinner blessings!

When this little baby girl was two months old she had open-heart surgery. She has been on a waiting list for a "good" heart since. The surgeon at MUSC just found a heart "good enough" for this little angel three weeks ago. She had a heart transplant three weeks prior and is now sitting at the dinner table eating with us, waving, and saying "hello." God sends dinner blessings!

Why didn't this woman sit at another table? God knows when the right time is to send us all "dinner blessings." Even if it is when your mom takes away your 25-cent Cherry Coke treat. God knows when the right time is to send us all "dinner blessings" when a mom of three Js realizes she has been away from "home" for almost a month tomorrow with her sick baby James.

I realized God sent her to my table to remind me that James can be normal. He may have a scar similar to this precious little baby girl (because you all know I asked to see her scar) but he can look normal. Who determines what "normal" looks like? God knows I need to continue to receive dinner blessings to remind me everything is going to be okay even if it takes me close to two years like this grandmother waited for her baby girl. Plus, who determines what milestone is important or normal? God determines.

Friends, take the time to sit down with your family and enjoy dinner together. Take the time to receive God's dinner blessings even if you need a minute to think about your blessing until your Cherry Coke distraction is taken away. Dinner blessings to you all!

P. S. By the way have you all been praying for pee yet? Just a reminder we need James's urine output to increase. :)

You have to Crawl B4 U Walk ~Dad
Friday, June 17, 2011 6:56 p.m.

The first thing I have to say tonight is that you can't leave our CaringBridge website without reading Jacqueline's journal entry from this morning. It was that strong. I remember when Jacqueline first went back to college. She would ask me to proofread her papers. It used to drive me crazy because it was hard for her to hold onto her thoughts through the paragraph. She became hurried and wanted to cover all topics of the conversation in one paragraph. I used to be pretty hard on her about slowing down, taking her time, and expounding her thoughts onto the paper. I told her people like the details. They need the adjectives. Most important, they need to be able to follow your thinking in a format that's easy to read. She worked on it and improved. She had to crawl before she could walk. In typical Jacqueline fashion, she wanted to hit the ground running. Now, we've fast-forwarded a few years, and she writes some of the most beautiful, meaningful prose I've read in some time.

So here we are with James. Being back home this week, I rarely had a conversation with any of my clients that the first question wasn't about James. Everybody wants to know how he is doing. I tell them he is recovering, and he's getting a little better each day. I can't tell you how many times this week the exact response has been, "You have to crawl before you walk." A good friend came and visited me today. He brought me a card and a gas card. He wanted to give me a better card but said the selection was pretty minimal. For some reason, though, this particular card spoke to him. On the cover it had three words, "inch by inch." In that moment, I had decided on my next topic for the CaringBridge post. Society teaches us that we have to have everything right now. Why take weeks to read the book when you can watch the movie in two hours? But think about it; how often do you hear people say, "The book was better?" They're usually right. We eat fast food like it's going out of style, but that stuff will kill you. How much better is a meal that's prepared slowly with the proper seasonings? The Italians say you have to cook with love, and consequently you love what is cooked.

So here is James. His progress is slow. They reduce his medicine in tenths of one cc. Think about a syringe and how small a cc. is. If they can go down one tenth per hour, in a day, that's a step forward for James. I personally want him to be off that medicine by next Friday, but I have to learn patience. I have to appreciate small victories. Every day we get a little better or a little worse. Every day that we get better is a good day. As long as James continues to show signs of improvement that means his organs are rebuilding and improving. As long as his organs are getting better, he will continue to need less medicine, less ventilator, less support. Does it really matter if it takes six weeks or six months? Not really because we are on God's time. We praise God that James is a little better. And we allow God and James to do their thing. On a side note, James's urine output has been solid all day. I am just saying!!!

Prayers For "Pee" are Working! ~Nurse Mom
Saturday, June 18, 2011 9:59 a.m.

Great news to report! J. J. spent several hours early this morning with James and came back with a good report. James's urine output is averaging fifteen units (ccs) per hour. It was averaging seven units before. Also, James's dopamine dosage has been reduced to .30, the epinephrine is .40 and blood pressure is holding steady. Praise God! Thank you all for your prayers.

J. J. enjoyed spending the morning with James reading him a book and talking to him. James opened his eyes and is alert more than the past. He is responding to us talking to him. Frick is excited about seeing him this morning, which warms my heart. Frack and I spent time with James last night reading books and saying prayers. He opened his eyes to see his sister and was watching her as she talked to him.

James's nurse from last night seemed to be surprised his urine output was so strong this morning when J. J. met with her. She was okay with it staying steady around seven units before. J. J. and I think James is laying there listening to us all talk and overheard the nurse say she didn't think he could sustain fluid output much higher. We think James is saying to us, "watch this!" He is proving to all of us what he can do when needed with the help of your prayers as well as God's help. I feel confident when we need something; we just need to ask God. That is what you all did for us. We asked for "pee" and we are receiving "pee."

We are heading out for the day to play, have fun, and of course visit Mr. James. Watch for an update late tonight. Have a great Saturday!

Power of Prayer ~Nurse Mom
Saturday, June 18, 2011 10:32 p.m.

Just settled in for the night and Frack is making the bed up for Frick. Thank goodness because I am very tired. Today has been a filled day ending with a 1 1/2 hour visit with James. Once again, James has had a good day.

J. J. wanted to hang around and visit with James until 10 p.m. "Mr. Analytical," J. J., wanted an hour's worth of urine output to analyze. Every ten minutes I would see J. J. go over to James's catheter and adjust the tube to watch the urine flow in the bag while counting James's total cc urine output. James's 9-10 p.m. hour cc urine output was 29 ccs. Yes, I just said twenty-nine. Two days ago it was averaging seven ccs per hour. Yesterday the average was sixteen ccs per hour, and then tonight, we watched his urine output reach twenty-nine ccs in one hour. Wow! Talk about the power of prayer friends. I felt a little silly asking you all to pray for pee two days ago, but I felt desperate. At times when I feel out of control and desperate with the circumstances, all I know to do is come to CaringBridge and ask you all to pray. Oh of the power of prayer!

Two days ago I realized the nurses and doctors kept mentioning for days that we need James to get rid of this fluid building up in his body. I watched James become very puffy and swollen day by day and knew we needed to release the fluids with urine. As of tonight, James's urine output has increased and his fingers and legs do not look as swollen. His middle area still looks swollen, as the fluids are hanging around and migrating to this area. Hopefully, the fluids are moving and exiting away from the lungs. Maybe soon we can proceed to the next step once all the extra fluids leave his body. Oh the power of prayer.

What is the next step for James if we can get the fluids to move and exit his body? I have no clue to be honest. We are just taking each day one at a time and waiting. After spending four weeks here in Charleston with James, I have learned one thing. I was telling J. J. tonight as we walked home from the hospital I have learned to listen to what the doctors and nurses say and take it all in stride. Each doctor, each nurse, has a different opinion and idea about James's condition as well as the best way to treat him. I respect each opinion and of course ask each one frequently. But I also learned to listen, digest the opinion, and then think about it for a few days. If I keep hearing the same opinion from different support providers such as, "We need this fluid to move out of the body," I start to take it seriously. I proceed with the next step of asking the Prayer Warriors to pray for specifics. For several days last week I watched James swell, even to the point that when a small tube lay against his body it indented his skin. I knew we needed pee and all the doctors and nurses (support providers) mentioning it were right. Our next step was to ask the Main Support Provider upstairs, God, to help James Pee. Oh the power of prayer.

We met with "Doc Level-Headed" today and we like him. He is very level-headed and able to give us the facts. We originally met him the first week when James arrived in Charleston. I didn't talk to him very much the first week, as you all know I was out of it during this time. J. J. was able to talk with him and has a better knowledge and opinion of him. He is a good doctor but is able to take the emotion out of the case. He agrees James is strong and confirmed this morning that James had a good week. Apparently James met several of the goals this week but guess what, we are still waiting on body output to be greater than input. Surprise! He did mention the solution to the output was due to a procedure called peritoneal dialysis. I hope I got the name correct. But Doc Level-Headed mentioned they would have to convince Doc Heart to agree to do this procedure if necessary. Of course, I asked why Doc Heart would need to be convinced to do the procedure. I was told Doc Heart likes the kidneys to do work and not be allowed to be "lazy." Dialysis would help the kidneys flush out the extra fluid and allow James's kidneys to be lazy. Doc Heart likes to wait things out and see if the body is a hard worker. After tonight watching James produce twenty-nine ccs in one hour I do think his kidneys are hard workers. I hope and pray they do not become lazy and have to have the extra help of dialysis. All the doctors stay concerned with avoiding infection, and dialysis creates another concern for infection. Oh the power of prayer

As I lay here and type I am listening to the rain pour from the sky. I am reminded of God's sense of humor. I am always looking for signs from God to let me know he is holding us tightly in His hands, especially during this difficult time of James being sick and stuck in the hospital. I have to lay hear and think that God's humor is James's body is going to pee like the rain flowing heavy from the sky tonight. Have you ever heard a person say once they hear water flowing they have to pee? Also, I remember a guestbook entry mentioning putting water on James's belly to help him pee. How funny! I don't remember it raining here in Charleston one single time in my four weeks of being here. It's kind of ironic don't you think? Like I said above, could it be a sign of us being held closely in the hands of the Main Support Provider (God)? We do read every guestbook entry, by the way, and keep up with it faithfully every day. Thank you for your entries.

It is getting late and I better go. Everyone is asleep here except me of course. I need to pump breast milk before I go to sleep as James is back on breast milk again. I think he is getting three ccs per hour. I could be corrected on that amount but think I am close. I will double check tomorrow just to make sure I have given my "number crunchers" (the analyzers) an accurate measurement. The analyzers in our world need to know the facts and we do need our analyzers. I definitely need my analyzer (J. J.) to help me stay straight even if he does check the urine output every ten minutes. :) Keep praying. Oh the power of prayer!

Father's Day ~Nurse Mom
Sunday, June 19, 2011 9:32 p.m.

Tonight's entry is dedicated to all the fathers, including our heavenly Father in the sky. Please forgive us all for not being perfect and appreciating you all day, every day.

Today felt like another day for me. I woke up early, showered, put on makeup and then ate breakfast. We were all ready to go to church, worship, visit James and then spend the day playing as a family, minus one important baby. J. J. quickly reminded me during the fantastic breakfast we shared this morning at the Ronald McDonald House it was Father's Day. J. J. hinted around jokingly to us that he sure would like to wake up every morning to an amazing breakfast like we enjoyed this morning: French toast, breakfast casserole, bacon, sausage, tater tots, muffins, biscuits, gravy, and my favorite, fresh fruit. What an amazing contribution by two caring ladies and their law firm employers this morning for the families.

During breakfast I remembered I purchased Father's Day cards last week for special fathers and forgot to mail them. What is wrong with me? The cards are still sitting in our room in the bag and I haven't even signed them. I also think about the kids and I attempting to purchase J. J. a Father's Day present last week, a new coffee maker, and decided to wait and let him pick it out. We have no present to present to one of the most amazing fathers I know. I need to call my dad and wish him a Happy Father's Day and let him know once more how much I love him and appreciate his support during this difficult time as well as the thirty-five years of my life. I know he is already awake since he gets up with the roosters and is normally awake by 5 a.m. To top the cake with humble icing, we woke up this morning, showered, dressed up, and realized at 10:15 a.m. during breakfast and conversation, there was no way we were going to make it to church on time. We are not going to worship our Heavenly Father who has blessed us the past four weeks with James's survival. This does not even include what he has done for us our entire life. I was standing in the Ronald McDonald kitchen this morning with my pretty blue dress ready for church thinking about all the things I have failed at already for Father's Day, and now I am missing worship. Remember it is only 10:15 a.m. This is going to be a day for me.

Should I call these faults? Even though we forget to mail our cards on time to you that doesn't mean we don't appreciate all you do and cherish the love you provide during difficult and easy times in our life. Even though there isn't a present to open or even a fresh cup of hot coffee waiting when you wake up in the morning, it doesn't mean you don't warm our heart when it feels cold. Even though we wait to call you late in the evening and not early with the roosters, it doesn't mean we don't love and cherish you. Even though we shower, dress up, and even put makeup on but forget to keep track of time and miss worship, we still rely on you when the clouds come storming in and the rain pours in heavy showers. Thank goodness you are there for us.

We are not perfect. The great news is you all still continue to love us and support us during good and bad times. When your baby is born premature at thirty-two weeks and you discover he has a severe heart condition, you continue to stick around and don't abandon your family. You hit the road early Monday mornings, go to work and stay away during the week so you can work and provide for your family. Even if the weeknights get lonely, you don't complain. You work seven days a week for your family business for at least twenty-five-plus years and try to find a way every Friday to make payroll. When your children turn sixteen you provide them with a car even though they promise to pay the insurance. Do they really ever pay? You even send your son to die on the cross for others' sins. You continue to answer our prayers for ridiculous requests such as pee.

Happy Father's Day to all you fathers out there who give so much and only get one day of appreciation. Some of you don't even get the one day of appreciation you deserve. Please know even though the mailboxes are empty, the coffee pot doesn't work, your cell phone rings late, and we continue to sin, sin, and sin some more; we appreciate and love you very much. We are not perfect, but the good news is we don't have to be for you to continue to love us unconditionally. Much love!

Another Day ~Nurse Mom
Monday, June 20, 2011 10:08 p.m.

The kids and I visited James several times today. It has been another day at the PCICU in Charleston. James was wide-awake this morning when I went in to visit. He was swinging his arms and moving his head. I was a little bit concerned he was going to pull his cords he was so active with his arms. The nurse asked me if I wanted her to give him some additional pain medicine as he had been awake most of the morning, but I told her I didn't know. She was the professional but he wasn't crying. My theory is James is finally realizing he is here. Since he is thirty-seven weeks gestational age, if we were still counting, he is becoming more alert. I told the nurse he didn't seem to be crying so I thought he was fine. I was told earlier it was good for him to be awake and alert. Also, I was told it was good for him to cry because it would help break up the fluids in his chest. Never did I think I would hear it was good for my baby to cry. Plus, several times last night and today he got sick and coughed up mucus. I am hoping this is a good sign. Hopefully he is trying to get all of the yucky stuff up and out of his lungs, etc. At least this is what I hope.

James's urine input was 100 ccs less than his output as of 8:30 p.m. This is a good sign as his fluids are releasing. This means he is peeing. Yeah for the power of prayer for pee! He was getting an additional thirty ccs tonight of plasma to help his blood clot. So for my number crunchers this would mean his output was seventy ccs more than input. His numbers for blood clotting are high. I think they are around 100 so the plasma will help. His body is producing his own blood thinner and making these numbers high. This is why James is receiving plasma tonight. We are not able to remove the black stuff in his belly button yet from the umbilical cord because of his body not being able to clot. He would bleed. The nurse said it might be tonight, maybe tomorrow. He has had this line in for a month now so we need to remove it to help prevent infection.

I mentioned to James's nurse tonight I couldn't tell a difference in the swelling in his middle area. I always look to see the swelling, thinking when I go in to see him I will be able to see a difference. I can definitely tell in his face, arms, fingers, and a little in his legs, but I cannot tell at all in his middle area. The nurse showed me tonight the swelling/fluids in James's sides as she touched his right side and pushed in gently to his rib. Oh my goodness. Just after a few seconds there was an indention in his side and she hadn't even felt the ribs yet. Finally, I saw with my eyes the actual fluid swelling on his sides. Finally, seeing the swelling everyone has been talking about made me feel very sad inside. I am a visual person and sometimes it takes something like seeing this indention for reality to sink in my brain. James looks so little to me now. I wonder how little he is going to look once the swelling goes down? When he arrived in Charleston they noted his weight was 2.7 kgs. I converted kilograms to pounds today on Google and discovered 2.7 kgs is five pounds, 15.23 ounces. He was born a very big boy to be two months early. Many of you have asked me how much he weighs now. I do not know. The PCICU doesn't look at weight yet. It seems like right now we are just watching the fluid levels settling around his lungs and heart.

Today has been a bit of a down day for me. Can you tell in my post? Mondays are always very hard. I know for you all, you probably feel the same way since most of you go back to work on Mondays. J. J. leaves early on Monday mornings to head back to Greenville. The kids are with me and I have tried to keep them busy and give in to things I usually don't do. Frick and Frack are getting wise to me, so I probably need to get back to the rules soon.

Please continue to pray. We need all the help and prayers we can get. God is ultimately in control and knows what He is doing. Sometimes this experience doesn't seem fair. But as I realize, everybody goes through an experience, or shall I say suffering in his or her life. Who am I to think I will be an exception? Today was just another day. As I told the receptionist in the PCICU today, it's "another day in paradise."

CHAPTER 10

Facing My Fears

No matter how steep the mountain—the Lord is going to climb it with you.
Helen Steiner Rice

Slow . . . Slow . . . Slow . . . Patience Please ~Nurse Mom
Tuesday, June 21, 2011 3:07 p.m.

It is mid-afternoon in Charleston and the heat and humidity is gearing up for a very hot day. The kids and I spent a little bit of time outside this afternoon playing with bubbles and water guns with a local youth group. You know I enjoy seeing a youth group come for mission work. I really miss seeing all the youth at St. Giles especially since they are leaving this Saturday for Mobile, Alabama for our summer mission for a week. This is the first time in many years I haven't joined them serving God's people in need. I guess I am experiencing the opposite end of service this summer, as I am the one who is getting served. Funny how things work out don't you think? I never thought I would be the one served this summer by others.

I visited with James a few times already today. Good news, James's blood is okay and clotting so the nurse is trying to pull his umbilical cord out today from his belly button. It is a slow process so he will not bleed. The nurse comes in every hour and tugs on it a little bit to loosen it. There is a line going into his belly button as well, so this line will be removed once the old residue from his umbilical cord is removed. Also, I met with a doctor this morning and asked a few more questions. James has met their main goal of getting his blood pressure stable as it runs 78/34 on average. He is also showing signs of his kidneys working as his urine output is producing positive numbers and his daily output is greater than the input. I think his output was around 150 ccs larger yesterday than his input. Also, the doctor wants to try to wean another medicine today slowly. She told me we had to move very slowly with James but that was okay because he was born a very sick little boy. I thought to myself, yes, slow, slow, very slow. Stay patient Jacqueline. Having patience is very hard. It is so hard but I am trying. Please God give me patience during this slow process.

I also had some tough questions I needed to ask somebody so I figured I would hit the doctor up this morning as I was starting to be eaten alive with answers to these questions. I am sure I have already asked the questions but now that I have been researching James's condition I needed to ask my questions again. Did James get this heart condition from me? Should I go to the doctor and get checked out and get an Echogram to look at my heart? I do have a heart murmur. Is this a genetic condition J. J. or I have and we didn't know about it? Are Frick and Frack safe? As I asked all these questions this morning to "Doctor Time" (she always has time for me when I ask questions yet seems to be working all the time), she assured me she didn't think this was genetic or a chromosome condition. Doc Time reminded me again James's condition is rare and unusual. Great, I thought, silently to myself. Of all things we catch a rare condition. James has mitral-valve and tricuspid-valve regurgitation. His valves are not closing all the way when his heart pumps so the blood flows both ways instead of one way in his heart due. I asked Doc Time again about treatment and she wasn't sure. Doc Heart is the surgeon and an excellent one by reputation. I am starting to think Doc Time and the other doctors are the "care providers" who make the decisions about James's daily care and getting his organs to perform properly. Doc Heart, the surgeon makes the decision on heart recovery and treatment. I am not sure that is correct, but that is my opinion after spending almost five weeks caring for James and learning the ropes.

I am not normally an anxious person so dealing with all of these questions has been hard for me to digest. I am normally the person who says to others, "stay calm everything will be okay and don't worry." You can imagine the need for me to ask these questions once, twice, and maybe three times just to reassure myself there wasn't anything I did to make James sick. As a mother, doing something to harm your child is unbearable. I remind myself when I start to doubt that God is in control and He has a plan during this difficult time. I did nothing wrong as J. J. reminds me on the phone again this morning because he knew where I was going with the conversation. I think with time I will slowly convince myself this is not my fault James is sick. This is part of some larger plan that I don't know and can't begin to understand. Stay faithful I tell myself!

Doc Time would also like to start reducing James's ventilator slowly. Yes slowly, so we can get him breathing on his own and off the vent. The current setting is on twenty-six again. Doc Time says James's lungs look like the fluid is moving slowly so we will try again.

God has a funny way of slowing us all down. I definitely needed to be slowed down but I wish my sign from the heavens above could have come in a different fashion than sending me a sick baby. Learning patience comes when you have no choice but to slow down. At this point, I have no choice but to be patient and slow down. There will be no quick or harsh moves made by me friends. Time goes by very slow for me now as I have difficulty some days remembering what day of the week it is. That is okay though, and I will take it as James is still alive and continues to take baby steps.

I reminded God last night in prayer I was getting tired but I know He has a plan with James. I begged him again to heal James and I would try to continue to stay patient and faithful to Him. Slow, slow, slow. Patience please.

"Changing Feet" ~Dad
Tuesday, June 21, 2011 7:15 p.m.

By the way, speaking of changing feet, football season is only ten weeks away! Patience. Patience!

My mom used to say that I only opened my mouth to change feet. I was always sticking my foot in my mouth about something. Yesterday was no different. I called the nurse yesterday to find out how James was doing. My first questions were about his urine output. She told me that he was having a good day and that we were expelling more fluid. My response was, "Great, we're still putting out. That's good." This caused the nurse to ask, "Are you talking about me or James?" (I'll let you read that again to get the joke) There I go changing feet.

So after telling the nurse that putting out was a good thing, I tried my best to ask another medical question that didn't sound so stupid. I asked about his blood pressure, his liver, and the tubes in his belly button. I managed to make it through the rest of the conversation without embarrassing the nurse or myself and that was a good thing.

Later in the evening I talked with Jacqueline and she told me James's feet looked really small. She said she could see the biggest difference in James's hands and feet. They appeared smaller. The change was most visible there. The fluid seems to be moving away from here first and back to the center of his body, slowly, steadily. I thought about the card that I got the other day that said "inch-by-inch." We're getting better inch-by-inch. Every day feels like an inch, and that's okay. In two weeks you've come fourteen inches. That's a little more than a _ _ _ _? You got it!

So today I began to recap our progress. We have taken a few steps forward. At one point James was on fourteen different medications. He has been able to get off of approximately five of those. He had a myriad of tubes plugged into almost every available vein on his body. By installing the pic line we got rid of three. We are in the process of removing two more from the belly button. They are even talking about removing one from his leg. That's five or six different tubes that he had going into his body that are now no longer required because of the slow steady progress he's made. Yes, it's taken over a month, a major surgery, almost losing him on three separate occasions, but the little rascal battled back. He is scrappy! Has it been hard? Yes. Are my nerves shot? Pretty much. Is the stress starting to get to me? At times. But then I remember the passage in the Bible where it talks about taking your troubles and laying them at God's feet and that helps. It helps to put my burden at God's feet and walk away. A lot of people have told me how strong I am. People have told me how amazed they are at our family's ability to remain faithful, and they attribute that somehow to our strength. It's almost like our strength has allowed us to remain faithful. As much as I would like to take credit for that, I can't. I think that reads backwards. It's not our strength that allows us to be faithful. It's our faith that allows us to be strong. When you're in a situation like Jacqueline and I are, faith ceases to be a choice. You become faithful out of necessity. The doctors tell you that there isn't much of a chance, that your child is very, very sick, and that they just aren't sure what to do, or how to fix him. As a parent, you don't have much to fall back on. You can't fall back on your strength because in that moment you're too weak to think. You're too weak to stand on your own two feet. That's probably why some of the most sincere prayers in history took place on the knees, because those praying were too weak in that moment to stand. The truth is, it knocks the wind out of you and leaves you with this tremendous overwhelming feeling of desperation. In that moment, instinct takes over. You look to the sky realizing that all else fails, and you say, "God, please help me!" It's not a matter of being strong, or faithful. You realize that in the end, He's all you have left. So we pray hard. We pray a lot. We lay our problems at God's feet. It removes the burden enough for us to stand up and keep going. In ancient Persia there was a saying, "Drop by drop a mighty river forms." So we continue to pray for specific things that will make James's health better. We ask for pee. Drop by drop, we ask for it. Until we've made it another foot (or a mighty river forms). Then we change feet. We move on to the next thing.

James's feet are changing literally. The swelling is going away because we're getting the fluid off of him. They are no longer dried and cracked because he's getting good oxygen saturation to them. His little toenails are going to need clipping before long because he's growing. The feet are a slightly pink color because his blood circulation is good enough to sustain them. Last, they're moving a lot more, because he's awake a lot more. His movement is more purposeful and more normal baby-like because he continues to improve. His feet are changing. By God's grace they're changing. One last thing he didn't inherit was that great big "Berry Toe." He was blessed with his dad's feet, which means he didn't have to try to oxygenate that big thing! God is good all the time. (LOL! Love you Jacqueline, just kidding, don't hurt me!)

I remember in the movie "Forrest Gump" he talked about shoes. He said, "You can tell a lot about a person by their shoes. Where they're going. Where they've been." He's right. In this case we can tell a lot about James by his feet. The direction he's going, where he's been. We have to stop for a moment and make note of these changing feet. They remind us of how far we've come. It's a play on words. When we've reached a certain level of success, we refer to that success as an amazing FEAT. It's important that we recognize James for his amazing feat—the fact that he's still here.

Our Father Who Art in Heaven ~Nurse Mom
Tuesday, June 21, 2011 11:44 p.m.

Our Father, who art in heaven, hallowed be thy name. Thy Kingdom come, thy will be done, on Earth as it is in heaven. Give us this day our daily bread. And forgive our debts, as we forgive those who debt against us. Lead us not into temptation, but deliver us from evil. For thine is the kingdom, the power and the glory. Forever and ever. Amen

When I am in a scary situation and face trouble, all I know to do is stand still and say the Lord's Prayer. I feel comfort standing still reciting a familiar prayer over and over. What do you do when you feel scared and out of control? As Jiminy Cricket says, "You just give a little whistle." *(Whistle is a code word for prayer)*

Tonight I went to visit James and say good night as I do every night. It was around 8:15 p.m. when I walked into his room. I noticed he was very fussy and swinging his arms around in the air again. The nurse was very attentive to him and this was her first night with James. I stood next to him, rubbed his head, talked to him, and tried to calm him down. I told him to be a good boy for the nurse, as this was her first night with him and we wanted her to know he was a good little boy. My back and left side of my stomach started to ache as I stood at an angle next to James's left side of his bed. I was there for almost 45 minutes, reaching over him to see his face and provide comfort. I try to get as close as possible when his eyes are open because he looks right at me as though he is trying to focus on my face and listen to my voice. The nurse came in and asked me if I wanted a chair to sit in, but I told her I'd rather stand up so I can comfort him and calm him down.

I was successful calming him down for a little bit and then he would start waving his arms around in the air and just look at me. Lots of bells and alarms started to sound as his ventilator alarm went off every minute. Medicine machines started beeping and the most unusual beep was coming from the heater on the ventilator. Something was wrong with James and I knew it. I stood there watching him and listened to all the alarms beeping constantly and the sweet nurse tried her best to keep up with everything and silence them all.

By 8:45 p.m. I started feeling anxious and impatient wondering why the Respiratory Therapist (RT) was not coming into the room to fix the machine. I normally don't get ugly or confrontational with the caregivers, as I know we all need to be respectful and appreciative for their care. I felt myself getting a little ugly and thinking I was going to cause a scene soon if the RT didn't show up soon. Remember in the Book of James it tells us all to "watch our tongues?" I cannot be there 24 hours a day to watch James so I depend on the grace of God and the caregivers' attentiveness to help James. Therefore, I try very hard to be nice and respectful to all, even Ms. O who cleans James room. Ms. O is one of my favorites by the way because she takes pride in her job of cleaning.

Suddenly, I looked up and saw James's heart rate declining. His heart rate reached 109 and I went out quickly to get the nurse. "Something is wrong and his heart rate is dropping quickly," I told the nurse. Several nurses and the RT rushed in to James's bedside and the doctor was called into the room quickly. They hurriedly "bagged" James. They breathed for him with a big green bag, and the RT checked the vent. The doctor discovered it is the ventilator and they decide to call for a new machine. The ventilator was overheating, we think, and having a machine malfunction. James wasn't getting enough air and he was trying to tell us.

Our Father, who art in heaven, hallowed be thy name. Thy Kingdom
come, thy will be done, on Earth as it is in heaven. Give us this day our
daily bread. And forgive our debts, as we forgive those who debt against
us. Lead us not into temptation, but deliver us from evil. For thine is
the kingdom, the power, and the glory. Forever and ever. Amen

My heart started to race and I felt anxiety coming over my body
as I stood and watched the doctor hand-pumping or "bagging" James
for air. The RT disconnected the malfunctioning machine and phoned
for a replacement to be brought immediately. Two other nurses quickly
prepared a series of five shots outside the room in case they needed to
bring James's heart rate back up. I walked out quickly and stood outside
the glass doors, staring at the adjacent wall.

Our Father, who art in heaven, hallowed be thy name. Thy Kingdom
come, thy will be done, on Earth as it is in heaven. Give us this day our
daily bread. And forgive our debts, as we forgive those who debt against
us. Lead us not into temptation, but deliver us from evil. For thine is
the kingdom, the power, and the glory. Forever and ever. Amen

Over and over I recited the Lord's Prayer to myself, as I did not
know what to do because I was scared. One of my favorite nurses who
was preparing the shots looked over at me and said, "Mom, his heart
rate is coming back up." She could see the blank stare in my eyes as I
prayed. She let me know it was okay to look back in the room instead
of the blank adjacent wall I was staring at deeply as I was praying.

I finally went back into James's room and stood at the foot of the
bed next to his Guardian Angel necklace hanging from his bed. His
heart rate was back up to 150. The doctor continued to "bag" him with
breaths. Another lady wheeled in a new ventilator for James to use so he
could breathe and replaced the malfunctioning machine. The woman
with the new machine asked if she could bring anybody anything else.
Quickly, I tell her to please bring me a beer. A beer? I don't even like
beer. What in the world was I thinking? I was completely stressed out
and the first thing I could say was "Bring me a beer!" Lord help me.

I told her I was joking and she looked at me with a weird grin. I told the doctor, "If I can make it through having a sick child, I think I can make it through anything." He agreed and nodded.

I couldn't take much more and headed home. Another nurse was performing an EKG on James and told me he needed to stay very still. I decided to leave and head home with Frick and Frack. I kissed James good night on his forehead. He watched me with his eyes. I told him I loved him and would see him in the morning. Friends, this is absolutely heartbreaking to leave one of your own behind in order to take two of your others home. You do what you have to do and ask God to keep the one left behind safe while you are gone. I told the nurse I would give her enough time to get the EKG results and lactic acid results back and I would call her at 11 p.m. for the results. It was now 9:45 p.m. and I had to leave.

The tests came back fine. Glory to God! James's EKG results came back fine as well and his blood gas level is stable. The nurse said everything that happened earlier was caused because of the malfunction of the ventilator machine. This malfunction caused them to stop his feeds earlier tonight. They thought James wasn't able to take the increase in milk from five ccs to eight ccs. James's blood gas number was poor earlier tonight and his heart rate had increased to 180. The doctors thought it was because of the feed increase, but they now think James's ventilator was going bad and caused all the problems. They are going to try to restart the feeds again around 4 a.m. if all stays good.

I don't know why any of this is happening. All I know is God has a plan. I am sharing everything with you because I often think God wants me to witness to you all His love and power (especially the power of prayer). James is truly a miracle and he continues to fight for us all even when his ventilator malfunctions. God continues to hold him in his hands when machines seem to fail. God continues to hold me in his hands when I seem to fail. All I know to do is "whistle" over and over:

Our Father, who art in heaven, hallowed be thy name. Thy Kingdom
come, thy will be done, on Earth as it is in heaven. Give us this day our

daily bread. And forgive our debts, as we forgive those who debt against us. Lead us not into temptation, but deliver us from evil. For thine is the kingdom, the power and the glory. Forever and ever. Amen

Fluid ~Dad
Wednesday, June 22, 2011 11:54 p.m.

Jacqueline met with the doctor today. We need prayers for the fluid in James's body to be removed. He needs this so his lungs can expand and send more oxygen into the blood. The fluid also gets in the way of blood flow to the kidneys and liver. By getting rid of the fluid, we get a compound effect. One, we get more oxygen into the blood. Two, we get more oxygenated blood to the vital organs. It speeds up tissue repair and recovery. The doctor states that we need to slowly bring James off of the ventilator, as time becomes our enemy. It creates scar tissue and does damage to the lungs because it's not our natural way of breathing. We need him off of this ventilator, and we need his body to make significant strides to get to the next surgery, which could a few weeks away. Please pray for these things. Thank you!

New Word: Edema (E-DEEM-A) ~Nurse Mom
Wednesday, June 22, 2011 11:58 p.m.

James had a pretty good day today. After this morning, his heart rate stayed consistent and fluctuated just a small bit. He looks great. I think he looked the best I have seen him in weeks tonight when I went to visit. He looks very tiny again and I think he looks like his middle area is starting to get smaller. Let's continue to pray his extra fluid, edema, is released especially around his middle area and around his lungs.

When I went to visit James this morning the nurse told me that Doctor "Go Get Mom" wanted to talk to me and wished to be paged when I arrived. Doc Go Get Mom was at the hospital the night James flew into Charleston and told J. J. to "go get Mom." She was the reason

J. J. called my two partners in crime when James was two days old and asked them to bring me to Charleston. My two partners in crime helped me escape the hospital in Greenville, check out after one and a half days post-cesarean, transport me to Charleston early that morning and well, lots of other crazy stuff I will save for its own journal. It is such a great story. I need to dedicate an entire journal to this adventure with my partners in crime.

I have to admit when Doc Go Get Mom asked the nurse to page her when I arrived, I was concerned. J. J. and I are normally the ones hunting and paging the doctors down in the hospital. Especially after the incident we had last night with the ventilator malfunction. I was very nervous. Thankfully, everything was fine and the doctor wanted to update me on James's condition. She reminded me how sick James is and told me the plan for the upcoming week. She did a great job of explaining his current conditions and helped me understand the next plan for James. I now have a plan and know what to ask you all to help me cross my fingers for James. Wait a minute. Did I say "cross my fingers"? I did. Oops. Sorry. I realize now if you are reading this blog you are probably a believer. A believer in medicine, yes. Also, more importantly a believer in God. So, since you are a believer in God we prefer to say, "Pray" instead of "cross our fingers." Another great story I will share soon. Heavens this blog is turning into a mystery novel for you all. Is the suspense starting to get to you with all these promised stories? A suspense novel is much better than a trashy novel so I guess I will be safe. Let's continue to pray.

Anyway, Doctor Go Get Mom told me James met last week's goals, which were all "baby steps" but we need him to start meeting larger significant steps in order for him to progress and help fix his sick heart if able. James was able to come off and stop the blood pressure medicine last week as well as remove two lines from his belly button. The black umbilical cord remains is still in his belly button but will hopefully come out and loosen soon since the two lines were removed yesterday.

James goals now are for all the extra fluid (edema) to move out of his body and for James to come off the ventilator. Wow! These are huge goals and definitely are not baby steps. The good news is James was able to sustain the ventilator setting at twenty-two today down from twenty-six. Also, tonight when I was visiting I noticed James ventilator had many pink lines appearing which means he is trying to take extra breathes over the vent. I hope this is a positive sign we will be able to reduce his ventilator setting from twenty-two again tomorrow and start helping him reach his "significant" goal of coming off the ventilator. We can continue to pray and not cross our fingers and ask God for these accomplishments for James.

Doc Heart would like to "stitch up" James's valves next. He is the surgeon. James is not a candidate yet for this surgery as he still has the edema. Remember edema is extra fluids around his middle area stomach, waist and even back. The surgery of stitching valves will require James to go on a bypass machine for his lungs and heart and will cause extreme swelling, which James cannot handle currently. Also, once the fluid is removed from his body we hope James will be able to breathe a lot easier as the extra edema will be gone from his lungs. Fluid around his lungs was described to me as someone sitting on your chest and every time you tried to breathe it felt like your chest was caving in. Isn't that a terrible image?

So tonight as I go to bed I think about edema and what a fancy word. I think about so many of us with "edema" around our waists and a dear doctor friend in Greenville who reminded me of his edema tonight as we laughed on the phone. It was so nice to laugh. I am not sure if I have given him a name yet. I will need to think about it real hard as he is so dear to me and trying to name him at this point would be very hard because he means so much to me, J. J., Frick, Frack as well as now James. He is married to one of my partners in crime, so you can imagine his character.

As I get ready to sign off and go to sleep I am smiling. I feel a tad bit of inner peace tonight for once. What a great feeling to have once again even if it last for a few minutes. Thanks to you all for everything! Blessings!

Song of Snores ~Nurse Mom
Thursday, June 23, 2011 10:02 p.m.

Frick and Frack are back with me tonight and are sound asleep. We were planning to go see James tonight but when I got finished returning phone calls after dinner, I came back in the room and Frick and Frack were knocked out. They were, sound asleep lying side by side in their twin-size, home-away-from-home bed. They spent last night with friends staying in the Isle of Palms and evidently are very exhausted. I decided to let them sleep and we will wake up early in the morning and go see James.

I bet James is wondering where I am tonight as he is probably expecting his nightly head rub and good night routine. I have to remind myself from time to time I have three children and not just one sick baby. Having a sick baby in the hospital can at times take over all my attention. As I listen to Frick and Frack sing a "song of snores," I remember they need Mom as well as James needs Mom. I could wake them up and drag them to the hospital but would that be fair to them? They wouldn't complain, I know, because they never complain when we go see their brother. They enjoy sitting in the PCICU waiting room playing with new friends and on the Internet. They do fight from time to time with each other as we walk the normal route from the Ronald McDonald House to MUSC along Jonathon Lucas Avenue, but other than the normal brother and sister "picking" they are amazing children and are doing very well for the ages of an eight and seven year old. Tonight though, they need rest and I am going to let them sleep and sing their songs instead.

Not visiting James tonight is wearing on me I must admit. I haven't spent much time with him today. This morning he slept throughout most of my morning visit. He would open his eyes when I talked to him, but I tried to not talk too much for once. He was sleeping soundly when I walked in his room this morning although the nurse told me he had previously been wide-awake and very active. Before I visited the nurse gave him extra medicine to relax him because he was so active and his heart rate increased a little. Plus, he likes to grab things with his hands and she was afraid he would grab his breathing tube and pull it out. It was a little loose and needed to be re-taped. So, this morning during my visit, I decided to not talk a bunch and let him rest and sing a song of snores for me while I watched silently. He looked so peaceful while he slept so I sat in the chair and watched his machines.

Since I am not able to visit tonight I called the nurse to let her know I was not coming. Isn't that crazy? I felt like I needed to let the nurse know why I wasn't coming tonight to visit James. Nightly visits starting around 8 p.m. are a part of our lives now and all the nurses know to expect me. I consider the 8 p.m. visit part of James's bedtime routine. Each night I squeeze hand sanitizer onto my palms, check his vital signs, talk and rub his head, read him a book, and say his nightly prayers. By the way, hand sanitizer is my new perfume scent now. I put it on all day long, especially when I am going to touch James. What do I do now since I am unable to visit James tonight and do his nightly routine?

But tonight, Frick and Frack get my attention. I am letting them sleep. One day when Frick and Frack are old enough I will share this story with them and let them read it. They will understand why we are doing what we have to do by living in Charleston and making these visits to James daily as well as the nightly routine. Frick and Frack will understand and realize I love them just as much as I love James, even though James seems to be taking the spotlight currently with his illness. I tried to explain this concept, the concept of family love to Frack a few weeks ago. I tried to explain that our family sticks together no matter what happens and our home-away-from-home was Charleston now because James needed us. James needs us to stay here with him and watch over him because he is sick. I told Frack I would never leave her, Frick or J. J. as well if they were sick. Since James is sick he needs me.

Frack is very smart, as most of you all know. She quickly interrupted me and let me know she did understand. She reminded me of a few months ago when she got the flu, had a very bad headache, and high fever and was very sick. She remembered I never left her as well. She even got to sleep in my bed because she was sick. It is funny to me what kids remember. Be careful parents, kids are watching, thinking, and remembering when we don't even realize it.

As I called James's nurse to let her know I wasn't coming in to visit, I started to ask questions. I thought to myself, "Gosh, I am starting to sound like Mr. Analyzer, J. J." He always asks for statistics, but now I know why. When you can't be there in person to see the numbers with your eyes you have to ask. The nurse told me James started a new medicine today (low dosage) to help his kidneys work harder. This medicine will hopefully help reduce the edema.

James's ventilator was reduced to a rate of twenty breathes per minute today at around 2 p.m. This is down from twenty-two. Thank God! He is doing well with the twenty breaths and his gas levels look good so far with this change. The lowest he has been on the ventilator a few weeks ago was a rate of sixteen. Let's beat that record and see how low we can go. The lower the rate on the breathe with the ventilator, the faster James gets off this machine.

J. J. looks forward to the day he can see James without all the tape on his face and tubes from the ventilator. I remember the day of the surgery I got to hold James and told J. J. I was looking forward to holding him more than anything. J. J. told me he looked forward to the day he could see James's face without the tape and tubes. This process of removing the breathing tube is called extubation. This is another medical term for you all. :) Hopefully J. J., your day of extubation for James will come soon because you sure do deserve it!

Time is ticking and it is getting late. Frick and Frack are still sleeping and I am getting sleepy. Please continue to pray for James. As I have said many, many times before, "I know your prayers are working and getting heard as James continues to fight to stay alive and get healthier." I am going to log off and start singing my "song of snores" soon. Unfortunately, I do snore. I have told J. J. the past year he was a liar and I didn't snore. But now J. J. has proof. That little "booger" took my camera and videoed my snoring here at the Ronald McDonald House after James was born about four weeks ago. Finally, J. J. had proof I snored. We got the biggest laugh out of watching the video. Good night to you all. Blessings to you and your families. Enjoy a restful night of "songs of snores."

Made it through! ~Dad
Friday, June 24, 2011 10:17 p.m.

Reading the guestbook today I noticed a guest that has been on my mind more than she and her husband know. Debbie and Jim Smith both taught me at different times during my childhood. I remember Mrs. Smith chasing Eric and me around the classroom ready to plant a great big lipstick print on our cheeks. She and Mrs. Gambill were the "teachers so nice, we had them twice." So for two years I got popped with a yardstick for splashing in mud puddles and harassed with the threat of a big old kiss on the cheek for misbehaving. Somehow we made it through. Years later, after I turned fourteen I had her husband, Mr. Smith, for freshman social studies, history, and economics. Among other things, he was a State Champion wrestling coach and not the easiest guy to please. He demanded a lot! There were a few days where I was asking for Mrs. Smith. Suddenly, her punishment didn't seem so bad! But he and "Sir Sid" must have done something right considering I'm in the process of getting my master's degree from Clemson in, you guessed it, social studies, history, and economics. Somehow I made it through freshman year too. I've had to put Clemson on hold for now, but I fully plan to get through that also.

Sometimes when I look back on different periods in my life, I wonder how I ever made it through it. But it's funny what we remember. Sometimes I think God puts events in your life and they stand out for us for some unknown, random reason. For example, both of these fine people had a daughter (while I was in elementary school) that had heart problems as a baby. I remember talking to my sister LeAnn about it. I remember them being in the Ronald McDonald House for a long time. I remember eating chicken and dumplings at Sparta Restaurant and it being one of the prime topics of conversation. I remember it in greater detail than I probably should for some unknown reason.

So we fast-forward more than twenty-five years and here I am in the Ronald McDonald House writing this update. Six weeks ago I was getting devastating news about my child and this heart defect. I remember the Smiths' situation crossing my mind, but I guess it took me a little while to really start remembering the situation. It took approximately twenty-eight hours. Because it was precisely when I boarded that plane bound for Charleston with no one to talk to that I stared out the window and began to recall the Smiths and their situation. I remembered bits and pieces, but the one important thing I remembered was the fact that their daughter, Megan, made it through. With God, all things are possible. The one scenario that I knew anything about ended in success. It was a huge deal to me in that moment. It remains a big deal to me tonight. She made it. She went to Appalachian State University. She was a good student in school. She was pretty and unless you knew what she had been through, you wouldn't know anything about that fight for her life they all went through in those first months. This gives me an incredible amount of hope. She made it through!

So what gives you hope? For my fellow church-going folk, they might answer God or Jesus. If you're a scientologist, you might say Tom Cruise, but for most of us God or Jesus might be the simple answer. But doesn't he work in magical ways to give us that hope? I have to continue this thought by talking about Ryan Wagoner. Ryan was a child that I had the pleasure of knowing pretty well as well as his mom and dad. For whatever reason, I have always felt like he was put in my path for a reason. He made a tremendous impact on me. Here was a child that couldn't walk, had a trachea tube that had to be suctioned periodically and he was sometimes difficult to understand when he spoke due to the severity of his illness. He had Werding-Hoffman disease. It was a form of muscular dystrophy that was supposed to take his life very, very early. Ryan lived much longer than anyone thought possible. In a sense, Ryan redefined for all of us what was possible. Ultimately, Ryan succumbed to the disease but not before he left his mark on the world. He impacted me and a lot of others with his unbelievable will power, his fantastic sense of humor, and his ability to defy the odds. He is a constant reminder to me that only God truly knows what is possible. God taught me this through Ryan's grace.

I'm a firm believer that God puts people in our lives at certain defined points in time to make an impact. Sometimes they walk along with us on our path for a long time. Sometimes, we only cross paths for a short while. However, it's amazing to me how certain people can make a huge impact to our spirit and are only with us for a few minutes or days in our entire life. Other people we can know for decades and see them in the street and can't remember their name. I do believe that God may have some sort of human highlighter or bold print He puts on people in certain moments. It's almost like He stops time for a moment and says, "Ok, ingrain this in your head. You're going to need to remember this year down the road." I believe He puts people in our paths for a reason. I believe that sometimes these people are there to guide you on your journey and help you along the way. Sometimes they're there just to let you know that somebody has been down this path before and you're not alone. I'm glad they're there. I'm glad they made it through and they continue to shed rays of hope that help light up the trail. They make the path a little easier.

It makes me wonder whom I may have impacted in my 38 years. It makes me wonder if I am inspiring others in some way or giving them hope, or shining a light. Jacqueline tells me that I can be a bit pessimistic. She's right. But I hope I leave a silver lining behind. Sometimes I wonder if I'm saying the right things, or setting the right example. I'm pretty sure I don't always get it right. I'm pretty sure I'm not supposed to. But I do think that we are in some way guided by a higher power (not Tom Cruise) into the right place at the right time and we are all given a chance to show God's glory by helping give someone hope. We all need hope.

Here I was, many years later, on a plane bound for Charleston not knowing anything even about my own situation. The only thing I knew was that Megan made it through and in that moment that was enough. Here we are six weeks later. I'm still in Charleston and don't have a clue what's going to happen. But I know Megan made it through and in this moment it's still enough.

James has had a good day. They have continued to up the amount of breast milk to sixteen ccs per hour. This is a tremendous step for James. Second, they were able to get him off of enough medication that they can now take out the IV in his leg. Another tube is gone! That's six out of fourteen tubes no longer required. (Rock on James) Last but not least, we were able to reduce the number of breaths on the ventilator from twenty-two to sixteen. This is a huge step for James.

So keep praying! Maybe one day we can all shine a light. We can talk about the love we saw pouring out from people. We can talk about keeping the faith that it takes to "make it through it." And we can give people hope that they can make it through it too.

Food for the "Soul" ~Nurse Mom
Saturday, June 25, 2011 12:49 p.m.

I started this morning working and drinking my 50-oz. bottle of water. Frick asked me how I was going to drink the entire bottle and if I needed him to help me. How funny. I told him I had to "cut my addiction" again so I was going back to water. Addiction? Frick had a worried look on his face. Frick understands the word addiction. It represents a bad word, as his vocabulary is extremely advanced. I have to cut my addiction of caffeine again since I finished my antibiotic yesterday and now will stop "pumping and dumping" the breast milk. Caffeine speeds up the heart when consumed and is passed through breast milk especially if you drink more than eight ounces. I definitely do not want to pass anything on to James that will speed up his heart rate.

The lactation specialist and I decided I would not save James's "food for the soul" while I was on the heavy antibiotic for my infections. Finally, after ten days I finished the dosage of antibiotics yesterday. My addiction of caffeine was "food for my soul" during the past ten days and seemed to help keep me going during the long days. I found myself during the day craving a Coke when I needed an energy boost. But now, I am now working on cutting out my caffeine addiction. James will need his "food for his soul" as his feeds are being increased again from sixteen ccs an hour to twenty-four ccs soon.

Last night for dinner we enjoyed lots of food for our souls. Palmetto Presbyterian brought dinner to the Ronald McDonald House for the families staying there. Dinner was very delicious and perfect! There is a family that has been at the House for at least two months so far. The dad is always in the kitchen cooking his own food and I rarely see him eating with the families. He is always cooking something "gourmet" and J. J. has often asked him his recipe secrets, as the smell is wonderful while he cooks.

The kids and I went downstairs for dinner. The funny thing was I finally saw this dad in the kitchen with his entire family. He said, "This is real food. This is soul food." He was fixing a plate of food to eat. I just smiled to myself and thought yes, this is food for the soul. This food was prepared by an amazing group of people who care so much. Thank you to all of you who prepared and set up last night's dinner at the Ronald McDonald House. Thank you to all the Saints in Greenville as well who have been feeding J. J. his "food for his soul" during this difficult voyage. The joke at church is Presbyterians sure do know how to feed you! We provide food for most events and functions at church. What a great thing. Food is such an important part of the day and provides us all with nutrients to keep us strong and have energy.

James is doing well today. His ventilator decreased to fourteen this morning. We have made a new record friends! This is the lowest setting on the ventilator yet. Also, James's catheter, or foley, was removed this morning. He no longer has the tubes coming from his right leg. Without the catheter James is now using his diaper for urine output. Yeah! He is getting sixteen ccs of breast milk and will soon be increased to twenty or twenty-three fortified with formula for nutrients. His soul food will be increased soon. What a wonderful report this morning! Also, the nurse said since James's output (pee) is looking good the doctors do not want to insert a drainage tube at this time. Thanks be to God for these wonderful baby steps this morning. I actually caught J. J. smiling from ear to ear in the room with James this morning. Blessings to you all! Thank you for the continued prayers of output, decrease in edema, and decrease in ventilator support for James.

Infection ~Dad
Sunday, June 26, 2011 7:11 a.m.

Last night, James started having trouble with his oxygen saturation levels. They had to go back up on his ventilator from fourteen to twenty. They also went back up on the oxygen percentage from twenty-one to thirty percent. A small part of his right lung seems to have collapsed a little bit and they fear that James has an infection. The doctors and nurses aren't sure about the infection because he's not running a fever. Still, he has taken a step back. That's okay. Mama told us all there would be days like this. So go to church and worship God. Say a prayer for us that James makes a quick recovery. Pray that he continues to get that fluid off of him and that the lungs, kidneys, liver, and vitals can turn back around and begin improving once more. Thanks to all!

"Bump" In The Road ~Nurse Mom
Sunday, June 26, 2011 8:24 p.m.

We have been driving along the road the past few days with steady progress and all of a sudden today we hit a "bump in the road." Our car hit a bump and now we have a flat tire that needs to be repaired.

Things started to get a little bumpy last night as I left the hospital around 9 p.m. and headed to our home-away-from-home with the kids. I left J. J. with James, as I couldn't take it anymore. James's vital stats were starting to act up last night and I couldn't sit by his bed and watch things decline again like last week. I was excited for the great progress we were making yesterday with the decrease in ventilator as well as getting the foley removed. So when things started to get bumpy last night, I felt exhausted. I tend to run to my bed and sleep when things get out of control. Exhaustion takes over my body suddenly. What do you do?

Today James's ventilator was increased back to twenty, his oxygen increased to thirty percent, and his heart rate went up to the 170s. He also has a new catheter/foley inserted tonight because his urine output slowed down. There are lots of new bumps in the road for Mr. James.

Doc Go Get Mom met with us tonight and let us knows James has an infection. We were told this morning we thought he had an infection but were not sure what kind or where. His cultures show he has pneumonia. He started to show signs yesterday of decrease in body temperature, higher heart rate, and lower tissue saturations. Sure enough there is fluid and infection in his lung. He started two antibiotics this morning. James is very tired and has barely opened his eyes today. He has been resting.

I didn't take the news very well this morning when J. J. let me know what was going on. I am ashamed to say I had a meltdown. Thank God J. J. was here with me and was able to get me moving this morning, as all I wanted to do was lay in the bed and cry. I think I was feeling sorry for myself and was ready to give up. Have you ever been dealing with a difficult situation and you just want to give up? I know I can't give up because there are so many people praying, helping, and James continues to fight even when he gets an infection. James needs us all to remain faithful, patient and strong for him during this difficult time. Plus, several friends and wonderful youth came down from Greenville today and took us to lunch to help me get my mind off the dirty, little, nine-letter-word: infection. I asked one of my friends several times if she thought everything would be okay if James had an infection. The word infection was one of my fears since I have been here in Charleston with James at MUSC. Today one of my fears hit me between the eyes like a rock hits a windshield on a car going sixty-five miles per hour.

My windshield shattered this morning when J. J. reported to me James probably had an infection. I lay in the bed, refused to get up and continually told J. J. I couldn't "take it anymore." I felt very angry with God for allowing us to have a great day with awesome progress and then hitting us with infection. Now that I have had a chance to repair my shattered windshield I know I should not be angry. When you get mad and upset about life who or what do you blame? I said a few things this morning I am not proud of during my meltdown, but thank God J. J. knows me well and understands how to handle me when I get to this point. J. J. knows to listen to me and let me get it all out and then he hits me with the tough love. He asked me this morning if I thought James would want me to give up?

I found the strength to get up out of the bed and get dressed. I found the strength to dress, walk to the hospital, and visit James. Also,

I had a good visit and lunch with friends as I mentioned above. I want to thank you all for remaining faithful to James as well as God and us. Thank you for praying. Please continue to pray, pray, and pray for this sweet little boy who was called "unique" tonight by the doctor. I do think James is unique. I think he is here for a very unique reason. I think James is teaching me as well as all of you lots of lessons.

The lesson for today is this: when your road gets bumpy do not give up. Let me repeat myself again. When your road gets bumpy do not give up. Remain faithful to God. Remain faithful to what is right. Even when your tire goes flat and your windshield is shattered, continue to get up and keep going. God is good, all the time, even in the bumps. Blessings to you all tonight.

Monday, June 27, 2011 11:11 a.m. ~Dad

We got word tonight that the infection has gotten into the blood stream. They are taking some pretty aggressive actions to try to get ahead of it but at this time we're just kind of holding steady. We're not really gaining ground on it. We need some more prayers and good fortune to go our way. Thank you.

"Warriors" ~Nurse Mom
Monday, June 27, 2011 12:13 p.m.

Yes, I am sad to report to you all that James has the dirty nine-letter-word infection. He has pneumonia as well as a blood infection in his body. His right lung is completely white, which means it has collapsed. A chest tube is being inserted. This means we are not allowed to go back and see James. Plus, a new case just came into the Unit so it is closed. Oh goodness. I know that report sounds scary but friends let's not worry. Let's pray. Let's stick to what we know best and pray to God to help us once again beat the odds and continue to strengthen Mr. James.

I am feeling very calm this morning, which may come to a shock to you all as well as me. I feel the peace of God watching over us as well as all of your prayers going up for James. I really cannot explain why I am so calm this morning because I thought I would be a disaster again. I feel inner peace as Dragon Warrior says on the movie *Kung Fu Panda Two*. Dragon Warrior talks about finding "inner peace" throughout the entire movie even when bad things happen. This infection has me extremely scared today but I trust the advice I read on the guestbook entries as well as my mom's advice. I am looking for inner peace as well as faithful strength.

Let's lay this down in God's hand and let him handle it. This journey the past few days has been way too much for me to handle so I am handing it over to God as well as you all, the Prayer Warriors. Last night around 1a.m. when I found out James had yet another infection, I didn't know what to do. We were sitting by James's bedside hearing the updates. I had no clue what to do. We decided to walk back to our home-away-from-home, take a shower, pump milk and most importantly call our "lifeline." You know on the show *Who Wants to Be a Millionaire* you always get a lifeline as a last resort. Our "Lifeline to God" is a dear pastor friend who has been with us every step of the way. I decided to call her at one in the morning last night to pray with us over the phone and help spread the word to others for prayers. Everybody needs to have a lifeline they can call in the middle of the morning if necessary. We are now waiting on updates and visiting with friends of J. J.'s from childhood. I will update you as soon as I know something.

Quick Update ~Nurse Mom
Monday, June 27, 2011 11:54 p.m.

James seems to be holding stable tonight. He has had a very rough go of things today. He has a blood infection as well called MRSA. He is being treated with strong antibiotics. His blood pressure dropped a little this morning so he is back on dopamine. His body is very swollen from the urine input stopping yesterday and his body was 100 ccs positive with input, so he has lots of ground to make up. When I saw him today for the first time I was upset seeing him filled with fluid again. His head was very swollen. Hopefully, the antibiotics will help the bacterial infection and we can get back on the road to recovery soon.

Please continue to pray. We really need your prayers for infection to clear up, swelling to decrease, and fluid intake to increase and James's body to recover. The past few days have been long days as well as nights, but I feel confident the sun will start shining again soon for us all. Keep the faith.

Another Dirty Nine-Letter-Word ~Nurse Mom
Tuesday, June 28, 2011 4:40 p.m.

James is stable right now and seems to continue to fight. I found out this morning he had another infection dirty nine-letter-word called stenotrophomonas. The doctors think this infection is in his blood as well. I reckon it is our lucky day. The good news is this morning James's ventilator was moved down from thirty to twenty-eight, and he still does not have a fever. Let's pray we caught this infection early or shall I say infections early. What a day. I will update you all again with more information tonight as I know more and will have more to say. Remember I said yesterday I was waiting for the sun to shine again? Hopefully tonight I will be able to report sunshine to you all.

CHAPTER 11

Light Shining in a Dark World

The Lord will watch over your coming and going both now and forevermore.
Psalm 121:8

Sunshine in the Darkness ~Nurse Mom
Tuesday, June 28, 2011 11:09 p.m.

I s it possible to feel sunshine in the darkness? Does it have to be nighttime to be dark? It is getting late and the sun has been down for hours. I look out my window from my home-away-from-home and see the hospital. The sky is dark and the streetlights shine a small speck of light along the sidewalks. I pray James has a good night for "Nurse Full of Joy" and that he remains stable during this dark night that fills his little body with several infections.

Some people are afraid of darkness, but I am not normally afraid of dark nights. I have always enjoyed going outside at night in the middle of the morning and looking up at the sky and admiring the stars. The stars are beautiful especially in the middle of the night with clear skies. Why should I worry now during nighttime, especially when it is time for me to come home and go to sleep? James is in great care and is watched with a very close eye from lots of loving and amazing people sent by God. Do not be afraid, I constantly tell myself before I go to bed for the night.

So, my question for you all is during these dark nights and dark times is can the sun still shine? Yes, I think so. Even during infections, surgery, and even parents waiting patiently in a hospital waiting room, the sun can shine.

Today, I was sitting in the waiting room visiting with my family and talking. I wondered when enough would be enough for James. Were we putting him through extra pain and suffering by continuing to fight for him, even when he takes a big step back as he has done the past few days? How many infections will we put James through in order to heal his little body? I asked my family, looking at my mom, if I was fighting too much for his recovery. When would I know it is time to give up, as he has been through so much the past six weeks? Of course, you can imagine how emotional I was asking these difficult questions. You can imagine how my sunshine this morning was quickly getting turned into darkness. The stars were no longer shining. How can darkness overtake the sun in the middle of the day?

As we were sitting near the back of the waiting room, I cried while my mom comforted me. She told me I had to continue to fight for James's recovery no matter how long it took. "Keep the faith," she kept repeating. Then a woman, a stranger, walked up and kneeled down in front of me. She handed me a yellow envelope. I had no clue what she was doing but gave her my attention as I heard her say, "I see tears in your eyes." Little did I know this lady was bringing me a yellow envelope full of sunshine.

"I know this is a hard time for you right now as I see you crying. Take this envelope and read what is inside. Someone gave this to me a while back ago when I was having a hard time as well. Do not give up, even when it gets hard. Now, take this envelope and read it," she said. She stood in front of me for what felt like a minute. Then, she looked at me again and said, "Read it." I looked down at the envelope and read the title. On the front of the yellow sunshine message read: Encouragement, Strength, and Hope. I opened the envelope and the words appeared again on the sheet of paper: Encouragement, Strength, and Hope. Then followed three Bible verses:

Psalm 18:1-3, 28, 35
Psalm 20:1-5
Psalm 23: 1

Wow! What a powerful message. What a powerful testimony from this lady who was a stranger sitting in the waiting room waiting patiently just like us. What a witness to God for this lady to come up to me and feel confident to share such a powerful message.

The sun can shine during dark days. God sends sunshine in yellow envelopes by his angels and messengers to us during darkness. God sends your mom and aunts to remind you to "keep the faith" and "do not give up." Remember encouragement, strength, and hope.

James's body has two infections but seems to be getting better and becoming stable again. The swelling is back, but James's urine output reached 30 ccs one hour today. This tells us his kidneys are working again. Urine output helps him get rid of the swelling in his tissues. A drainage tube was inserted in hiss left side but does not seem to be releasing the fluid. The fluid fills his tissues and is not sitting in a "pocket" in his body. Urine output, or shall I say pee, seems to be the best route for fluid release. James's heart rate is back in the 150s and blood pressure is running 65/35. His temperature is low and he needs the heat lamp to regulate his temperature. He still has not run a fever yet. Also, tonight his ventilator was reduced to twenty-six, and hopefully around 4 a.m. he will go to twenty-four. All of the setbacks are caused from the two infections in his body. According to the nurse and doctor, his vital signs have improved so we think the antibiotics are working. We will have to wait and watch the cultures taken to see if the bacterial infections are clearing up and getting better. Sometimes it takes seventy-two hours for the cultures and bacteria to grow to see results. The good news is we know what bacteria James has so we can use the correct antibiotics to treat the infections.

The days seem pretty dark sometimes for me when things like infection hit. As you read a few days ago J. J. had to "get me moving" when I found out infection hit James's body. I do think I realize now, that even during these days when the sun stops shining and darkness seems to appear, I need to stop and feel encouragement from my family and friends, strength from God, and hope for the future for James. During these sunshine-less days and nights I need to remember to keep the faith and continue walking along these streets with specks of streetlamp light and brightly shining stars.

Thanks be to God for you all. Thanks be to God for your prayers. Thanks be to God for the sunshine!

I Saw the Sun Today! ~Nurse Mom
Wednesday, June 29, 2011 11:58 p.m.

Today was a beautiful day in Charleston and the sun was shining. James had a good day and seems to be feeling much better. Also, I have great news. James's foley was removed this morning and his little body is continuing to produce output and pee. Yeah! A culture was taken today and we will find out tomorrow if bacteria continue to grow. We are hoping and praying for a negative result showing no growth of bacteria. James's "crib" received a new addition today: a mobile. It warms my heart to see James open his eyes and watch the mobile with go around and around. I can't wait for him to see his monkey mobile attached to his crib at home in Easley.

James has discovered he likes to suck on a pacifier. I found myself standing next to James's crib today holding his pacifier in his mouth while he sucked. This is a great sign that James will and can suck on a pacifier. Sometimes babies with breathing tubes "forget" how to suck. When his breathing tube comes out we will have to teach him how to suck and swallow so we can feed him with a bottle. I am trying to get a "jump start" on this milestone now by working with James and a pacifier. I told him tonight after standing for thirty minutes holding his pacifier in his mouth we were going to have to talk. I laughed and told him he was going to have to learn to keep the pacifier in his mouth on his own and not expect me to stand next to him all day and hold it in his mouth for him. I giggled and told him we raise independent kids in this family. I think I am already starting to spoil James by rubbing his head, holding his little hands and now holding his pacifier in his mouth for him. I guess he deserves a little pampering right?

I spent the afternoon and night with J. J.'s mom, sisters and nephew. It was good to see them and laugh during dinner. J. J.'s nephew is growing up so fast. I remember many years ago when J. J.'s nephew would come and stay with us for a week during the summer. Wow, how time flies! Enjoy every day, as we do not know what the next day will bring. I am trying to learn this lesson and enjoy every day and be thankful for the "baby steps" blessings.

The ventilator setting went up today from twenty-four to thirty-two Yes, I know that sounds discouraging but the volume on the ventilator went down from fifty-five to forty-five at the same time. This is very complicated I know. I didn't realize until today there were two number settings along with the oxygen level setting on the ventilator. You can imagine how disappointed I was when I realized we went up on the breaths-per-minute setting. The Respiratory Therapist (RT) explained to me the difference between the two levels. The volume measures the pressure sent to the lungs and most of the children in the PICICU are set on forty-five. So with this in mind, even though we went up to thirty-two on the breaths per minute given to James, we went down on the volume and pressure put on the lungs from fifty-five to forty-five today. Are you still confused? If so, it is okay. I have been here seven weeks and look at these numbers every day with my eyes and I still get confused. Sometimes knowledge can be our enemy as ignorance can be best so we do not over analyze these numbers.

I am heading to bed tonight with a smile on my face. Isn't that great news? Today was a good day and I was so happy to feel the sunshine on my face today as I walked back and forth to the hospital and Ronald McDonald House. Thank you all for continuing to be faithful with your prayers, guestbook posts, and support. We could not do this journey without you all. You will never know how much your support and prayers mean to us. I can't imagine riding this roller coaster alone without you all as well as God. A rollercoaster has never been fun to ride alone. Having your friends and family sitting next to you always makes things better.

Thank you all again and Happy Birthday to a very special man serving alongside the St. Giles Youth today in Mobile, Alabama, doing mission work on his birthday.

Quick Note ~Dad
Thursday, June 30, 2011 7:52 a.m.

This is just a short note to say that James is continuing to improve. His foley has been removed and his kidneys continue to function at a very good rate. He is on a full dose of nutrition which is the number one thing that will help him grow, get stronger, and most importantly, fight off infection. You will see this nutrition become more and more of prayers focus. Chest x-rays looked about the same today as yesterday so not a tremendous improvement there but his gas tests have started to improve so maybe we can tweak the ventilator down a little bit. Currently it's at thirty-two breaths per minute and twenty-five percent oxygen. The pneumonia has set him back. Hopefully we are starting to see signs of the antibiotics working. The liver seems to be working a little better. They haven't run any tests to check but based on the amount of stool from yesterday and James's overall color; they feel pretty confident that those numbers should look better. His nurse said that he is completely off of the dopamine and his blood pressure looks great.

So our little Jedi seems to be returning again. Please continue to pray. We still have a long way to go but we're headed in the right direction. To quote Bartles and Jaymes, "Thank you for your support."

Angels are among us! ~Nurse Mom
Friday, July 1, 2011 12:30a.m.

The PCICU unit closed early this morning before I got a chance to go see James for my normal "good morning" visit. James seemed to be a tad bit grumpy this morning or so I heard through the grapevine. J. J.'s mom went to visit him this morning and told me along with the nurse he was a bit fussy this morning. The nurse told me on the phone James needed to rest, especially since he was fighting infections. I decided to run my errands early this morning and let James sleep because he seemed to be giving me a sign I needed to take "Jackie" time as well and rest.

My first stop was to Mt. Pleasant to get a pedicure and manicure. It has been so long since I treated myself. I had been trying for at least a week to go get my "feet done" and every attempt was interrupted until today. As I arrive at the nail shop I walk in and sign my name on the waiting list. I was taken immediately and seated in a chair facing a wall with a mirror. I place my tired and blistered feet into a tub of hot lathering water, closed my eyes and took a deep breath. Then my mind started to wonder. I wondered how James was doing as it was noon now. My mind started to travel. I thought about James and started silently asking myself if he wondered where I was this morning. I missed my "morning visit" with him and immediately started giving myself the guilt trip for taking time for myself. I opened my eyes, looked straight across the room at the wall in front of me with the mirror. What do I see in the mirror? There is a wooden cross made out of 2x4s nailed onto the wall directly behind the pedicure chair and me. How odd. Have you ever seen a 2x4 wooden cross nailed on the wall in a nail shop? You always see pictures of hand-painted nails or nail polish on the walls in nail shops. If you don't believe me check out a few nail shops this week and let me know.

A cross? I take another deep breath and think to myself it is ok to treat myself. It is ok to take quiet time and relax even if I miss my morning visit with James. God is watching over James and knows I need time to myself today.

As the nail technician starts working on my tired feet I hear a voice coming from my right side asking me about my handmade bracelet attached to my right arm. This soft angelic voice asked me about my bracelet and what it said. Frick and Frack and I visited the Children's Atrium at the hospital a few weeks ago and made handmade bracelets with beads and letters. My bracelet spells the names of my three children in birth order. My bracelet reads *JVCKJULIVJ<3MES*. Does this sound Greek to you? The atrium was out of As so the kids and I decided to use Vs for As. Also the <3 is a heart bead for the A in James's name. James gets a "special" A. This bracelet is very hard to decipher if you do not know the secret code.

I proceed to tell this sweet angelic voice James's story. I tell her about his heart and how sick he is and how we have been here in Charleston for seven weeks. Suddenly she silently reaches in her purse and hands me a card. The card reads:

But THEY THAT wait upon THE Lord shall renew their STRENGTH. They shall mount up with wings as eagles, they shall run and not be weary, they shall walk and not faint. ISAIAH 40:31

This is another angel friends. God is sending me another angel to help my weary soul get through this time of troubles. We begin to talk, laugh, and witness to each other the strength and power of God. As we continue to talk I feel comfort as well as feel my tired feet turning into stronger feet; stronger feet for this walk. I noticed my feet looked beautiful again. They looked just like I felt before this journey. My feet started to look beautiful. They looked beautiful because I use to take time for myself. Beauty is truly found inside and not outside even if your toe nail is cut in half by your seven-year-old daughter stepping on your foot.

During the conversation we discovered James's name is very similar to this sweet angel's family names as well. This is not a coincidence I am sure. The cross on the wall in a nail shop and now I am sitting next to an angel. This angel immediately tells the nail technician she is going to pay for my services today. Wow! I am so blessed. I told her it was hard for me to accept gifts from others, as I am the one who likes to give and not receive. I explained to her that it was very hard for me to accept her gift but I know I needed too. She explained to me that God wants us to "bless" others and give, and sometimes we need to take the blessing and receive from others. It is very hard for me to take from others as I always enjoy helping and giving. God is truly humbling me as I learn to accept nail service gifts as well as dinners from others when I want to be the one giving.

"Did you notice the cross on the wall," the angel asked? I smiled and let her know I did notice it and I truly believed in signs as well as angels. "You are an angel," I told her.

Friends, angels are among us. Open your eyes and notice. Angels are in the hospitals giving yellow envelopes of sunshine. Angels are buying pedicures and manicures while sitting under wooden 2x4 crosses nailed on walls in nail shops. Angels are among us and sent by God to clean our tired, weary blistered feet. God knows when our feet are tired. God knows exactly when he needs to send an angel our way to remind us to "wait," and he "renews our strength."

Please open your eyes. Please notice the angels among us. You never know? You may be the angel sent from God to somebody. You may be the Angel serving in Mobile, Alabama, at 5:30 a.m. at a soup kitchen on your free day. You may be buying an "overly priced" seafood dinner. You may touch a life of a weary traveler with tired feet. May God continue to bless us all with angels. Much love and appreciation for you, James's angels!

Dear God ~Nurse Mom
Friday, July 1, 2011 10:31 p.m.

Dear God,

I am not going to try to understand your plan with James. I am going to try to remain faithful, strong, and giving to others during this "storm" and journey to heal James heart, organs, and body. It is very hard for me to continue to stay strong week after week and remain faithful to you. I know I have to turn everything over to you and trust your hands to continue to hold us tightly.

I wonder why this is happening to me and ask "why me" tonight? My heart aches to see James shake and not have answers to why he is shaking. My heart aches to see J. J. upset tonight and on his knees next to James's bed holding James's head. I pray for you God to heal James's body. I beg you God to heal James's body. What do I need to do in order for James to be healed? Give me a sign please. I beg you.

I listen to the doctor say tonight, "If you show any cardiologist in the world James's echograms they would not believe it." I thanked the doctor for telling me this as this is proof to me you have a plan. I know you are holding James tight in your arms for a reason. I hope and pray you will not take his life away from us here on earth. I don't want to be mad at you God. I hope and pray James will one day read this blog and realize he is a miracle baby.

Things seem like they are getting worse for James since the infection struck his body. At times, I don't know what to think. I don't know what doctor or nurse to listen too. I try to stay patient and faithful and look for the positive signs and progress with James. It is so hard. I continually read the Book of James in the Bible looking for ways I can witness to your love and grace. I continually recite the Lord's Prayer looking for comfort and peace. Do you want me to witness and testify to others? Is that why I am going through so much suffering? You know I said before James was born, "I can handle anything; a job loss, financial ruin, just please do not give me a sick child." God, you know I love my children most. God, you know I love all children. Please help me. Please hear my prayer along with others for healing for James. Please forgive me for all the sins I have committed and things I continually do that are wrong.

What do I need to do God for James to be healed and healthy? Love, your faithful servant even during the storms (I think).

Measure ~Dad
Sunday, July 3, 2011 11:20 p.m.

Jacqueline looks at James and tells me how he's doing. She looks at his skin color, his facial expression, and the way he moves his foot and assesses whether he is better or worse, happy or sad, and tells me what we can do to help. I, on the other hand, cannot tell by his skin color. I can't tell by the way he moves his foot, or by his facial expression. The only way I can tell is by measuring anything and everything. Jacqueline and the nurses give me a hard time about this. I'm borderline Obsessive Compulsive Disorder about the numbers. I always ask the same questions. How was his input versus urine output? This tells me how James is doing with the edema or fluid. If he's "negative" that means he has more fluid out than going in and that my friends is a very good thing. If he's positive, then he's got more going in than coming out. Jacqueline looks at him and says, "He's more swollen.

Literally, she could tell that his belly was forty centimeters, up from thirty-eight the day before. That's two centimeters people not much but she could tell. My next question, how have his blood pressure and heart rate been? It doesn't really matter if the heart rate reads 153 or 173. The bigger concern is the stability. They don't want to see a lot of quick fluctuation. Steady changes over time are okay. Blood pressure can be impacted by his feeds, his medicines, and his support. It usually reads pretty close to the same. The question is, what support did you change to keep it there? Sometimes they go up on support. Sometimes they go down. Jacqueline can look at his skin color and tell how his heart rate and blood pressure have been. When it's going well, his skin color looks whiter and less shiny she says. It looks less shiny? Yes, less shiny. I don't get it. You have to ask Jacqueline. Recently, the critical measure that I've been paying the closest attention to is James's urine output. Through last week, he had a foley in with a tube that filled a bag at the foot of his bed. My little game with James was to see how much he could pee in an hour. We would measure his output on an hourly basis and measure it against the amount of fluid going into his body via medications, feeds, and flushes. A flush is the solution that carries the medication into the blood stream to make sure it gets to the appropriate organ and provides the most benefit. Then we would measure the output versus the input. Currently, James needs about 22 ccs of output per hour to match what he has going into his body. Sixteen of these ccs are feeds, which are looked at a little differently. He's on a full regimen of nutrition, which is important for healing his organ tissues and the rest of his body. Anyway, last week they took the foley out so I know longer had this game to play with James. I was happy it was gone for James's sake, but I sort of missed our little game. There's not a lot to do and James is not much for conversation. Jacqueline says it's because he has a feeding tube and a breathing tube. I think it's just that he's the strong silent type. (The nurses are pretty sure Jacqueline's right on this, haha) Anyway, the nurse today suggested that I could still play my game with James by weighing his diapers. Jacqueline said my face lit up like a Christmas tree. I have to admit I was pretty happy about that. The nurse and I also played another game where we guess what James blood gas numbers were going to be. His numbers actually ended up coming back better than either of us predicted. To someone from the outside looking in, they might think that this is the stupidest thing they've ever heard. But it lifted my spirit to see him get out more than he put in. It lifted my spirit to see his blood gas numbers come back better than expected.

These are all measurements. They are hard and fast numbers and generally speaking, numbers don't lie. The doctors and nurses have different opinions on James. Some have a lot of hope for James, like Doc Optimistic. Other doctors like Doc Detective and Doc Honesty have a less optimistic opinion. The numbers don't have an opinion. They measure the day without regards to opinion or point of view. My good friend Sylvester used to say that "The truth don't like me. It don't like me or dislike me. It's just the truth." Numbers speak the truth. And for someone who can't tell how things are going by looking at the skin color or watching his foot move, the numbers provide a bit of truth for me to know how James is doing.

Then, a strange thing kind of happened that redefined truth for me especially about these numbers. College football season is just around the corner. The NFL draft has already happened and the colleges have entered summer camps, which open huge recruiting opportunities to them. These coaches have every statistic known to man on these athletes. They provide height, weight, forty-yard dash time, shuttle time, max bench press, number of reps with 225 pounds on the bar. They list last season's stats and the year before that. They list team record, strengths, weaknesses, other colleges recruiting them. They will tell you everything under the sun about the player, except whether or not he can play football. See, it doesn't matter if you're six feet two inches and 225 pounds and run the forty-yard dash in 4.3 seconds if you don't have the will power and drive that it takes to be a champion. It seems you can measure everything except for the size of a kid's heart. At least that was what the analyst said interesting choice of words. I'm into measuring everything under the sun including the amount of urine in a diaper, but it's not going to give me James's outcome. I can't measure the fight in James. I can't measure his will to be a champion.

Doctors can't measure it either which is probably why every doctor or nurse that comes in to help take care of James tells us that he has really surprised them. They talk about those first days and can't believe he's still here. They can't explain it. All the x-rays or ECHOs in the world can't measure the will to live. And my son has a strong will to live. The doctor last night said, "Any cardiology doctor in the country who saw James's first ECHO would not believe he's still here." The only explanation that we can give is that he has a strong will to live. "He can do all things through Christ who strengthens him." In the end, it's not the numbers that know his truth. They can't even explain why he's still alive. So why is he still alive? Only God knows and thank God for that! Thank God he holds all of us in the palm of his hand. All thanks be to God for that and for another successful day of life. Amen!

A tough "Bible Study" Named James ~Nurse Mom
Monday, July 4, 2011 12:32 a.m.

Have you ever done a tough Bible study? Maybe you are in the process of studying a famous Beth Moore Bible study as I write. Maybe you are reading a "self-help" book currently. Maybe your life is a Bible study. Boy do we all have our own stories to tell.

What are we looking for in Bible studies: Answers to our difficult life questions, Guidance for decisions, or just pure biblical knowledge? Several of the Nurses at the Unit here in MUSC are joining together for a weekly Bible study. I am always curious and find myself asking the Nurses, "How is your Bible study going?" hoping to learn a "new" life lesson and hoping to find answers to my questions. I find myself lately and constantly asking others questions about God. I ask difficult questions such as, "Do you think God punishes people? Do you think God has a plan? Am I not faithful enough? I thought I was a faithful servant and if so why is James sickness happening to me?" I find myself searching for answers in the Bible. What is my lesson to learn? Will this be a tough Bible Study with James heart condition for me with a tough lesson in the end?

As I listened to the youth and leaders preach this morning during the St. Giles Worship Service in Greenville they reminded me of one of the most important Bible studies written and preached: Seek justice, love kindness and walk humbly with our God. The youth and leaders reminded me this morning about how important as well as fun mission work and good works are to perform with others. I listened to their stories of anger for injustice to kids, hope for the future, and love for each other and the sick. Even though tears fell from my eyes as I listened to their testimonies this morning my heart warmed. My heart warmed to know this mission team gave up a week of their summer to serve others and had fun. My heart warmed to hear about the mission team praying with the homeless. Oh, how my heart warmed when my "shower singing partner" shared her story of her love for others as well as the power of prayer. What I would give to rewind the youth mission teams trip and hear the prayer the youth team shared with the homeless concerning James's health. How powerful!

In the Book of James there is a Bible passage that states God does not show partiality to anyone. Everyone is created equal. The Youth proved to me their love was not partial this past week with either the rich or the poor. All the Youth wanted to do was serve, serve and serve some more. Even on their free day the Mission Team wanted to go back and serve. This was very powerful! This makes me so proud to say I know these young people as well as their leaders.

So, what is my lesson I am supposed to learn with James? What is my "Bible study"? Is God trying to teach me a lesson from this journey? Is God trying to teach the doctors, nurses or even you with James? I don't know. James's nurse tonight Nurse J doesn't know either. Of course you know I asked her. When I walked into James room tonight he was sleeping wearing his homemade T-shirt made by Nurse J saying, "Jesus Loves Me." I can't wait to take his picture in his t-shirt to show you all. It was very nice to talk with Nurse J and share faiths about God. What a blessing! I am such a lucky woman to be surrounded with such wonderful nurses, doctors, caregivers, Family and Friends.

This journey with James is going to be a "tough Bible study" for me. I don't have any of the answers to the questions. I don't have a videotape I can watch or a YouTube video to catch up on if I miss a lesson. I do have a support group, perseverance, a Bible and most importantly faith. I plan on continuing to be faithful and perform good works even when the "tough Bible study" gets hard, long and tedious. I plan to read the scriptures over and over until I find comfort, understanding as well as inner peace even if the outcome is not "my plan" but "God's plan." I will not quit. I may be mad but I will not give up and I will make it. I will handle whatever I am given and I will handle it with God's grace.

"JAMES" That is the name of my "tough Bible study." Thanks for joining me along this journey and staying faithful in prayer. Remember, we need pee. We need James edema to reduce and help his body as well as James's organs become healthier. Blessings to you all tonight! Thanks for sticking with us during the difficult times. Thank you for sticking with me during my "tough Bible study."

CHAPTER 12

Limitless Hope

Hope is one of the theological virtues.—*C.S. Lewis*

Big Boys Don't Cry ~Dad
Monday, July 4, 2011 6:58 a.m.

"Hanging on in quiet desperation is the English way." These words from Pink Floyd describe my thoughts to a tee last night. Last night, when I came to visit James and tell him good night, Nurse J and I had one of those difficult heart-to heart talks about James's condition. She didn't tell me anything that I didn't already know. She just wanted to make sure I had a clear understanding of where we were. Where we are is not a very happy place. In the PCICU, time can be a friend or an enemy. Right now, James needs time to heal. But he needs to get a move on with the healing. Every day that he stays the same could become more and more problematic. Every day he goes with the ventilator on its current settings, there is a threat to cause more and more damage to his lungs which means he's going to need more support, which means he's going to get more and more damage to the lungs. It is of ultimate importance that he begins to get more fluid out than in. Over the last two days he has been "positive" which is not a good thing. We have seen his little belly grow from thirty-eight centimeters to forty centimeters to 41.5 centimeters. All of this is retained fluids that are making it harder and harder for James to breathe. All of this news is very difficult to hear but I prepare for it like a prizefighter. I know I'm going to take some shots so I prepare for the worst. I already know the stakes. I know the situation. So when Nurse "J" told me last night that we were "positive" almost 150 ccs, I didn't break. I looked at her, told her I understood the situation, told her I would continue to pray, said my good night, and left. I didn't break. Not a tear was shed. I knew the stakes and it was time for me to be tough. I needed to be strong in that moment and I was. I went home, laid down in the bed, pulled Frack up so tight that she was almost right underneath me, and pulled Frick in tight enough to get my arms around both children and I slowly faded off to sleep while the children watched *The Deadliest Catch*. (I don't know what it is about crab fishing that my kids love, but they can't take their eyes off of it).

This morning I woke up bright and early. I said a little prayer, took a shower, said another little prayer, drank half my cup of coffee, refilled my cup and trekked on over to the hospital. I already knew the answer to my question before I asked but being "OCD" about the numbers I had to ask. "How positive were we yesterday?" Then it happened, the unexpected. The thing I wasn't prepared for as the nurse replied, "Oh, Nurse "J" wanted me to tell you, she looked at the numbers wrong last night. James was a negative 150 not a positive." Then in that voice that women get when they're talking to a baby she said, "Baby James had a good day yesterday." The moment overwhelmed me and I broke. The tears (of joy) flowed freely without restraint because I didn't have time to gather myself and hold back. I apologized to the nurse because I really didn't know what else to say. I told her I thought it was stupid because she was giving me good news, so why am I crying? I just told her that the moment overwhelmed me. It seems I had already prepared myself for the worst and God sent me a definitive reminder that this story isn't over not by a long shot.

During the course of the last two months there have been a handful of moments where I prepare myself to losing James. God does a funny thing. He whispers in my ear "J. J., you're doing well with the faith, you're doing good with the love, but where is the hope?" It seems I still have a lot to learn. God gave us faith, hope, and love and the greatest of these is love. However, we really need all three. At face value it would seem hope would be the easiest of the three. I mean, you have to have hope. But this is the one that gets me. In my effort to be prepared for the worst, in residing myself to losing James, the only thing I lose is one of the greatest gifts God has given us hope. I'm reminded of what my hero Jim Valvano said, "Don't Give Up, Don't Ever Give Up!" If Jacqueline has her own Bible study of James, here is one Bible verse from my boy "James" Valvano. "Don't Give Up, Don't Ever Give Up."

So anyway, back to that "God-awful" image of me crying like a baby in front of the nurse, respiratory therapist, God, and everybody, a funny thing happened. James smiled. It was the first time I've seen him smile. I'm not sure it really was a smile, maybe it was a twitch in his lip, or a pull from his ventilator tube, but it looked like a smile to me. I thought in the moments following that if a tear would make him smile, I would cry a river. I got on the CaringBridge this morning and one of the messages from someone I don't know read simply "Jesus Wept." In a sense he has already done the very same thing. Jesus died on the cross for our sins so that we wouldn't have to. He suffered so that we could overcome death and sin. He cries so that we don't have to. If it allows us to smile, he would cry us a river. He loves us like a father loves a son.

Jacqueline went home yesterday for our church service at our home church for the first time in many weeks. It was the Youth Mission sermon. We look forward to this sermon more than any other. A lot of the Youth spoke yesterday and a lot of profound ideas and words were spoken, but one in particular resonated with me. One of the leaders asked one of the Youth to carry the large wooden cross in at the start of the service. She said, "I don't know, isn't that cross too heavy." His response, "Yes, the cross is always heavy."

He's right you know. The cross is too heavy. The task is too great. There is too much hurt in the world. Even good news can be too overwhelming to hold back the tears. No matter how much good we do, there is always more that can be done. All the hurt that we see and experience does make us angry. It's more than we can bear. And Big Boys Do Cry. Even Jesus WEPT. But never forget that when the hurt becomes too great, when the anger takes over, when the cross becomes more than we can bear, that we have faith, we have love and we have hope and hope is a wonderful thing!

Good Morning from Charleston ~Nurse Mom
Wednesday, July 6, 2011 6:45 a.m.

Good morning to you all! I am awake bright and early this morning and realized I didn't post an update for you all last night. The kids (Frick and Frack) and I were in the bed last night by 10 p.m. It was an early night for us all in Charleston. Frick and I watched the new episode of *The Deadliest Catch* at 9 p.m. together and then we went to bed. I am not sure why this is "our show" but Frick and I love to watch this show together. I use it as a "life learning lesson" as one of the characters is recovering from a drug addiction or dope as Frick calls it. I decided to let him continue to watch this show with me so I can explain and answer all of his questions especially the questions about drugs. The day Frick asked me what dope was and why this guy on the show was doing it I figured it was time to have the "bad drug" conversation. Hmmm? Yes, I know. Frick is only eight years old but you have to start early now days with teaching your kids about the world especially drugs. You have to answer your kid's questions as well as prepare them for what is out in the world even if they are only eight years old.

The birds are chirping outside our window, Frick and Frack are still sleeping peacefully and James is on schedule to get his RA lines out this morning. Wow! What a day in Charleston or should I dare say a good morning? I almost feel normal as I have already pumped James's "liquid antibiotic" food, showered and preparing to "dress" up. The rumor around James room No. 8 is once his RA lines come out and everything is running smoothly I may get a chance to start holding him. Wouldn't that be a great morning? Yesterday, step one was complete as James visited the CATH Lab around 9:15 a.m. for an insertion of an additional PICC Line in his right arm. Now James has two PICC Lines and the two RA lines inserted into his heart should not be needed. Of course I will have to hold him with his ventilator inserted into his mouth so he can breathe but friends I will take whatever I can get at this point. I am learning to be very patient as well as appreciative for what God allows me to enjoy with Mr. James even if I have to wait eight weeks to finally hold James for a second time. Can you believe it has been eight weeks already? Boy time flies by when we are having fun.

As I think and type, I look around our "shoe box" room. I see a scooter, a bicycle, two twin beds pushed together to make a king-size bed, dirty clothes laying on the floor in a corner, a small dorm size refrigerator and a sink full of dirty "liquid antibiotics" pumping equipment. Maybe I need to get busy and start cleaning and organizing? Maybe I should just get back in the bed and cuddle with Frick and Frack while they sleep? I am learning to remind myself to "STOP" and enjoy the kids more. The clothes will sit for another hour until I wash them. The "liquid antibiotic" pumping equipment will get washed, as I need it clean next time I pump. As far as the bike and scooter, I am sure they will get ridden and moved today once the kids awake and remember they are here to enjoy.

James's little body is still full of extra fluid settling around his waist and tummy. We need the fluid to move out of his body and tissues through his pee or urine (correct term). I find myself now asking J. J.'s questions since he is back at work this week. "Are we positive or negative with output"? Last night when I left visiting James the output was close to even to the input. Keep in mind James received a large dose of blood yesterday ranging around 45 ccs as well. James had a "huge" diaper when I arrived last night to visit. J. J. you would have been excited. I think the diaper weighed over 100 ccs! I thought about how excited you would be to see the diaper on the scale. What is my life turning into when we start to get excited about diapers weighing 100 ccs? Also, the funny thing about the diaper situation is after the sweet Nurse changed James diaper he urinated in the new diaper again before she could close it up. So, J. J., there was two diapers to weigh at the same time. Sorry love. Sorry you missed this one.

I look back and reread my post as I get ready to save for you all to read. Oh wow this post is reading all over the place. There is not one single thought or discussion; so much for my writing skills. I seem very scattered and "all over the place" with this writing. Hey. Scattered and "all over the place"? Yes, that sounds normal for me? You all know how I am "normally" all "over the place" and going, going, going. Yeah. I am getting back to normal. Today is going to be a "Good Day in Charleston." I feel normal again. Blessings to you all for a Good Day!

P. S. ~Nurse Mom
Wednesday, July 6, 2011 7:26 a.m.

P. S.—Just wanted to let you all know I am back in the bed cuddling with the kids. Yes, I am enjoying Frick and Frack. My chores are waiting. Let's take time to "smell the roses" and even enjoy them even if it takes eight weeks to hold your baby for the second time. Schedule your vacations now friends!

Support ~Dad
Wednesday, July 6, 2011 7:57 p.m.

It's funny how we use little terms to make things seem different or less severe than they actually are. In the military you may hear them use the term "brought to justice." This is code for "He's dead, we shot him dead! Or you may hear them use the term "dispatched the resistance." That means we killed a whole bunch of them, and the ones that were left stopped resisting. In the hospital they do the same thing. Instead of referring separately to the three towers of fluids, feeds, flushes, and pharmaceuticals being pumped into James body, the fourteen tubes and lines running into or out of James's body, the heat lamp over his head, the respirator and suction devices with all their settings instead of reporting on all this separately, they simply give it the code word SUPPORT. If we have to increase medications, vent rates, or install more IVs, we don't refer to it as these separate ugly truths, we dilute it by saying, "We had to increase the support being provided." This sounds a lot better than, he's not breathing as well, his lungs are more damaged, his hearts not pumping as well, the organs are failing, etc. We simply say, "We increased our amount of support."

Well, I'm happy tonight to report that we have decreased the amount of support required to keep James going. First and foremost, he has finally made some progress with the edema. The fluid is starting to come off slowly but surely. He was down about 60 ccs today, but it was visible even to the naked eye, that a lot of this was coming from his middle area. They have been able to go down on his ventilator in three ways. First, they've reduced the number of breaths per minute from thirty-four all the way to twenty-six without negative impact. Also, we've been able to reduce his oxygen percentage from 30 percent to 25 percent. Last, we've been able to go down on his tidal volume (the amount of pressure given in each breath) from fifty to forty-five. These are all signs of progress. Perhaps most importantly, James got the two RA lines that were stitched into his heart, removed today. This means two fewer chances of infection. It also could possibly mean that Mama (and Daddy) gets to hold him. If he does well over the next day or two, its possible Jacqueline could get her hands on him. Bless his heart if they ever let her hold him again, she may never put him down. I can't say as I blame her. She's been through months and months of Hades. The payoff was supposed to be at birth; she reminded me that at birth, you're supposed to get to hold the baby. When she didn't get to hold him, she felt like a precious moment was taken away. I guess at that time, the trees were being pruned. But I can't help but rejoice in how beautiful it's going to be when she does finally get to hold that child. Just the thought of this warms my heart. She deserves this moment and more.

I'm anxious for the day when we don't require all of this support. It's not just James that has required support. We may not be on ventilators, or three towers of medicine, or a heat lamp but we have needed truckloads of prayers, friendly favors, kind gestures, and well air conditioning. You might laugh, but Charleston gets hot during the summer. The amount of support we have received via meals being prepared, kind friends fixing "comfort food", the many kind gestures, the gifts, the cards, the creative ideas, the coverage from co-workers, understanding work-places, financial assistance, medical advice, phone calls, visits, high school friends and college roommates that visit and take our children out for the day, guestbook entries, Facebook comments, gift cards, posters with coins attached for the vending machines, hauling our kids back and forth, allowing our kids to stay at your home and making them feel like it's your home (I'm talking about you Bird family), setting up CaringBridge sites, smuggling my wife out of the hospital in the middle of the night, or being in the waiting room in Charleston before I could even get there. God has richly blessed you to be a blessing to us. Alleluia!

I had dinner with some dear friends from church tonight. I took the leftovers with me and can't wait to have them again for lunch tomorrow. It was her grandmother's beef stew. That's special isn't it? Grandmother's beef stew is always a special dish with love always being the primary ingredient. We had a good laugh when I told them that my Jewish grandmother had a special dish too. She made the best baked ham you've ever put in your mouth. Yes, Jewish grandmother baked ham. I'm not joking, it was delicious. During dinner we talked about the "St. Giles Way" and our community of faith. What we talked about was providing a tremendous amount of "Support." We talked about making sure that the support doesn't go away after the first week or two. They have made sure that our support has not gone away. They have made sure that our family's ventilator settings, towers full of medicine, and the warmth in their hearts has never waned. It has always been fully loaded for whatever needs may rise. But all this support, as good as it is, is nothing without prayer. The best, most important, most wonderful thing, are the prayers that have been sent our way.

James doesn't seem to require as much support today as he did yesterday. As for me, I'm still requiring buckets of it. I know that prayer works because I have no other plausible explanation for being able to continue on. People say to me, "I don't know how you're doing it." My response to them is that I don't know either. The only explanation I have is that as parents, husbands, etc., we do what we have to do. Right now my plate is full and I live fifteen minutes at a time. I can't think about the future or the past. I don't have time. I can only think about the present, right here right now. If you think about it, that's what God tells us to do. "Do not worry about tomorrow. Today has enough worry for itself." I go back to a blog I wrote very early on about Philippians 4:13.

"I can do all things through Christ who strengthens me."

This is the only explanation I have for being able to get through these days. That along with a ton of support being provided by you. So while James continues to improve, baby step by baby step, please don't reduce our support. We still need full ventilation. We still need a gamut of favors and charity. We need prayers by the truckload. If you can help us with this part, I'll take care of the air conditioning. My friends that fed me and kept me company tonight reminded me of a key fact. They told me that one day I would be able to pay it back not by paying anything back, but by paying it forward. I look forward to those days!

Out of the Mouth of Babes ~Nurse Mom
Thursday, July 7, 2011 11:55 p.m.

"Dad", Frick said on the phone tonight to J. J. "I just feel like our family is in turmoil." Wow! I thought as I listened to Frick talk to his dad on the phone and covered my face with my hand lying down on the bed next to Frack. Turmoil? Frack says to J. J. on the phone tonight, "Mom hasn't told us tonight if James is better, Dad. I think James is getting sicker. Mom is covering her face with her hand and told me she just needs a minute to herself. I think she is crying." A minute? Yes, Mom needs a minute I thought.

"You don't love me anymore Mom," said Frack tonight as we were walking to the hospital to say good night to James. Wow! Frack doesn't think I love her anymore. Really? "You get to see James all day," said Frick as he questioned why I said I didn't want to be here in Charleston either seeing James sick. Wow! Frick thinks I am okay with being in Charleston just as long as I get to "see" James all day.

What am I doing wrong? This comes straight "Out of the Mouth of Babes." I try so hard to make things as normal as possible for

Frick and Frack, and now they say we are "living in turmoil" as well as think I don't "love" them anymore. Yes, we are living in a state of confusion, disturbance, and commotion but I am trying to make things easy and fun. I spent several hours today taking Frick and Frack to the Charleston Children's Museum. I sat patiently as the kids wanted to play once again with the golf balls and buckets in the museum. I helped the kids check out their food purchases in the kid's grocery store at the museum. I even bought them slushes and popcorn at Target this afternoon as we shopped for them new bicycle helmets and bike locks so they can safely ride their bicycles to the hospital when we go see James. What else in the world can I do to show them or shall I say "Frack I love you," and Frick, "we can make it through this turmoil."

Yes, James is sick. James is very, very, very sick. It isn't easy on any of us. Especially when I walk into his room tonight to say good night and I see his ventilator is moved back up again to thirty from twenty-six. It isn't easy on any of us when the doctors don't know what is going on with James and take blood to run liver enzyme tests, culture tests, urine tests, etc. Can't I get a break God? Can't I get a "pass" for once, even if it is just from Frick and Frack? I came to reality that James was going to give me a run for my money, as I am on this journey with him and his illness but I can't take my other two children now feeling turmoil and unloved.

Frick, I am so sorry we are living in Charleston in turmoil. I wish it was different. I wish we were back at home like you told your dad on the phone tonight. I wish we could sleep in our own beds or "cozy" beds as Frack says. I wish we could play with our friends, eat dinner together when Dad got home from work and then brush our teeth and go to bed. I am so sorry we have to live this way. Hopefully soon we will all be able to go home Frick and live a "normal" life again with James at home with us.

Frack, I do love you very, very much. I tried to cuddle with you today and I did rub your hair just like I rub James's hair every day when I go see him. Just because you are not a baby and wear diapers like James, I still love you. Just because you are not sick and in the hospital, Frack, I love you just as much as I love James. It may seem like

I love James more at times but he is sick and I cannot leave him alone. I have to at least say hello to him and let him know we need him to keep fighting. We need James to keep fighting and stay alive for us all.

This is out of the mouth of babes. Kids do often say remarkable and insightful things. It is hard for me to get over these things the kids said tonight because all I ever wanted to do in life was be a good Mom. I want my kids to feel and know they are loved. I don't want to live life in turmoil. I want to live a normal life, eat dinner together at the dinner table, watch movies together, play in the yard and yes, even brush our teeth in our bathroom sinks at home.

Right now, with James's sickness, things are crazy. Right now, with James's sickness, we are experiencing extreme confusion. Eight weeks of living in Charleston and not knowing what kind of report we will get from the nurse and doctors day by day is extremely disturbing. I am powerless and not in control of anything.

Can I get a break God, please? Fill my kids' hearts and minds with love, comfort, and peace. Fill my kids' hearts with healing. Frick and Frack need James to heal. Frick and Frack need "normal" soon. James needs to come home with us healthy. I need a break; send me good news. James needs his right lung to heal. James needs his ventilator settings to come down and get rid of all the infections with negative cultures. The fluid is slowly diminishing, so God please continue to release fluid from the tissues in James's abdomen so his lungs will work correctly. Heal his enlarged liver with the high bilirubin levels. Heal my spirit, as I need my kids to feel peace and love.

James II:14 "Faith without Works is Dead" ~Nurse Mom
Saturday, July 9, 2011 2:50 a.m.

> *"What good is it, my brothers and sisters, if you say*
> *you have faith but do not have works?"*

While I was pregnant I pondered what I was going to name the baby. J. J. continuously asked me what we were going to name him.

I knew I wanted to name the baby a "J" name since everyone in our family has a name that starts with J (J. J., Jacqueline, Jack, and Julia), but I wanted the baby's name to have meaning. I wanted the baby's name to have a special meaning as well as be a "Biblical" name. I immediately knew I was using my dad's first name, Robert, as he is very special to me and I love him very much even if I am his "second favorite daughter" as he calls me every time I call his phone. So, all I needed was a meaningful Biblical name. I questioned Doc Mission about Biblical names during a Youth Conference at Montreat. I emailed two Bible scholar friends at church their opinion on Biblical names a few months later. Both of these scholars said James. They both said James because the book of James in the Bible represented "faith and good works." After I received the scholars' responses by email I went straight to my Bible and read the Book of James. Faith and good works; "hmmm" I thought. James is perfect. Finally, I sold J. J. on the name James and he agreed without discussion we would use Daddy's name Robert as well. Faith and good works; two very powerful meanings!

Can faith save you? Yes, faith can save you. Many of you have mentioned you don't know how J. J. and I are able to handle this tough situation with James's illness. Many of you mention the inspiration you feel from this journey with James and the power of prayer. I credit all of these comments you make to faith in God. I have no clue what or how I would be able to handle this journey with James without faith in God? Sometimes during the day when I am standing next to James's bedside watching him breathe and rubbing his head, all I have to hang onto to keep me standing is my faith in God. I know God has a plan. I know God is in control. Even during my darkest times, please know I am trying to remain faithful to God and trust in him. I realize there is a reason for my hurt and suffering with James. I pray that God will hold me up and let me stand next to James's bedside. I continue to remain faithful even during the rollercoaster rides. I pray even though today is tough, I have faith tomorrow will promise lots of good things. God gives us support as J. J. mentioned a few days ago in a journal. God keeps us faithful and standing during these difficult journeys in life.

*"If a brother or sister is naked and lacks daily food, and one of you
says to them, "Go in peace, keep warm and eat your fill," and yet
you do not supply their bodily needs, what is the good of that?"*

Today was a great day visiting with a dear sweet friend today. We
spent the day visiting James, lying around in my room at the Ronald
McDonald House talking and resting our eyes. The most adventurous
part of our day and reason for tonight's blog was tonight though. As I
was finishing up a visit with James around 6:15 p.m. tonight, I walked
past the PCICU waiting room on my way to the elevator. My friend
and I had plans to go to a nice dinner tonight with the kids. Her treat!
She was waiting for me with the kids back at the Ronald McDonald
House. As I walked past the waiting room I noticed a family I knew
from the PCICU standing in the doorway with all of their belongings.
When I say belongings, I mean five large black trash bags, two large
suitcases, three bags of cold refrigerated food, two American flags,
one bag of the girls' toys, a Dalmatian puppy, one makeup bag, a
plastic bag filled with shoes, a box of Lucky Charms cereal and many
more bags. This family was now homeless. The father had lost his
job several weeks ago and now they were homeless. Homeless, yet I
say because they didn't "watch their tongue." Remember, you have
read about me mentioning our tongues and how they can get us in
trouble. Now this family was homeless and had all of their belongings
on a hospital cart and lying around in the waiting room because they
didn't "watch their tongue." All of a sudden I saw the two little girls
come around the corner. They were five and three years old. Oh,
how my heart ached friends when I saw the two little girls Frick and
Frack had played with for the past eight weeks. If you know me well
you know children and youth are part of my "beating heart." What
in the world would this family do? They couldn't sleep in this waiting
room. They didn't have a car so they couldn't travel anywhere. I was
pretty sure they didn't have the support like J. J. mentioned earlier.
But remember this:

> *"If a brother or sister is naked and lacks daily food, and one of you
> says to them, "Go in peace, keep warm and eat your fill," and yet
> you do not supply their bodily needs, what is the good of that?"*

I had to do something. I had to do something to help this brother and sister in need. How could I turn my back and walk away and go to dinner with my friend while this family sits in the waiting room with everything they own? They even had their frozen chicken legs in a plastic bag. How could I turn my back to these precious two children? How could I walk away not knowing these kids do not have dinner? The box of Lucky Charms isn't going to fill these "Children of God's" bellies. You know Lucky Charms need milk, right? I watched the mom cry and watched her oldest daughter walk up to her and spill her cereal on the floor. "I'll be right back," I told the mom. "I need to go let my friend know plans have changed," I told the crying mom. As I reassured her everything would work out, I noticed everyone else in the waiting room was watching but was quick to turn their backs to this family in need. It was obvious this family was homeless. "I will be right back. I will come back and take the kids to dinner for you," I reassured her. "The kids can eat their fill for dinner," I said. At least I knew the kids would not be hungry tonight I thought.

What would you do? Should I have just turned my back to this family? Should I have acted like nothing happened? I called my "jury" to get a verdict. I call J. J. and tell him the situation. I tell my "Green Analyzer" friend as well. I call my "Trusty Logical Advisor" and get his opinion. My "Trusty Logical Advisor" asks his "Consultant" his wife of course (we all know the wife has the right answer) and gets her opinion. My jury confirms I need to help this family.

We loaded J. J.'s car with all of the family's belongings and took the mom to a hotel two blocks from the hospital. She and I unloaded the car. It took two trips in J. J.'s car from the hospital to the hotel to get all of their belongings in the hotel lobby.

I am happy to report the family slept in a comfortable bed, warm, or shall I say cool, since it is so hot in Charleston. They received a free continental breakfast in the morning. The homeless family had their bodily needs supplied for the night. As for the "Green Analyzer" Frick, Frack, and me, we finally ate dinner tonight around 10:30 from the Burger King drive-thru because the drive-thru "comes first."

Friends, I beg you. Please do not be caught sitting in a waiting room turning your backs to naked brothers and sisters and going in peace to a nice dinner. Please, please do not turn your backs to children in need. I am not suggesting you give your money away to people. I am just suggesting you help others when you see a need. I am suggesting if you have $100 extra dollars given to you by a saint in a tissue box or even a "love offering" collected at a very, very special church, you give back to someone in need. And you especially give to someone who needs shelter. I am suggesting if you are sitting along with four other men in a hotel lobby and see two women carrying five large black trash bags, two large suitcases, three bags of cold refrigerated food, two American flags, one bag of the girls toys, a Dalmatian puppy, plastic bag full of shoes, one makeup bag, a box of Lucky Charms and many more bags, you have no clue what is in there until you get up off your behinds and help lug the items into the hotel lobby for two women. I am suggesting you continue to be faithful in God during your trials and journeys as well as provide good works to others.

> *"What good is it, my brothers and sisters, if you say*
> *you have faith but do not have works?"*
> *James II:14—Faith without Works is Dead*

Thank you James for continually showing me daily God has a plan for us. Thank you for helping me to continue to be faithful in God as well as showing me opportunities to provide good works to "Naked Brothers and Sisters." I love you James!

Sunday, July 10, 2011 10:07 p.m. ~Nurse Mom

Welcome to the world James! Today, July 10, 2011, was your due date. I thought about this day yesterday over and over in my head. I knew you would be delivered early but had no clue you would be delivered two months early. I never expected you to be born a sick little baby either.

The day you were born was a very scary day for your dad and me. Luckily, we had lots of friends who were able to come to the hospital and visit and pray with us during this scary time. The last few months of my pregnancy I felt very sick and was put on bed rest by my doctors. As I lay in bed, all I could think about was how excited I would be when you were born and I got a chance to hold you. Little did I know it would take many, many weeks after your birth before I got a chance to hold you in my arms!

The nurses and RT reported you had a good day today. This morning a new, larger breathing tube was inserted in your throat and went down to the top of your lungs to help you breathe. You were put on a paralytic medicine this morning to paralyze you during the procedure. Throughout the procedure your vitals stayed stable and you did very well. Also, the RT told me this afternoon that the x-ray taken today shows improvement in the upper lope in your right lung. Praise God! Hopefully, the infection in your lung is getting better and we will be able to lower your ventilator rate again soon. Today, your rate went down to twenty-four from twenty-six after they inserted your larger tube. Also, I noticed today your oxygen is back to 21 percent, which is room air. This improvement came down from 25 percent. Your gas levels looked good as well today. What great "due date" statistics for you, my precious sweet baby James. Your vital signs remained very stable all day today and tonight as I sat in your room. The only thing that bothered me was the smell in your room. Your new medicine to help break up the mucus in your lungs smells like rotten eggs. When this medicine is distributed, it stinks up the entire room like someone has bad gas. The youth at church and I could have lots of fun with this new medicine you are taking. Imagine the looks we would get at church during a Sunday morning service if we leaked some of this smelly medicine out into the congregation and then proceeded to release the sound of a whoopee cushion. Oh, how much fun would it be to play this prank?

I know you were born on May 17 instead of July 10. Even though you are almost eight weeks old today, the previous weeks I still held onto your gestational age and continued the "count down" until your due date arrived. Today, your gestational age countdown came to an end for me as you were supposed to be born today. Even though most babies are never born on their actual due date, I still held onto this thought after you came early. So, with all of this said James, Happy Birthday!

Finally, tonight at 6:41 p.m. on July 10, 2011, I was able to hold you again in my arms. I waited an hour for the doctor to come back into the unit so I could hold you in my arms. While waiting, I thought about a mother laboring, waiting for the birth of her baby. I wasn't able to hold you tonight until the doctor came back to the floor, in case something went wrong. As soon as "Doc Humble" came into the room, he immediately apologized for making me wait. What a respectful thing to do. I quickly told him it was not a problem. "All I have is time and don't mind waiting," I said.

Everything went perfectly tonight as I held you in my arms and your vital signs didn't change a bit. In fact, your vital signs showed improvement while I held you safely. You slept the entire ninety minutes that I held you. As I held you James, I watched your heart beat and your little chest rise. I rubbed your leg and held onto your toes. I tickled your neck and watched you smile at me and play "possum" with your eyes, peeking at me to make sure I continued to rub your head. I held your little hands and counted your fingers and toes. I did all the things a mom would do when she holds her baby for the first time. Even though it has taken me almost eight weeks to hold you two times James, I will always cherish today. Today, your due date, I was able to hold you in my arms and smile as a new mother would do when she holds her baby for the first time. Today James, I was able to look at you in my arms and look past all your cords, ventilator, and scars on your tummy. As I held you tonight James, and looked at your face, I saw a healthy baby through my eyes. Things seemed normal and I smiled just as a new mom would do when her baby was born.

Even though today is not your birthday I will always remember our ninety minutes together. I will never forget my eight-pound, six-ounce little baby. When a baby is born they always weigh the baby. Yes, James! You were weighed tonight after I held you for the first time since birth. I got to see them weigh you. This was a first for me since you, your brother, and sister were born by C-sections and your daddy was always the one to see you guys be weighed. Blessings to you all!

Three Little Birds ~Nurse Mom
Tuesday, July 12, 2011 12:46 a.m.

"I rose up this morning and smiled up at the rising sun." I started my walk to the hospital this morning in my pink Sketchers, my "endurance outfit," and approached a busy intersection I needed to cross to get to the hospital. While I waited for the cars, transit buses, and ambulances to stop at the red light so I could sprint across Calhoun Street, I felt the warm sunshine on my face. I approached the MUSC Cancer Center. Birds chirped at me from the parking garage. The sound of the singing birds reminded me of a story J. J. told me a few weeks ago as we walked this same route together to see James. He told me a story about "three little birds."

On J. J.'s way to see James, early one morning, he noticed three little birds playing together. The three little birds seemed to follow J. J. frolicking with one another as he continued to walk the familiar path to the hospital. The three little birds would chirp, play with each other in the air, and then quickly return to the trees planted along the cemented sidewalk. These three birds seemed to be following J. J. and telling him a silent but joyful message with song. The song by Bob Marley sings like this:

"Don't worry about a thing. Cause every little thing, is gonna be all right.
Singing don't worry about a thing, Cause every little thing is gonna be all right!"

As I approached the MUSC Cancer Center on my right side I noticed the birds singing from trees that J. J. pointed out a few weeks ago. I continued to walk, feeling the rising sun on my face, and I saw faces of cancer patients exiting their cars for treatment. The valet attendants opened doors for the feeble as well as healthy patients. I thought about this powerful, silent, joyful message coming from God's creation: birds. Three little birds who sang, "Don't worry about a thing. Cause every little thing is gonna be all right."

How true is this message? Everything is going to be all right. I remember over a year ago my mom was diagnosed with stage three ovarian cancer. I spent time with her in the hospital in Norfolk, Virginia, and then in Elizabeth City, North Carolina. When she was able to go home after a week in the hospital recovering from an infection, I went home with her to help her with her treatments and her PICC line. When she lay sick in the hospital bed, her bald head and pale face sick with infection, I told my aunt I didn't know if my mom was going to make it. I also remember being terrified of hospitals. How was I going to stay with mom alone in a hospital and make sure she received the care she needed if I was afraid? When I was a child, five years old, I spent two weeks in Kings Daughters Children's Hospital in Norfolk, Virginia, and remember events from this unpleasant experience. I was going to have to pull up my "big girl pants" and face my fears of hospitals in order to take care of mom.

I was reminded by the "three little birds" today as I passed the MUSC Cancer Center to not worry about a thing. Cause everything is gonna be alright. How many times during the week or even during the day do we let our fears turn into worry? A sick parent struggling with cancer and then infection; a valet attendant fighting traffic to park cars; a daughter scared to enter a hospital alone due to a bad experience as a child; and even a mom living in Charleston patiently waiting for her baby's heart defect, enlarged liver, and fluid-filled lungs to heal. Life brings lots of fears and worries to us. Can you hear the "three little birds" singing a message to you?

Now, I am happy to report my Mom is cancer free and is in remission. I no longer have a fear of hospitals. Imagine that? My fear of hospitals is gone. I walk into the hospital now with a smile on my face saying good morning to the information desk receptionist. I smile and greet my new friend in the black scrubs that I see every day at least once, wheeling patients in and out of the hospital in wheelchairs and hospital beds. My quest in life is now to find out his name. I am happy to report to you all these three little birds reminded me today along my walk with the rising sun shining warmth on my face to not worry about a thing. Cause everything is gonna be alright.

Remember God is in control. Remind yourself this when you get sad about a challenge you are facing even if you find yourself crying. I was reminded a few days ago as I was visiting James with a pastor friend. God is in control and he is going to provide you with the help you need to make it through difficult times of worry and journeys. Even if you can't see the "three little birds" along your walk, open your ears and listen for their chirps and joyful songs. Blessings to you and "Don't worry!"

Purple Popsicles ~Nurse Mom
Wednesday, July 13, 2011 12:31 a.m.

"Have you been sucking on a purple popsicle," I asked James today. "Your lips are purple." No, James isn't able to eat grape popsicles yet but his lips do turn purple time to time and he gets a purple ring around his mouth. Having a purple popsicle today would be a great idea though as the hot, humid temperature in Charleston was 96 degrees not counting the humidity.

As I educate myself on congenital heart disease I now notice James shows signs of heart disease from time to time such as purple lips. I remember a nurse in the Unit telling J. J. and me a month ago, "Sometimes being intelligent and educated about the disease can be harder for a parent of a sick child rather than being ignorant." The comical nurse sat down with J. J. and me for over an hour one night educating us on James's condition and where we could research correct and accurate information on the Internet. I think I agree with Nurse "Comedy," as now I find myself asking questions concerning oxygen saturation, D-Sat (decreased oxygen saturation), oxygen perfusion and continuous positive airway pressure (CPAP) treatments. Ignorance can be a good thing from time to time. Now, if you like to snore at night (as my friend "Bubba the Bear" does) and stop breathing during your sleep, then these terms, at least the CPAP term, are not Greek to you. Yes, you are familiar with a CPAP machine as you enter the world of "Darth Vader" at night to sleep while you strap your mask onto your face to sleep. Hopefully soon, James will be able to receive CPAP treatment when he reaches a setting of 10 on the ventilator.

This morning I was visiting with James when he became restless. James is not a restless baby. He normally lies in bed, sleeps peacefully and gives you a smile from time to time. His morphine drip was reduced by half to .1 mL thirty minutes prior. That's when James started to get restless. "Of course it has got to be the morphine reduction," I thought. I walked out to find his nurse to let her know I thought something was going on with James. You know, since I am "Nurse Mom" now. I've been on the payroll for eight weeks, plus the eight, almost nine, years of prior experience with Frick and Frack. I know everything about medicine, congenital heart disease, lung functions, livers, and even restlessness now. I am a pro! I am getting my on-the-job training daily in the PCICU at MUSC and my degree from Wikipedia. Oh sorry, Nurse "Comedy," I forgot to mention my degree was also coming from Cove Point Foundation as well.

After leaving a few "presents" in his diapers, James began to D-Sat and his heart rate decreased. Here we go with the Greek words again. With this said, I will educate you on D-Sat and oxygen saturation. Oxygen saturation, or dissolved oxygen (DO), is a relative measure of the amount of oxygen that is dissolved or carried in a given medium. It can be measured with a dissolved oxygen probe such as an oxygen sensor or an optode in liquid media, usually water. In medicine, oxygen saturation refers to oxygenation, or when oxygen molecules (O_2) enter the tissues of the body. In this case, blood is oxygenated in the lungs, where oxygen molecules travel from the air and into the blood. Oxygen saturation, or O2 sats, measure the percentage of hemoglobin binding sites in the bloodstream occupied by oxygen. Thank you Wikipedia!

Oh, my friend "Mr. Worry" started to creep back into the room when James showed signs of D-Sat., especially since I noticed James was sucking on that darn purple popsicle again. Where are my three little birds? Why can't I hear them chirping and singing a joyful song this morning? Remember, we are not supposed to worry when life sends us trials. Gosh, now I am going to have to start taking my own advice and practice what I am preaching. "Don't worry about a thing, cause every little thing is going to be alright," I started to hum to myself in my best Bob Marley voice. The purple popsicle must have tasted good as I noticed James's face was purple all over. Thank heaven for "Nurse Calm" today. She handled the entire situation excellently and was so calm as she laid her hand on James's head to calm him down. She didn't complain once about all of the presents James delivered in his diaper for her this morning, especially since she wasn't even James's assigned nurse. "Nurse Calm" was filling in since, James's assigned nurse was delivering her own presents in the Employee Lounge.

As I send you a report tonight James is doing well. The purple popsicle stain went away soon and he was able to quickly recover from this morning's D-Sat (you know what that means now right?) and decided to stay calm the rest of the day. His ventilator was reduced to twenty and his feeds increased from sixteen to twenty mL today. Yeah! Praise God and he seems to be doing okay with the new settings. James's CO2 levels were elevated today at seventy-two but did decrease from seventy-eight yesterday. That is a venus gas. The gas levels were around 7.36 today and his blood pressure looked good at an average of 92/50. James's heart rate bounced around a little this morning but is staying around the 160s tonight. I am not sure about the urine output today, but I think James was about even around 6 p.m. I will find out tomorrow morning how today's total outcome ended. I hope these numbers help my analyzer friends out there. I haven't forgotten about you guys and girls and know you need numbers to stay informed.

Purple popsicles are delicious! We just don't want to wear them on our faces like James does sometimes. When we bring James home, J. J. has promised me a great big party and celebration at our house. If God decides we need to wait until December for James to come home, we will wait patiently. Remember, God is in control. All are welcomed to celebrate the safe delivery and arrival of James! I promise you even if it is in December we will all enjoy purple popsicles. We will have purple popsicles at the party and remember this journey, the trials, and how we handled it with grace and patience. Even if the weather is twenty-five degrees outside instead of ninety-six degrees, we will serve purple popsicles in celebration!

Blessings to you all as always! Thanks for reading and continuing to pray for James's healing of his lungs, edema, liver, and leaky valves in his heart.

Love Wins? ~Nurse Mom
Thursday, July 14, 2011 11:49 p.m.

Last night I realized I had not written a journal entry for the day to update you all. I had a friend from Greenville come to Charleston yesterday and spend last night with me at the Ronald McDonald House. I thought I would take a break from the reality of my life and have fun with my friend. Yes, I did have fun with her as she always makes me feel youthful. I thought, "If I didn't write a journal entry last night then somehow, maybe, I could take a step away from the reality of my life right now." Taking a step away worked for a day, but the reality came back all too quickly—just like it always does. How do you get away from your own reality? How about Calgon? Like the commercials, do you ask it to take you away?

The reality of my life is back now as I spent time with James tonight and my friend is gone. My youthfulness has waned and I am back to being a 35-year-old-blonde (again) lady with an adorable, sick baby. He is so cute and I just want to pick James up, hold him tight in my arms, and take care of him. But, the reality of my life is this: James is sick. Point blank, James is sick. Just when I think we are making progress as we "rode" a setting of twenty on the ventilator for the past two days, this morning we returned to twenty-eight due to his high carbon dioxide levels. James's liver is still enlarged and his lungs still look hazy. The dopamine medicine drip is off and his blood pressure is a tad bit lower, running around 62/40. There are so many things going on right now I can't even begin to start to tell you the numbers.

Nothing bad or uncommon I should say. There is nothing James does not continue to fight against and stay strong. Don't get me wrong, James is stable with a good heart rate, oxygen saturation, and blood gas. So please don't panic. I am just frustrated with the slow, small progress. I grow very discouraged when we seem to move backward with things such as the dirty nine-letter-word infection as well as increasing the ventilator settings when I thought everything was okay.

I am tired. I feel very beat up again. I miss J. J. He and I have not been able to spend much time alone together in a while and I really miss him. I miss his laugh, his hug, and his assurance that everything is going to be okay. He has been in training all week for work and had to leave around noon last Sunday to head to the training. He normally stays with me Sunday nights and gets up around 4 a.m. on Monday morning to head straight to work. J. J. is my rock and always seems to make things better even if he has to do something silly to make me laugh.

I know I need to remain strong and keep hanging in there for James. When I am in his room with him at the hospital he knows I am with him. When I am standing behind him and start talking to him he tries his best to turn his head around to see me. This breaks my heart. It absolutely breaks my heart because I know James knows I am there with him rubbing his head, holding his hand, and even watching his breathing. When he is awake I will not leave him alone until he goes back to sleep. James is so sick yet he continues to fight. He continues to fight day after day after day.

I find myself starting to feel anger and coldness. I get very angry with the current sickness and just want to fix it. I want to fix James. Being a mother and standing by day after day after day, watching your sick baby, is absolute torture on earth. I say torture on earth because I just finished reading Rob Bell's new book, *Love Wins: A Book About Heaven, Hell, and the Fate of Every Person Who Ever Lived*. Bell talks about the dark, hot place being on Earth and how people experience their own Hades on Earth at times. I feel like I am experiencing Hades on Earth as I stand by and watch James in the hospital. I feel like this must be Hades. I feel helpless and can do nothing, absolutely nothing, to make James better. A mom is supposed to help take care of her sick baby and make him better. There is nothing I can do to make James better but wait, and wait, and wait. Did I mention pray? Tonight I feel too tired to even pray. God help me and please forgive me.

I anger myself wondering, "why me?" I grow cold trying to put up a wall to block my sad and scared emotions. I cry all morning when I hear James has a blood clot in his neck on his right side. I watched his neck swell within a ten-minute span last Wednesday morning and knew something was wrong. All I could do was stand next to James and cry as I watched his little eyes look at me and say, "Help me Mom; help me."

So Rob Bell, I have a question for you? In your book you talk about heaven, Hades, and the fate of every person who ever lived. I believe in heaven and look forward to the day I see it. I feel like some days I am in hades, and my fate right now seems pretty dark as we battle James's heart defect, enlarged liver, fluid-filled lungs and now a blood clot in his neck on his right side. You say in your book love wins. I believe in love because right now I am so dependent on J. J., the love of my life, but he can't be with me every day. I try to love everybody, even loud, rowdy six graders in Youth Group, who seem to be my favorite. All I ever wanted to do in life is love, love, and love everybody in the world. So Rob Bell, if love wins in the end like you say in your book, why in the world don't I feel like it does? I don't feel like love is winning right now. Look at me.

Help me God. I need you to remind me I am going to be okay. Give me strength like I talk about to others. Give me the patience I preach about often. Answer my prayers even when I am too tired to pray. I know you are in control and I know you have a plan. Show me how love wins in the end, amen.

Keep It Together ~Dad
Saturday, July 16, 2011 1:12 p.m.

"Success consists of going from failure to failure without loss of enthusiasm." James must know something about Winston Churchill that his mother and I do not. The hits just keep coming and he keeps overcoming them with an increase in confidence. Jacqueline and I die a little more with each setback. He has overcome so much in his short life. It's hard to fathom a child so small being challenged on a daily basis with the likes of blood clots, pneumonia, MRSA, heart failure, liver failure, kidney failure, and lung failure, yet, here he is still alive and breathing. That's not to say there isn't a great deal of assistance, but he's still breathing. We heard today he might have another infection, but he was able to stabilize his temperature without any help. The doctors put him back on the antibiotic as a precaution. So far today his numbers look good and his first culture test for bacteria was negative. It might take forty-eight hours for the infection to appear. Or, we're hoping he may have taken care of this one on his own. At this point we don't really know. What we do know is James has overcome a very difficult surgery on his heart, two infections, and a blood clot. His kidneys have recovered, his liver appears to be improving (though it still has a ways to go), his lungs appear to have improved, and his tricuspid valve seems better now than it was. It is hard to believe we are almost nine weeks into this. It feels like so much longer. In nearly sixty days James has overcome all of this with the help of doctors, nurses, family, church family, co-workers, a community of Christ—most of whom we don't even know personally—therapists, prayer warriors, some very special stuffed animals, and one cricket named Scott. So when they told me today he might have another infection but they're not sure, I felt a little odd whistling my prayer on the way home. I turned it over to God to keep from losing my mind. I succumbed to the fact that there will be ups and downs and it is all in God's hands. The truth is none of us are in control, which is probably a very good thing. God showed me James's strength. He is stronger than I think he is and these doctors can only go as far as James and God will allow them to go. Indeed James has been able to achieve and overcome. He accomplishes all things through Christ who strengthens him.

So when thinking about James's accomplishments, I thought about something bigger for him than his small domicile inside the PCICU. I spoke with one of my best friends from high school. He and his family now know my family and me. His kids know my kids. Sadly, an event such as this should not be the reason we've reconnected, but thankfully, he and his wife have visited twice. Last weekend our kids played in the ocean and it was an awesome time. It wouldn't have happened if not for James. On our way back to the car my roommate said to me it made him sad to know it took something like this to get us together after all these years. I told him he was right. The most special thing to me however, was that we could spend years apart yet come back together like we hadn't missed a beat. You don't find friends like these guys very often.

I have done very little to try and maintain these relationships. I get so wrapped up in my own self-centered little world. One of our friends talked about how our church came together, united in prayer, over James. Wow, what a statement. You guys at St. Giles have no idea how much we miss you. I really look forward to the day when I can catch up with you all, give your kids a hard time, play a little basketball, watch the little ones climb the trees in front of the sanctuary and the brick wall to the prayer garden. I look forward to seeing the moms chase the kids, trying to get them from the sanctuary to the car so they can go eat lunch or get home in time for the game. I look forward to hearing about Clemson, South Carolina, Auburn (Tim), Georgia, as well as talking about how bad my Wolfpack are doing and how good my Ducks are. I'm hoping I don't miss all of this fun this fall! I have seen my co-workers get behind me and give selflessly of their time so that I can find balance between work and home. All of these changes are good changes. All of these changes make us better Christians. We're doing more of what we're supposed to be doing.

I guess the change I can speak to the most is within me. I've always been a little cocky. I don't know if it's a defense mechanism to cover up insecurity or what but it's true. I'm a little cocky. But there is nothing, and I mean nothing, that will put you on your knees in prayer faster than what we're going through right now. There is nothing that will get you to pray harder, longer, more sincerely, more heart-felt. Sometimes the tears just flow. Before, I would have covered my face and maybe left the room before I let anybody see the tears. I would have viewed it as a sign of weakness that should never be seen. I have been humbled to the point where I really don't care who sees. I realize that everyone understands this hurt. Nobody sees this as a sign of weakness but rather a sign of love that brings out their kindness and compassion. My second flaw is that I'm also a little too self-centered. Whenever someone tells me a story, I love to recollect a story from my past that relates to their's. I also like to focus on my problems and not bother with everyone else's. This experience has shown that I need to be more giving of myself to others. I need to pay attention to others because you just don't know what is going on in the person's life next to you. This week, on Thursday afternoon, one of the instructors at the banker's school came in and asked the lady in front of me to step outside. The lady got up and walked out. I knew it was something bad when the instructor grabbed up the lady's books and belongings. In one action, it let us all know she wasn't coming back. This wasn't just a personal call from a co-worker. While she didn't say what happened, I knew it couldn't be good. It turns out her grandmother passed away. Oh, I thought, that's not so bad. She was probably in her mid 30s. It was time for her grandmother to go. Only I would have been wrong. She lived with her grandmother and helped take care of her. She called her grandmother that morning to make sure everything was okay. She was nervous about leaving her grandmother for a week for fear that something might happen, but realized this school was a big deal that shouldn't be passed up. So she took the opportunity. On Thursday her grandmother passed. I've heard that her reaction was heartbreaking. The old me, before my personal event with James, would have been to possibly say a little prayer and do very little else. What a jerk! But isn't that what most of us would do? I don't really know her. "It's none of my business," I would have thought. The problem with that is this: being kind to people is my business. The kind thing would be to get involved and to send a simple card that lets her know she's not alone, that everybody hurts, and that it will be okay in time. The kind thing would be to let her know that somebody she doesn't even know was impacted by this and cared enough to send a small note saying as much. This is what the new me is going to do. I wouldn't have done this if not for James. I will never be able to pay back all the kindness that people have shown me throughout the past nine weeks. However, I can try to listen to the lessons I'm learning and pay these kindnesses forward.

So I take the lessons as they come and appreciate the things James is accomplishing. I look back over the last sixty days at the impact he's made. I know that my kindness fails in comparison. The good news is that I'm now humble enough to be okay with that. It's not a competition. Rather, it's confirmation that we are all part of God's plan. James is a huge part. Jacqueline is a huge part. Even I, yes cocky, self-centered, flawed me, get to be a part of God's plan. I know two things to be true. One, God has richly blessed my family and me. Two, "to whom much is given, much is expected." I know I've got to do better. I know I can do better. How about you?

Peace to you all!

Venti Caramel Macchiato ~Nurse Mom
Monday, July 18, 2011 10:30 a.m.

As I walked into the PCICU Unit this morning around 7:45 a.m. I was greeted with amazing smiles. Nurse "Full of Joy" seemed surprised to see me so early since I like my sleep and 7:45 is a very unusual time for me to be up and going. It was nice to be greeted this Monday morning by Nurse "Full of Joy." She has an amazing smile that lights up a groggy, humid, Monday morning. I noticed another one of my favorite nurses sitting behind the nurses' station smiling as well holding a white coffee cup with green writing. I thought, "I wonder if "Nurse Newlywed" is drinking a Venti or Grande from Starbucks this morning?" A 20-oz Venti Caramel Macchiato sounds perfect, especially for a Monday morning. Starting my Monday off with freshly steamed milk with vanilla-flavored syrup, marked with espresso and finished with caramel sauce sounds yummy! This might be exactly what I need to start the week. Then I realized, "I can't have caffeine." Darn! Remember, I am trying to cut my caffeine addiction so James's "liquid antibiotics," or breast milk, will stay healthy and caffeine-free as to not increase his heart rate.

Good morning friends and family! I am back. Did you miss hearing from me this weekend? I completely stepped away from the reality of having a sick child this weekend. I didn't check emails. I didn't return phone calls. I didn't answer my phone. I didn't log onto the CaringBridge website the entire weekend. I needed a break from my very own reality. If you remember from last week I was feeling beaten up and too tired to even pray. I was watching the clock all day Friday and waiting patiently for J. J. to arrive in Charleston. I knew I wasn't able to take on anymore, or shall I say anything else, for the day and I knew I desperately needed to spend time with J. J. alone. It is amazing to me that a person can feel so beaten up and not have the strength to continue. I can't believe I felt so defeated last Friday. I told myself I knew I was a strong person, but my 20-oz. Venti Caramel Macchiato was empty. I needed a refill. I needed a refill soon and quick. Last Friday was like we used to say twenty years ago at the full-service Exxon stations to the gas attendants, "fill her up."

When J. J. arrived Friday evening he was very disappointed to find me asleep in my room. "I thought you were excited to see me and were waiting on me to get here. How can you be sleeping and excited to see me," J. J. questioned. I quickly discovered J. J. was upset and angry at me because I was sleeping. He thought I wasn't excited to see him. I responded with groggy eyes to his questioning with sobs and tears. Depression set in pretty fast last Thursday. Friday was even worse. All I could do to manage making it on Friday while waiting for him to arrive was to sleep. I don't drink alcohol. I don't exercise (which I should) and I don't scream. Remember, a few weeks ago I admitted to you all sleep is my coping mechanism for stress and depression. Some of us drink alcohol, some of us exercise, some of us eat, some of us shop, some of us pray, some of us scream, some sleep. The list goes on and on. You know the list. We all cope differently with stress. I sleep.

J. J. was quick to understand and realized fairly soon he needed to intervene. J. J.'s reaction was perfect! He knew we both needed to spend quality time together and relax. We needed to remember and experience how much we each loved one another and step away from the reality of James's sickness. This is exactly what we did over the weekend. We found ourselves sitting on the beach Saturday watching the waves crash along the shore. We visited the local cupcake store and enjoyed dinner at a downtown delicious restaurant named S.N.O.B. This was a great recommendation by the way, "green analyzer" friend. We even slept in.

J. J. and I realized we still needed to take time for each other this past weekend and enjoy ourselves, even if James was sick and Frick and Frack were, well you know, Frick and Frack. They have been at "Aunt Debbie Camp" since last Sunday and probably haven't even missed us. J. J. and I realized we needed to constantly nourish our relationship as well. It is sad to say a sickness prompted this need of husband and wife nourishment. We had one of the best weekends enjoying each other in our eleven years of marriage as well as five years of dating prior. We filled each other's 20-oz. Venti Caramel Macchiato.

So, as I walked into the Unit this morning greeted with smiles, visions of Caramel Macchiato helped remind me of the refreshing, relaxing weekend. When I walked into the Unit I saw Mr. James sleeping peacefully on his tummy with his little legs tucked up close to his belly. What an amazing site. To see a baby sleeping peacefully, especially a baby as sick as James, is remarkable. His heart rate is starting to decrease again and come back down around the 170s today. This weekend his heart rate increased over the weekend to the 190s. Remember, we like to see his heart rate around the low 150s. Also, James blood pressure looked better this morning as his blood pressure had dropped as well over the weekend and he was placed back on Dopamine medicine this weekend. We had a little scare last Friday thinking James was starting to get another infection. He started running a fever around 101 during the night and his heart rate and oxygen saturation increased around the high 90s. The doctors gave James more antibiotics at the threat of another infection. As of this morning, most of the cultures (forty-eight hours running) are showing a negative growth of infection. His lungs still show a positive culture for growth though, with the same infection as weeks before. It is thought this bacteria is colonized and not growing. Especially since his right lung still looks collapsed and hazy in the daily x-rays. But, the good news is James has been on his belly for two days now and seems to be loving it. Putting a heart patient on their belly is a great step. It helps take the pressure off of the lungs from the heart.

We are hoping and praying James's lungs will improve with this step. The ventilator machine and stats looked great last night as the pressures from the lungs were running around the low twenties and Mr. James was able to start breathing on his own again at the twenty-eight breaths per minute setting. We saw lots of pink lines last night for breaths for James. We are not sure about the blood clot that appeared last Wednesday in the right side of his neck. In order to do another ultrasound the tech would need to turn James over on his back. Since James is doing so well on his tummy the ultrasound of his neck may be delayed and the Heparin medicine drip may continue to help with clots. James's 20-oz. Venti Caramel Macchiato is getting filled this morning with "tummy time."

Today is a new day. Today is Monday and J. J. is at work again. I am in Charleston and Frick and Frack will return tomorrow to Charleston from "Aunt Debbie Camp." James is enjoying "tummy time" and seems to be having an okay day so far. Starbucks is booming with business at the hospital coffee shop and Nurse Full of Joy is still smiling while "Nurse Newlywed" continues to sip on her coffee and take care of the many babies in the Unit. My empty cup has been refilled with an amazing weekend with my wonderful husband. I hope you all will take the time this week to fill your cups, with either a Venti 20-oz. or Grande 16-oz. Even if you need to take a small amount, and refill your cup, please do. Please do not get to the point as I was last Friday: sleeping, coping before I took the necessary time to "fill myself up." God doesn't intend for us to be this way. God richly blesses us with whatever we need. So, go in peace knowing this is what God wants us to do. "Fill her up," even if it takes a Venti Caramel Macchiato. Blessings to you all for a wonderful week full of strength!

Things are Looking Up ~Nurse Mom
Thursday, July 21, 2011 11:22 p.m.

Tonight's post brings good news to you all. James is having a good week and his ventilator setting is now down to sixteen. Yeah!

Hopefully, we will be able to continue to reduce his ventilator setting and get off of this machine soon. Taking James off the ventilator will be a huge step for us. His lungs seem to be clearing up and the x-rays from earlier in the week look better. The right upper-lobe in James's lung doesn't look as hazy or collapsed as before. Within the past twenty-four hours James has been taken off two medicines. He is off fenoldopam and dopamine. These medicines helped his heart and blood pressure. Soon the doctors will try to wean the Bumex as well. When I left tonight James's blood pressure was around the 70s/40s and was looking good without the medicine. His heart rate has also decreased and is running in the 170s. Our goal for his heart rate is in the low 150s but we will take the 170s for now. We hope to reduce his Morphine but this must be done very slowly because of the side effects. We need James's lungs to continue to improve and help wean him off of the ventilator. We need James's liver to improve and his bilirubin levels to continue to drop. The last time I asked James's bilirubin levels they were slightly under ten. This number has been as high as twenty before so this is a step in the right direction. Please continue praying for good days for James and steady improvement. Things seem to be looking up for us. Thanks be to God!

Searching for the Signal ~Nurse Mom
Friday, July 22, 2011 2:59 p.m.

As I looked over the flyer for the Montreat Youth Conference (MYC) theme this week, "Searching for the Signal," I began to ponder the selected theme. Every year during the summer for a week the youth of our church go to Montreat, NC, for a week of inspiration, empowerment, and community. The youth and four adult leaders from St. Giles are currently at Montreat this week "Searching for the Signal." What a deep topic. What does this topic mean to the youth, the leaders? J. J. and I drove up to Montreat Wednesday evening for a surprise visit and worshipped with the Montreaters. What does this theme mean to me, I thought while visiting with the youth at the back home meeting in Montreat. The description for the 2011 MYC flyer reads as follows:

"Gathered on this journey, we aspire to provide and model faithful ways to live out the call God has for each of us. Although the path ahead may seem filled with uncertainty, we will reveal a bearing for the journey. Leaving as so journeying disciples of Christ, young people will be empowered to spread a hopeful message by word and deed."

The words uncertainty, bearing, and sojourning mentioned above speak to me in a silent way. Since I left Montreat Wednesday night I have been racking my brain with these words. I have been thinking about the signals God sends me, J. J. and the youth. I ponder about the signals I am supposed to be getting along this journey with James. I wonder if I am missing any important signals or signs sent to me. How nice would it be if God would just send us an email or text message with instructions on what he wants us to do. Can you hear it? My cell phone is beeping, notifying me I have a new text message. It's from God. "How r u doing today? Cont. 2 sty strong. I have a plan. Rmbr to pray daily. love u. God." Did you see the new email in your inbox today from God marked "urgent message?" Maybe it went like this: "Dear Faithful Servant, please remember to attend worship this Sunday morning at 10:30 even if you are tired. Also, when the offering plate comes around don't forget to tithe ten percent, even if you haven't paid your electric bill yet. Please respond immediately with prayer and let me know you received this email." It would be nice to have specific, written instructions from God through text and email. How nice and convenient it would be to receive specific signals from God with no searching.

Going back to the three words that race through my brain from the Montreat theme I think of uncertainty first. My life is extremely uncertain right now. Walking into James's room at the PCICU every day brings a new challenge and uncertain response to treatment. Doc Hope talked to me today and let me know he is uncertain of the treatment for James. There is talk of open-heart surgery for James to stitch the leaking valves, but the risk is extremely high. We continue to hope and pray James will not need the surgery this soon and will be able to improve without the help of a high-risk surgery, including the use of a heart and lung bypass machine. Everything seems to be improving; very slowly, but improving. The bilirubin level was down to 8.2 this morning, the lowest it has been. Praise God! Doc Hope knows how frustrating this situation is for J. J. and me but also feels the same way as James's doctor. Doc Hope wants to help heal and fix James quickly.

The word patience seems to continue to play over and over in my head like a broken record on a record player. The beginning of the week things were moving very fast with positive changes on the ventilator and Doc Hope was pushing James to better health. This morning the right lobe in James's lung has collapsed again so we will probably continue to slow down and not push James as fast. Doc Hope is absolutely amazing and is a great reminder to me that doctors are human. His honesty and humbling attitude reminds me that we put doctors on pedestals sometimes and think they should always have all the answers. When things go wrong we want to quickly blame the doctors or nurses. In the end, God is in control and the doctors and nurses are placed here on Earth to work God's magic. Doctors and nurses are human like us. As my dad always says, "they put their pants on the same way we put our pants on." Not being able to plan my weeks where I will be or what I will be doing brings uncertainty to my life.

I think all the time about the way people act, especially when times become tough. I go back and remember the story of the man, a dad, who stayed in the Ronald McDonald House alone. His baby girl had heart surgery and his wife left him to go get drunk. She couldn't take the pressure of having a sick baby with yet another surgery. I remember seeing this dad walking around the House as well as the hospital all alone. My heart ached for him having to handle the situation by himself. His daughter coded three times and had to have her heart shocked to restart all in the same day. The amazing truth was how he handled the situation all by himself and conducted himself in a very strong manner. The day of joy for him was actually Father's Day when he was able to take his daughter home from the hospital. He was carrying his daughter around the house showing her off to everyone and getting ready to head home, a single dad, on Father's Day. The bearing in which he handled himself as well as his daughter's situation was with grace. I pray to God and ask him to continue to give me a bearing of grace, hope, and love as well.

The final word sojourning keeps haunting me silently in my head the most. I wasn't quite sure what this word, sojourning meant until I looked it up on the Internet. According to the Farlex online free dictionary, sojourning means to reside temporarily, a temporary stay, a brief period of residence. "Oh my heavens," I thought as I discovered the meaning of this word, sojourning. I have been thinking over and over in my head for the past few weeks about my temporary home-away-from-home residence. I wonder if I am doing the right thing by staying in Charleston. I wonder if our family should move to Charleston. I wonder if I should rent a house. Where should J. J. and I live to be able to make this journey doable and possible. Frack tells me on the phone early this week "I want to go home Mom." I had to think quickly and ask myself about my "home." What home is she talking about? Our home in Easley or our home-away-from-home in Charleston. She was talking about her home in Easley. Charleston is her sojourn, a temporary residence. Charleston MUSC is James's sojourn, his temporary stay, a brief residence.

As I close today's blog with positive news and report on James's slow progress, I want to remind you to continue to "Search for the Signal." Continue searching for the signals even on days when words continue to silently haunt your mind for meaning and you are waiting by your cell phone for God to text you his plan. Remember to open your Bibles and read the word of God. As I was reminded last Wednesday night in Montreat by words from the theme, discipline draws you closer to the signals from God. The discipline of reading scripture as well as prayer draws you closer to God and his signals. I think we have the prayer part down, as I have been begging you all to pray, especially for pee. After I talked to Doc Hope today and walked home from the hospital listening to my three little birds sing, I wondered about James's next step. All of a sudden I heard a loud beep. Yes, it was a new text message. Is it God? Is God sending me a text message about James's condition? Is God telling me about my sojourn or bearing? I opened my text message instantly to read my signal. "Slow down, calm down, don't worry, don't hurry, trust the process," said the text. It was a quote from author Alexandra Stoddard. Of all times, a youth from church sent me this message. Wow! God does send signals to us through text messages. God uses his angels on earth to text us when needed.

Blessings to you and wishes for success this week while you are searching for the signal. Stay quiet, rest, and be at peace in order to hear your signals.

CHAPTER 13

Home-Away-From-Home

A bone to the dog is not charity. Charity is the bone shared with
the dog when you are just as hungry as the dog. Jack London

Home Sweet Home ~Nurse Mom
Saturday, July 23, 2011 11:50 p.m.

I am home tonight in Easley. Nurse Mom is taking a few days off from Charleston and resting at home. Yeah! I decided to drive home today and spend a few days with Frick and Frack. After Frack told me last week she wanted to go home I knew I needed to head west, drive the three-and-a-half hour drive and come spend a few days at home with them. It is hard to believe I have been in Charleston with James more than nine weeks now. Wow! Does it seem that long to you all? J. J. is in Charleston this weekend watching James along with his mom, Barbara. As I left the hospital this afternoon I told them to keep a very close eye on my baby since it was very hard for me to leave. Don't ask me how many times I have already called J. J. today to find out how my baby is doing. The answer is quite embarrassing. Even though James is sick and in MUSC Hospital, he is not my only baby. Frick and Frack, even though they are seven and eight years old, they need me as well. I have to stop myself at times and remember that I have three children. Even though James needs me so do Frick and Frack

As I type, Frick and Frack are snuggling while sleeping in my bed and I am running the dishwasher. Yes, I still know how to run a dishwasher even though I haven't cooked in four months. Can you please contact Martha Stewart and ask her to give me a few cooking lessons so I can polish up on my cooking skills? I know, I know, I am such a softy by letting Frick and Frack sleep with me in my bed tonight. I thought they earned the right to sleep with their Mama. Frack wasn't happy because she was stuck on J. J.'s side and Frick got the middle of the bed tonight. "Why can't I sleep in the middle Mom," Frack asked. "Remember Mom, my stomach hurts and I may get dehydrated again like last time I slept in your bed. I really need to sleep in the middle tonight Mom," pleaded Frack. Dehydrated? I don't remember her getting dehydrated. How do you reckon I explained the sleeping selection arrangements tonight? Especially since Frack is "always" right and now her stomach hurts and she may get "dehydrated' if I don't let her sleep in the middle. If you don't believe me about Frack "always" being right, just ask Mrs. Wooten, her first-grade teacher last year. (Side note: Jennifer (Wooten), I loved the "Always Right" award Frack received last year at school. What a laugh). Even though at times I feel like I am losing my mind with the questions of an always right seven year old, I got smart. I decided a while ago that Frick gets picked for special situations on odd days and Frack is picked on even days. For example, today is July 23, an odd day of the month, so Frick gets picked for special privileges like sleeping in the middle of the bed with Mama. Now, you may be thinking that is a lucky pick, but when it comes time to say the blessing or feed the cat and I don't have a volunteer guess what I say? What is the date of today? Is today an even or odd day? Today is an odd day so Frick you are the lucky camper. Now, go feed the cat, or say the blessing, or like tonight, you can sleep in the middle of the bed. This is a wise trick my friends. Please feel free to borrow my trick when needed, especially if you have a Frick and Frack of your own at home who think life isn't fair and argue over who sleeps in the middle or who gets to push the buttons on the elevator at the hospital. Did you ever want to push the buttons on the elevator at the hospital when you were little? I don't think I did, but remember, I hated hospitals.

Today was a steady day for James and he looked fantastic. I was able to hold him today for almost two hours. Thanks be to God. James LOVES to be held. His heart rate decreased to the low 160s while I was holding him. This is great news! Also, when the R.T. handed James to me to hold, she handed him to me without a blanket. For the first time I was able to hold him and feel his skin. We placed a blanket over his little body to keep him warm, but I was able to feel his skin with my arms and hands while I held him. If you have noticed, I changed the photo on this blog tonight from a picture from today while I was holding James. By the way, "Nurse Picturesque" took this shot for us today. Good call Nurse Picturesque on placing it on the blog. I realized when you said we needed to put it on our blog today you had found us online. Have you figured out who is who, with all of our nicknames we give you, the caregivers, doctors, and nurses of James? Now we need a picture of you on here. :)

J. J. wasn't ready to hold James today and wanted to wait another day to hold him. We have to be very, very careful when we hold James because of his breathing tube. At times, it is quite nerve-racking when he is moved from the bed to our arms because we have to not pull the breathing tube out of his mouth. The R.T. that works magic on James's lungs was working today so I felt very comfortable with her handing James to us. "R.T. Magic" has done an amazing job on James and hopefully will be able to reopen his collapsed right upper-lobe on his lung again. No pressure "R.T. Magic." No pressure. We do need to get James off the ventilator soon and will need his lungs to function fully. His ventilator setting is still on sixteen, which we are thrilled with but would be ecstatic to see it lower and have James breathing on his own. Maybe we need to change the prayer of pee to the prayer of breaths. We still need pee, though, to reduce the edema hanging around James's waist and his enlarged liver.

It is a good feeling to be home tonight. As I stand in my own bathroom I realize my room at my home-away-from-home is smaller than my bathroom at home. I am not sure what that says about us having a bathroom that large or what that says about us living in a room so small in Charleston. Today when I left Charleston I noticed the two twin beds pushed together to make a king-size-bed took up almost half of the room. Wow! I am going to enjoy my own hair dryer, large bathroom, king-size-bed filled with Frick and Frack, and yes dishwasher, for the next few days. Oh how sweet it is to be home. Home sweet home!

Thank you God for giving us all James. Thank you for giving me Frick and Frack and reminding me of my small blessing that I take for granted everyday: dishwasher, bathroom, hairdryer, and bed without a hole running down the middle (two twin-size-beds pushed together). Thanks be to God! Hope your weekend is going well. I will see my St. Giles friends tomorrow at worship.

Sleep Inn ~Dad
Sunday, July 24, 2011 6:25 a.m.

I love the new photograph Jacqueline chose for the blog. I have always loved her smile. And let's be honest, her smile doesn't get much bigger than it was yesterday when she held James! Also, I loved her entry this morning. I couldn't help but get a little perspective on Frick and Frack. I'll bet they were in hog heaven yesterday having their mom home and to themselves.

Speaking of moms, I spent yesterday with my mom. We hung out with James in his room for a couple of hours. Mom was able to hold James for the first time. A funny thing happened. Her smile was almost as radiant as Jacqueline's was when she got to hold him. Mothers being able to hold a child is a Christmas-morning-type gift from God. There are certain presents you get on Christmas morning like soap-on-a-rope. You politely say thank you and move on to the next gift. Then there is the Christmas morning you wake up and the new bike is under the tree or the new Oregon Duck football jersey. A mother holding her baby is like getting the new bike, or that new football jersey. Only in James's case, I think it was more like getting that new BMW under the tree. It was a rich moment in time and you don't know how relieved I am that Jacqueline got this moment yesterday because now I don't have to buy her a BMW for Christmas!

So, here my mom is holding James with a smile as big as I've ever seen on her face. I look up at his numbers and they are almost as beautiful as the smile. The heart rate has come down to 152. That's great! The blood pressure is 78/36. That's great! His CO2 level is around forty-one percent. That's also great! I look at the ventilator rate of sixteen and think about how far we've come. The top number measures fluid pressures at the top of his lungs. It used to stay around 30-35 and sometimes bounce up over forty. Now, it stays around 19-23 and sometimes bounces up to twenty-seven. Lower pressures are a wonderful thing. I look at the tower (no longer towers) of medicine behind his bed. James is down to three medications. He is on Milrinone to help his heart squeeze, Bumex to help his kidneys, and Morphine for pain. He is down to .2 ccs per hour on the morphine. We are almost off that as well. I look at this child and reflect back to those first hours in Charleston. Here was this six pound baby with fourteen, yes fourteen different tubes running into or out of him. Now I look at him and see a pic line on each arm, a breathing tube, and a feeding tube. That's it. His legs and his body are tube free. Admittedly, he still has scabs where they were removed, not to mention the scab from his first surgery. Believe it or not, I think they're beautiful. The scabs remind me of how far we've come, and all we have been through to get to this point. I'm reminded that chicks dig scars! I sure hope so for James's sake!

My mother held her grandson as I stood by keeping guard. It occurred to me this is special. I soaked it up for a few hours until hunger took over. We waited for the RN and RT to return and help James back into his bed. They put him on his belly and he slept like a rock. Bless his heart; he couldn't keep his eyes open.

Mom and I went to dinner last night and I had pork tenderloin and an ice-cold beer. Beer is a pretty rare indulgence for me, but I must admit, everything tasted a little sweeter last night! Mom and I talked and laughed, and had a nice little toast to James. That was it for the toast: cheers! It was nothing more, nothing less. That was all that needed to be said. We enjoyed our meal and shared one of the most, if not the most, delicious desserts I've ever had. Afterward, we went back to the Ronald McDonald House, packed a change of clothes, and headed back to the hospital to see James one more time. James looked beautiful and peaceful. His heart rate was 152, blood pressure 69/32 and CO2 look good. His ventilator settings looked the same.

Doc Optimistic came in to talk with me about James and answer any questions I might have. He and Doc Heart met earlier in the day to discuss James. They don't know what to do with him at this point. He has made a strong comeback and then has kind of leveled off at the end of the week. It's a constant reminder that he still has a long way to go. He's still pretty sick. We still need him to get better. We need his improvement to continue moving forward. Doc Optimistic and I discuss different surgery options and he reminds me that it could come as soon as a couple of weeks. He reminds me that it's extremely high-risk but that it all depends on James. As long as he can continue to improve on his own, they will allow it.

We want to be patient and allow him time to be as well as he can on his own. In Doc Optimistic's words, we don't know how strong James can be. We were interrupted with that infection last time. We have yet to see how far he can go. We need to give him every opportunity to achieve. I start to feel the pressure of the situation again. Then Doc says, "But just look at him now. Look at how much better he is. He is in a much better place now than he was." I look at James. I look at the numbers. I look at the equipment surrounding his bed. I look at the three remaining medicine bags. We have gone from fourteen tubes to four. We have gone from more medicines than I could count coming at him harder and faster than I could keep up with, to three medicines slowly entering his body to help him. I looked at him breathing on his own over top of the vent and thought to myself, none of us know how strong this little man is. None of us know what is ahead for him. But I know this: James is awfully determined to live for some reason. Or should I say, God is awfully determined for him to live for some reason, because he shouldn't be here. Yet here he is. He's beautiful.

My mom hugged me and I hung on to her just a little bit longer than usual. It was an enchanted moment, a happy moment. I thought about Frick and Frack and how they must feel to have their Mom home. I had a feeling that they would probably be sleeping with their Mother tonight. So when my Mom asked me at dinner if I wanted to pack a bag and stay with her at the Sleep Inn, how could I resist. So for the first time in a long time, I slept through the night. I woke up feeling refreshed and energized. I felt rested, better, stronger. I'm willing to bet Frick and Frack do too.

So my advice to sleep in. Take a nap. Enjoy some quiet time where you can rest. Find a way if at all possible to leave your worries behind and find peace. Rejoice in the many blessings that have come your way and try to think about those instead of all your worries or problems that need fixing. Let the grass grow another day. Leave the dishes in the sink one time. Spend a little time lying out by a pool or find a nice hammock. Watch a baseball game through the back of your eyelids! Find some time to relax. My second piece of advice: call your mother. Ask her how she's doing and tell her you love her. For most of us, when we were little, she was the first one we went running to when we were hurting. And if I've learned anything through this, it's that we all hurt sometimes. Even mothers! So what have we done to pay them back for all those times we went running with scratched knees for Neosporin and Band-Aids? How many tubes of cortisone cream did your mom rub in during your lifetime? Call your mother and tell her thank you, and if time permits, stay overnight. Instead of getting up in the morning in a hurry to get things done "sleep inn."

Searching For The Signal" Part II ~Nurse Mom
Tuesday, July 26, 2011 3:46 a.m.

As I arrived in Charleston tonight around 11, I realized I was sojourning back to my home-away-from-home still "searching for my signal." When I arrived at MUSC the unit was closed for a surgery case and I was not able to visit. The little voice in my head told me to drive my van back to the Ronald McDonald House, unpack and then drive back later to visit James once the unit re-opened. I wasn't about to go another day without seeing James even if I had to come back to the hospital later in the night to visit.

Around 12:15 a.m. I made it back to the Unit and found James wide-awake waiting on me. What a wonderful welcome to come back and see my sweet precious baby. The caregivers hugged me tonight upon my return. "Nurse Paparazzi" greeted me in James's brightly lit room No. 8 when I arrived. They said, "James, your mom is here." Nurse Paparazzi was the first caregiver in the PCICU at MUSC to discover our blog. She is hot on my trail, a faithful blog reader and is actively seeking out the connections in the blog between the secret identities and real names of those mentioned. She enjoys a mystery but likes the challenge of figuring out who is who. She questions me about the identity of Doc Hope and Doc Optimistic hoping to get a clue or confirmation from me concerning their true identity. My lips are sealed!

Nurse Paparazzi and I talked for several minutes tonight about the latest happenings while I rubbed James's head. He watched me intently with eyes wide open. I wonder what James thought about as he watched his Mom and Nurse Paparazzi go on and on laughing and talking?

There are still no text messages from God. Still no urgent emails received telling me what to do next. I am still wondering what signal is going to strike and get my attention to help me understand the plan with this uncertain journey, or walk in the wilderness I am on with James. Doc Optimistic recently mentioned a new surgery option over the past weekend to J. J. for James. We are still uncertain at this time on the best treatment for James and will need to remain patient and wait to see what James is going to do and how far he is going to allow the caregivers to push him for recovery and healing.

Nurse Paparazzi informed me tonight the weekly plan consists of trying to wean Mr. James off the morphine drip this week. He is on a small dosage currently and during this week they are going to try to take away this narcotic slowly with good intentions to help reduce withdrawal side effects. Also, we hope and pray James's right upper-lobe in his lung will re-open and allow us to reduce the ventilator setting again, even if it takes slow adjustments. James's ventilator setting is still set on sixteen.

Later, James started to fall asleep and I grew tired. The clock ticked and tocked and I noticed 2 a.m. was growing close. Rest time was near so I whispered James his nightly prayers and told said my goodbyes to my new sojourn caregiver friends. Flashes of lightning briefly brightened James's room while complementing thunder pounded the night sky. Finally, rain had arrived in Charleston. The 100-degree weather was quickly turning into a nice, cool 77 degrees through with swollen raindrops and flooding.

I walked down the silent hallways of the hospital and rode the elevator from the fourth floor to the first floor seeking a quick hospital exit to my van parked outside on the street next to the Children's Emergency Exit. As I was turning the last turn to exit the hospital lobby I saw a lady I met a month ago. You may remember me telling you about her. I was waiting for my famous ride back to the Ronald McDonald House in the police car and sat in the lobby talking to this very sweet and caring lady. She is an employee at the hospital and works second shift on the second floor.

I turned the last turn out of the hospital when I recognized her face and smile. She has one of those faces you can't forget. I immediately asked her if she remembered me from a month ago. To my surprise she said "yes" and asked me how my baby James was doing? I felt my heart warm when she said James's name. She remembered his name. I asked her if she knew how to get out of the hospital since it was now 2:15 a.m. and the door was locked. It was pouring rain and the street was flooded.

"Are you riding with public safety," questioned the lady. Public Safety was the cop car that picked me up last time we met and drove me home. "No, not tonight," I said. "I have my van parked outside on the street tonight," I replied. Although the woman's shift ended a midnight, it was now 2:15 a.m. and she was waiting for the rain to stop before she walked to her car across the street. The road between the hospital exit and parking garage was covered with ankle-deep flooding. The rain didn't appear to be stopping anytime soon.

I told her I would drive her to her car in the parking garage so she wouldn't get wet and have to walk in the deep waters. "God is good," she replied. I said, "all the time." Once again I asked her if she knew how we could get out of the hospital and immediately I felt her warm, dark-skinned hand take a hold of my hand and hold on tight. "Follow me," she assured me.

At this moment, walking hand and hand with my new sojourn friend, I realized the signal I had been searching for was now found. Walking next to this stranger, following her lead and holding her warm, soft hand was the signal I was looking for over the past week. Yesterday, I enjoyed lunch with the youth from St. Giles and found myself basking in the sun while talking outside with good friends. Once again, someone brought up the topic of "Searching For The Signal." I mentioned to "Youth Golden Boy" and "Youthette Smiley" I was still searching for my signal. "I am still waiting to see my signal appear," I stated.

"We are the signals," said Youth Golden Boy while Youthette Smiley just smiled (of course) and nodded. Profound! "We are the signals," quoted straight from the mouths of babes once again! Remember, "God is good?" My new friend said, "God is good" immediately after I told her I would take her to her car so she wouldn't have to cross the river outside Yes, Youth Golden Boy, we are the signals.

Here all along I was waiting for God to send me a signal concerning my journey, concerning my sojourn, concerning the wilderness I am experiencing with James's illness. All along, I was a signal. I shouldn't be waiting for the signal; I should be shining the signal. I am a signal to others. Just like Joshua in the Bible. Tonight I led and helped this lady cross the river, the River Jordan. I told her to stay under shelter. I walked through the ankle-deep water and drove the van to dry land to keep her safe from harm.

The Israelites lived in the wilderness for forty years due to their lack of faith. When Moses was 120 years he died and God choose Joshua to be the new leader. This was God's commission to Joshua:

Now then, you and all these people, get ready to cross the Jordan
River into the land I am about to give to them. Joshua 1:2.

We are signals. We don't need to sit by our phones and computers and wait for God's text messages or emails for direction. We are signals. We need to continue to be faithful when we are in the wilderness and stay strong and courageous. I need to stop waiting for a message or signal and start being a signal. This wonderful sweet lady helped remind me tonight what Youth Golden Boy told me yesterday. It doesn't matter what color our skin is or where we are from. Grab someone's hand, even if it is different from your own, and help them find their way. God is good—all the time. Yes friends, even when your nine-week-old baby is "chronic" and humans are not sure how to fix him, God is good—all the time.

> *"Slow down, calm down, don't worry, don't hurry, trust the process" Alexandra Stoddard.*

Trust God! Blessings!

Good News ~Nurse Mom
Thursday, July 28, 2011 12:25 a.m.

Yesterday, James had a fever of 102, which broke late afternoon and James's elevated heart rate (high 200s) started to decline slowly. These signs concerned the caregivers and I heard the dirty, nine-letter-word "infection" again. The caregivers drew James's blood and tested his urine, which showed a possible urinary tract infection. James seemed a little fussy yesterday when I walked into his room. The nurse gave him Tylenol as well as an extra dose of morphine for comfort. Even though this sounds bad, good news is coming from today.

The good news is James's fever broke and his heart rate decreased within hours. Thank you for all the prayers. I held James the past two nights. Like all babies, he loves to be held. Tonight, however, was the first night James was awake when I held him. He spent twenty minutes looking at me and staring at my face and the overhead lights. This morning, James's ventilator rate was reduced from sixteen to fourteen. Praise God! His chest x-rays looked better this morning so the caregivers decided to decrease the rate. Also this morning, James's morphine drip was removed. Yes, they cut off his morphine drip. Further, the Bumex drip was cut off. So, in the beginning of our journey James received fourteen medicines via drip. As of today, James is on one medicine drip, milrinone, which helps his heart squeeze. I guess he will be on this medicine for a while.

An echocardiogram was taken today and "Doc Resolution" stopped by tonight to talk briefly with me about James. Doc Resolution told me the echogram showed slight improvement in James's tricuspid valve. Yeah! Also, we talked briefly about Doc Heart's idea and professional opinion on the next surgery for James. There is thought of doing a different surgery instead of the original plan of stitching the valves. The surgery to stitch the valves would be an open-heart surgery and James would be placed on a bypass machine for his heart and lungs. This surgery is extremely risky for James. The second surgery consideration would insert a valve replacement and be less risky. I could tell Doc Resolution is a thinker and likes to resolve problems and issues. He mentioned it would be best if James was a tad bit bigger before they performed the surgery. I asked him the ideal size James would need to be for the surgery. He said, "fifty pounds," and then chuckled. My throat kind of bulged with a lump when I heard him say fifty pounds, as James is only eight pounds currently. After Doc Resolution laughed, I said with a smile on my face, "how about ten would that work?" Yes, ten pounds probably would be okay, but the bigger James is the better. With this said, James's feeds were increased to 27 ml/hour today with extra calories added. For all the number crunchers and analyzers out there reading, 30 ml equal one ounce. James is almost taking a full ounce every hour through his feeding tube.

Good news to report today. Please pray for James's ventilator rate to continue to decrease. Please pray for James to come off the ventilator soon and help continue the tricuspid valve to improve as well. Fluid is reducing and the edema is getting better slowly. Prayer is a very powerful thing. As "Nurse Conversant" said today, "James is doing amazing. Keep the prayers coming as they are working." Nurse Conversant was impressed with James's progress. It has been almost a month since she has taken care of him. She was extremely knowledgeable and familiar with James's condition. She impressed me with her educated, quick response to my fifty million healthy questions concerning James and his condition. She was patient when I warned her I had a silly question. "When will James start getting his shots," I asked. Nurse Conversant was quick to answer with a perfect answer. After James gets out of the PCICU he will be moved up to floor 8D. This children's floor helps educate parents and continues to watch over the patient before they are allowed to go home. Oh, home sweet home. This is in my dreams! Good news today. Let's continue to pray for continued good news and good reports. Blessings to you all!

Hazelnut Cream ~Dad
Sunday, July 31, 2011 5:20 a.m.

This morning, I woke up to the rising sun, thanked the Lord for things he's done (to steal a line from Toby Mac). I went downstairs and fixed that first cup of coffee. Usually, I take it black with a bunch of sugar. On special days, when the mood hits me, I like to add a little bit of hazelnut cream to make it just a little better. Now, one might ask, "they make truck loads of hazelnut cream, why not just put it in your coffee everyday if you like it better?" It's a fair question I guess, but I like to keep it special. It's that little added touch I get on special days. If I used it every day, it would become ordinary and not as special.

Given the day we had yesterday, and the days we have had over the last two weeks, this morning called for hazelnut cream. The caregivers turned James's ventilator rate down from fourteen to twelve yesterday morning, took lactic acid levels at 4 p.m. yesterday, verified that he was doing well, and turned his vent rate down to ten. Oh, did I mention ten is the goal for the ventilator? When we get to ten, that's as low as they go. We still have a bit of work to do on the pressure, but as far as number of breaths go, that's it. Goal!!! Now, before we all get too happy, I have to tell you that he didn't tolerate ten. They had to increase to twelve last night after his blood gas at 4 a.m. His CO_2 and acid levels were too high. He just isn't ready for that yet. So, they raised it back to twelve. I leaned over his bed and prayed. I felt a little disappointed to be honest, but then I looked at the vent rate again. It said twelve. Do you know how great that is? Two weeks ago he was at twenty-eight.

In two months this child has gone from being air-lifted in an emergency effort to save his life. He all but died on the runway at the Charleston Airport. We were told that he may only have hours to live. One of the nurses told Jacqueline that all the nurses were so on edge the first night because they fully expected him to code at least once, if not several times. By the grace of God he never did. Two months ago, James had fourteen tubes either running into or out of him. He had more medications than we could count pumping into him and a long road that we didn't even think might be possible. Now let's fast-forward nine weeks. He's on one IV drip of milrinone. He's taking on full feeds. His kidneys work like a champ! His liver numbers have decreased from twenty down to under seven. We need to be at four. His ventilator is now down to twelve. For a brief moment, we made it all the way to ten.

So the question becomes, what did I do this morning with my second cup of coffee when I found out his rate had been turned up to twelve? I took it black with some sugar and a little bit of hazelnut cream, and again, I thanked God for the blessings.

As I sit here typing, Frick is laughing in his sleep. His feet are on his mother, his head is on Frack's arm. I don't know what he's dreaming about but he's happy. Frack is so zonked that she's "catching flies." That's what my family says when you sleep with your mouth wide open, snoring like a grown man. Bubba would be proud. I can't wait to send her to Montreat to see who can out snore who! Bubba and "Mama J" are not allowed to retire from Montreat until my kids get through youth group! And that includes James you guys! The point of this is simple: Jacqueline being down here in Charleston and the rest of us being in Greenville is not easy on any of us. Thank God Grandmother can fill in, get the house organized, cook dinners, do a much better job than I can of cleaning up, and keep things as normal as possible for the kids. But at the end of the day, it's different. I can't sleep as well with Jacqueline not there. You would think having the bed all to myself, being able to sleep with the fan off and the TV on (the way I like it) instead of the TV off and the fan on (the way Jacqueline likes it), I would sleep better. Unfortunately, it doesn't work that way.

In talking with Frick, he has had similar problems. Frack told her Mother yesterday that she would come stay with her in Charleston, that she would rather have her than all her friends. Being separated like this takes its toll. It's hard. It's hard on all of us. So these two weekend days when we're all together, seeing the kids sleep soundly, hearing Frick laugh in his sleep, these moments are also special. They are more important than the ordinary day. This also warrants some hazelnut cream.

In this life, we all go through hardships. We have people talk behind our backs. We have people do dishonest things, or not live up to their word. We get our feelings hurt by friends. We make mistakes at work that we worry about too much. Sometimes we're not all that we can be and we blame ourselves for coming up short. My mother had an expression that I always thought was a little cheesy. "Don't let the turkeys get you down." Taking a step back from ten to twelve on the vent could get me down. But I'm not going to let it, not today. To focus on that would be a failure on my part to notice the improvements in his heart, his lungs, his kidneys, and his liver.

Is James where we want him to be yet? No! But then again, how many of us are? How many of us have reached our maximum potential? Most of us probably haven't, but we're getting there. We make efforts to improve ourselves every day and so is James. He continues to make improvements. He takes on full feeds, which are critical to gaining strength. He drinks calorie-laden, fortified milk and takes a multivitamin. The other day my dad asked if he was walking yet. I laughed. He's not walking yet, but he's a little better today than he was yesterday. And he was a little better yesterday than he was the day before. So for this we are thankful. I'm sure that if you look, and you won't have to look very hard, you too will find some blessings to celebrate in your life. You too can find a reason to be optimistic. You too can find a way to improve yourself every day. And you too can fix your coffee and if you want, add a little hazelnut cream.

Riding The Roller Coaster, Again ~Nurse Mom
Sunday, July 31, 2011 8:09 p.m.

By this time, you would think I am used to riding the roller coaster ride of good news, bad news, good news, good news, bad news with James and his illness. Even though we all know roller coaster rides are fast and furious, we always know there are times when you ride slowly to reach the peak. Sooner or later the ride balances out and is over. Today was a different day for me. The roller coaster ride hit me pretty hard and I started to feel very anxious and stressed while the ride was going down. Today, the roller coaster ride hit the peak and started to come back down for us with a bad news report.

Yesterday afternoon, James was able to move to the ventilator rate of ten breaths per minute and his heart rate was in the high 160s. The roller coaster ride was very fun and moving quickly. We received very good news and reached a ventilator goal rate of ten. We were so happy to see ten on the ventilator rate and hear from the nurse that James seemed to be tolerating the rate well. Also, his heart rate started to come back down as well. Last night, we all enjoyed dinner out as a family, laughed, and had a good night's rest. Late this morning J. J. and Frick went to visit James as Frack and I started making a scrapbook for her. I decided Frack and I needed a project together and thought scrapbooking would be a good hobby for me to pick up while in Charleston. Plus, Frack loves arts and crafts.

J. J. and Frick returned back to the room at Ronald McDonald House late this morning warning us of the ride reaching the peak and starting to go back down. "James has another fever and wasn't responding well to the new ventilator rate of ten. His chest was retracting (drawing back and in during breathing) and he seemed to struggle breathing on the rate of ten. They moved him back to sixteen," J. J. reported. Normally, I stay positive and just go with the ride. Today I felt stressed, frustrated, and downright discouraged when J. J. gave me the news. I started to feel angry and very mad. Here we go again, I thought. Can't we just get a break, Don't I deserve a break? Haven't I gone through enough?

I was doing well up to this point for the past few weeks from restraining from crying, up until today. I thought my tears had dried. Today, the tears just flowed down my eyes as I sat outside with J. J. on the front porch facing Lucas Park. Frick was riding his scooter around the park and Frack was swinging on the swings. We finally reached ten on the ventilator and today, bam, we're back up to sixteen. Plus, now James has yet another fever of 101. I want answers. I want to know what happened and why this is happening? "What did the doctors say," I questioned J. J., "What does this mean?" I sobbed. J. J. was trying so hard to comfort me when all I wanted to do was spit fire and break something. J. J. tried to hug me, but I didn't want a hug. Have you ever been so upset that you felt very angry and mad? "Why can't we just get a break," I questioned again.

I need a break. I need good news for more than a day. I need for the roller coaster ride to stop reaching the peak and then going down very fast with bad news. We need for James to continue to improve. Being away from home now for ten-and-a-half weeks is starting to break down my strength. Being away from my family daily is starting to hurt my soul. Why can't I just go home and leave James behind, I've often asked myself, Why do I feel like I will be abandoning James if I leave? I am his Mom and know he needs me, especially when his fever spikes and he looks at me with his sweet little eyes trying to tell me he feels bad. I find myself saying to him, "Just tell Mommy what is wrong. What do we need to do to make you feel better?" God, I wish I knew what James needed to help him. Standing by his bed, helpless, is not something I would wish on any mother having to watch. Especially, when they are on a roller coaster ride of good news, good news, bad news, good news, I would not want that for any mom.

J. J. reminded me this afternoon as I was sobbing to look where James has come so far. Yes, he has come a long way. He wasn't expected to live past two days. Yes, he is fighting and continues to fight even when the fevers hit, the ventilator tube comes out and the machine malfunctions. Patience has it place and boy am I trying to be patient. I tell myself all the time to be thankful for his slow, baby step progress. Be thankful for him being alive and still with us. God, it is so hard especially on a day like today when the roller ride starts back up and starts to go down.

I am patiently waiting for the nurse to call us and let me know I can come back over to the hospital tonight to see James and get answers to some of my questions from the doctor. There was a very sick baby who came in tonight and the unit had to be closed. It was hard for me to leave James awake and looking at me. His head felt warm with the 101-degree fever. His big eyes watched me. Please continue to pray for us. Please ask God to help me sustain my control and faith as I go up and down on this roller coaster ride with James.

God, please give me the strength to continue and keep riding this ride of health with James. Please give me the strength to ask my questions and be comforted with the answers. Life is so hard right now and you know what I need. Continue to watch over James and hold him in your arms. Help James's ventilator numbers come back down and strengthen his lungs to be able to function without this machine. Watch over his small but enlarged heart and reduce the leaking of his valves. Grant us peace and comfort to handle the fast, furious falls of the ride and uplift us and help us praise your name during the steady ride. Soon, this ride will be over and hopefully your will and plan will send us home with a healthy, beautiful baby. Blessings to you all!

Weaving in Faith ~Nurse Mom
Tuesday, August 2, 2011 12:51 p.m.

As a parent, the past few days were extremely hard. I found my faith slipping. I felt discouraged and beaten with bad news. James has had a rough two days to say the least. Fevers, increases in ventilator support, high heart rate, bad blood gas reports and now this morning the news of change in milk.

James will no longer be using breast milk because his stools are too loose. Some of you may think this change of milk is not a big deal. I would probably agree with you if it was somebody else's baby and mom dealing with this change. "It could be worse," you probably think. But, since it is my baby and all I have heard up until this point starting eight almost nine years ago when Frick was a baby, breast milk is the best milk for babies and helps increase their immune system. I felt like it was very important to make sure James drank breast milk. So, now with the nutritionist wanting and needing to switch James to formula, I feel absolutely sick in my stomach and want to cry. But once again, the tears are dry. There are no tears to fall.

As James's mom, pumping breast milk is one of the only things I am able to do to help him. Yes, it is very time consuming, and quite a pain at times, but it gave me meaning and a purpose and most importantly gave me a sense of helping. Standing by James's bed day after day watching him and not being able to help him feel better, as a mom you need something to do to feel like you are helping. Even if it is something as small as pumping breast milk. I have finally been able to kick my caffeine habit just in order to make sure his milk is perfect for his body. And now, the milk is not needed. I am not needed.

What should I do, completely quit pumping? Should I continue to pump just in case they decide to put him back on it? Should I just continue to pump feeling like I am helping even if I am not? James is not gaining any weight and his protein levels in his body are low. I would have not had a clue he was losing weight because when I look at him he looks bigger. He definitely looks longer. He is measuring at 50 centimeters. When he arrived he measured forty-two so I know he is getting longer. The nutritionist explained, "His arms and legs (extremities) are not getting bigger. He has very loose stools and he is not able to absorb all of the nutrients with loose stools. We need him to grow and absorb the nutrients. His protein levels need to be up around six and they are currently very low around two-and-a-half. The protein levels have been dropping as the stools increase. Breast milk is our number one pick for food but it is running right through his body.

Yesterday, James had a rough day. His gas levels tanked pretty quickly. His heart rate went over 200 and he continued to have a slight fever as well as loose stools. Doctor Go Get Mom, one of my favorite doctors, thought he may have a gastrointestinal (GI) bug and probably was dehydrated. Especially since James was having a bunch of loose stools, we thought he might be dehydrated. James's medical team drew new cultures to check for bacterial growth and infection. Thank God, nothing has shown up yet as a positive growth. The dirty nine-letter word is still absent. Stool cultures were tested to see what was going on with the runny stools, and James had an ultrasound of his belly to see if any pockets of fluid were present. His gas level was very bad yesterday and his ventilator support increased back to twenty-four breaths per minute. The roller coaster ride got very fast and turned downhill yesterday for me quickly.

As of lunchtime today, James is still on ventilator support of twenty-four and his heart rate is down to 175. He has a pack of ice on his head to keep his fever down and regulated. Surgery is looking closer than we thought since he had this step back, a big step back. The doctors are considering different options but we are unsure of when and what surgery will be performed. Doc Heart is out of town this week so the discussion will probably begin again next week when he returns. He, along with the other wonderful doctors, will talk as a group to decide what the best surgery option is for James.

Performing another surgery to fix James's heart will be a very high-risk event for him. We could lose him. But after the past two days of setbacks I think the surgery will be on the table sooner than later. We just need for James to feed and grow for when we have to pull the plug and take another shot at surgery. We need James to grow stronger and gain weight. We need his protein levels to increase to normal.

Friends, I ask and beg you to continue praying for James. Please continue to ask God to keep James pain-free, safe and continue to lead the doctors to the best possible solution to fix James's heart. It appears to continue to make his lungs sick and unable to come off the ventilator. Your prayers are very powerful as I truly feel God hears all of your prayers. Your prayers as well as the love and knowledge provided by the caregivers are what is keeping him alive. Please ask God to give me comfort knowing I am helping James even if my milk is not needed right now.

I continue to remind myself to stay faithful and find comfort in God during this extremely tiresome journey, especially during the past two days when the roller coaster has begun to speed up and come down off the peak very quickly. During this difficult time, we all have to continue to as the ancient proverb says, *"weave in faith as God will find the thread."*

CHAPTER 14

Walking Through the Valley

When walking through the valley of shadows,
remember, a shadow is cast by a light.
—Barclay, H.K.

Names and Faces of Many ~Nurse Mom
Wednesday, August 3, 2011 11:35 a.m.

Have you ever filled your mind with so many questions, concerns, facts, names, and yes, numbers, (number crunchers) that your mind goes blank? Names always get me. I am forever trying to remember people's names. Calling someone by their name is so important and meaningful and now I can't remember half of the names of people I meet and continue to see on a daily basis. I see faces and hear names of sick babies and hurting parents daily. Oh how I wish I could remember all of their names so I can continue to pray for them and ask God to give them strength, healing and comfort. Oh how I wish I could take away some of their pain. I wish someone could take away some of my pain.

Tonight as I was standing at the Nurses' Station with Nurse Picturesque I noticed there was a new baby in room nine to the right of James's room. I noticed an older couple, probably grandparents, in the room standing around the crib looking at the baby. Nurse Picturesque and I were chatting and laughing as usual and I was asking her about how much longer she thought I had at MUSC in the PCICU. You don't want to know her answer by the way. Also, I was giving her a hard time because it had been several weeks since she has taken care of James.

"You don't love us anymore," I teased her. I told her she is not fighting hard enough to get him during her shift.

I noticed this older Hispanic couple and the woman was crying. How familiar I am with those days of standing next to the baby's crib just crying and crying, praying, and wiping my eyes with tears flowing. I couldn't help but look again and watch this older couple. Why would anybody want to continue to watch and see someone in pain? Then, as the couple walked out of the room, I noticed the man's eyes were bloodshot and full of water as well. I swallowed deeply and felt my heart hurt for this family. Here was yet another family affected by a heart condition on an innocent baby.

This site of hurting families, babies, and moms is really starting to fill my mind. My mind is filled with more questions, concerns, facts, names, and numbers. "Why is this happening to me," I asked a pastor friend on the phone. "How long do you think I will be here," I questioned Nurse Picturesque. "Is a heart transplant one of the options now for James," I asked the doctor. "What is your baby's name?" I asked the grandparent couple so I could pray. I am happy to report, however, James's heart rate is down to the 160s tonight.

There is so much hurt filled in the world today along with questions, concerns, facts, names, numbers, the list goes on and on. There is so much darkness happening that I seem to notice it all the time now. Even J. J. states, "Your journal entries are so dark Jacqueline." Yes, I do agree they are dark, dear; but I am honest, truthful, and say what I feel. For some reason, dark times are happening now. All the sickness I am around, all the names and faces I see seem to be hurting and seem to be dark.

This morning, I started to really worry about myself. I told myself, "Jacqueline, you have got to snap out of this funk you are in. Yes, James has had two bad days but snap out of it." I even found myself wishing James's condition would be a live or die situation. How terrible. I can't even believe I just admitted that in print. I felt myself ball up emotionally today as I started my walk to the hospital this morning. All of a sudden, I realized I was at the hospital right outside the Children's Emergency Entrance. Have you ever been walking and quickly realized you were at your destination? Your body was so numb from all of the deep thinking, questions, concerns, numbers, etc., that you didn't realize you were walking? It was like time just stopped still during the walk. It was like time stood still for me the past two-and-a-half months. I sometimes still find myself writing May 2011. I am still living in the month of May when James was born.

My question to you tonight is what are we called to do during these dark times? What does God want us to do? I have been thinking about this question all day. How do we pull ourselves out of the dark times, snap out of it and fight the "D" word nobody likes to talk about: depression? We all have dark times at some point in our lives: a bad day at work, financial insecurity, fear of college, job loss, relationship issues, and yes, a sick baby. Do we continue to walk around all day wondering, asking questions, and crunching numbers? Do we let the darkness continue to heavy our shoes or even load our backs full of bricks? Do we walk around all day and let the pressure build on our shoulders like shoulder pads or even throb our heads with pounding headaches?

Well, I do have an answer to one of my questions tonight for you all. I am not full of complete darkness tonight, J. J. I found the answer this evening. My afternoon and evening were filled with light. The darkness of questions, concerns, numbers, facts, and names were filled with the light of God's love through community, yes, community.

Community with others helps provide light when darkness sets in. I spent the day talking to friends, laughing with clergy, watching a beautiful baby boy interact with his parents and grandparents and broke bread over dinner with saints, true saints. What a gift of lightness provided to me. The best thing about community is that it can be free. Community doesn't cost anything at times. Thanks be to God for this gift.

So tonight, as I returned back to the Ronald McDonald House after an afternoon and evening filled with lightness, I noticed the same grandparent family from earlier sitting at the Ronald McDonald House table eating dinner. The granddad's eyes are no longer red and the grandmother no longer has tears flowing down her face. They are sitting in community with their family eating dinner. I walk up to them and introduced myself. I pray that one of them is able to speak English, as I do not know how to communicate in Spanish. I wish J. J. was here tonight so he could speak to them in Spanish. He always makes an effort to speak to the families at the Ronald McDonald House in Spanish. J. J. says we should now always expect that everyone in America can speak English.

I introduced myself and asked them the name of their baby. As I talked, the young girl at the table translated what I said to the other family members in Spanish. "Is everything okay with the baby today," I asked. I discovered the baby's heart rate was slowly increasing today and the family is very worried. Darkness is starting to fill their lives. I told the young girl about James's heart rate the past few days and how it reached 210! Then I told her how it was down as low as 159 today. I tried to provide comfort and encouragement to this family as their young interpreter translated my words for them. I tried to offer community to this family even if we don't speak the same language and our skin is not the same color. This is a gift, a free gift, God provides us all.

In closing tonight I offer community back to others. The community I received today was priceless and exactly what I needed to help me make it through yet another day that started off dark but ended with light. Tonight Lord, I pray for Jose, the baby of the Hispanic family staying at the Ronald McDonald House. Yes, Jose. I remember his name. Please watch over him and help lower his heart rate. I offer virtual community to a new friend in Berlin, fighting leukemia with stem cell transplants. You are winning my friend. You are winning because you see the light in the darkness. Your beautiful blue eyes shine light to me through your daily video postings of encouragement and strength. Tonight, I offer community by prayer for a robin carrying three little eggs in her nest. God, please let the bird sit patiently with comfort and safety on her three little eggs so they can hatch in perfect timing. In your perfect timing God. I pray for an Upstate family who is providing community to others in honor of their sweet little baby given to God a few weeks ago in heaven. May God continue to offer you comfort and provide you strength to offer comfort back to other hurting families suffering from heart defects. May your little "Rose" continue to bloom to others through your serving hands, friends.

I offer community to you all reading this blog. I want you to know we all experience darkness. I share my darkness with you hoping you find comfort knowing we all struggle with darkness, even this smiling youth director who loves to laugh. The good news is God gives us the gift of community to share with each other, to help each other, through these times. I pray you all are a part of a community that helps you during the dark times. I pray you all feel God's love and feel the light it provides.

Remember faith, hope, and love. The greatest gift is love. Community is love. Blessings to you all for a glimpse of light in your life today!

He Can Take It ~Dad
Friday, August 5, 2011 9:29 p.m.

What can you live with? What can you live without? We all have our needs. We all have our weaknesses. For some, it's a pack of cigarettes a day. If you talk to someone who smokes, they will probably tell you that they need their cigarettes to keep from going crazy. Some will tell you they need an alcoholic beverage or two after work to chill out from a hard day at work. Well, I'm here to say, no you don't. But don't worry, I'm not judging. I didn't need that piece of sweet potato pie tonight either. Nor did I need that third cup of coffee or third Diet Coke. I didn't need any of it. I wanted it because it's a weakness for me. I tell you this because without that cup of coffee in the morning it's harder for me to focus and function on my job. My body can't seem to tolerate missing out on caffeine. It misses it. It responds by feeling tired, giving me a terrible headache, and making me intolerable to my clients and coworkers. I'm kind of like Doc Jekyll, I turn into Mr. Hyde pretty quick. I just can't tolerate being without caffeine. Now deep down, we all know this is not a true statement. My body could survive without caffeine, but adjusting to it requires feelings of pain, frustration, anger, anxiety, and depression. The same exact feelings can be described for someone trying to quit drinking, quit smoking, lose weight, or cut back on sugar. The body reacts in a predictable, awful way.

The same can be said for James and his adjustments. It seems like everything we do for his good has some kind of negative side effect. For example, we have given him blasts of antibiotics to help his body fight off infections. The problem is that these antibiotics kill all bacteria. Yes, they kill the bad bacteria, but they also kill the good bacteria that aid and assist the digestive system. His body first responds to the change, but eventually there are some negative side effects. The same can be said for the ventilator. Yes, it helps James to breathe, but it may cause lung damage and can lead to lung disease. So what do we do? This is the constant question that our doctors and nurses must weigh and measure. Unfortunately, a lot of times we have to take some bad along with the good.

I hear the doctors and nurses refer to James's ability to tolerate the change. It makes me ask the question referencing the first paragraph. What are you willing to tolerate? What can you live with? What can you live without? The last two months has been a give and take with support for James. The doctors make the decisions based on what they think James will tolerate. Sometimes they're right; sometimes, they're wrong. But when they fail, they back up and punt and try again. So it is with the last few days that we have had to back up and punt. We have lost a good bit of ground on the ventilator and based on what I saw with his fluid pressure tonight, I expect, we may lose a little more ground. We are still having problems with his right lung collapsing. It just can't seem to tolerate the amount of fluid and mucus clouding the opening.

James has also lost a good bit of nutrition. Having to cut that off was another setback for him. He may have had some small infection. It may have been parts of his digestive system were inflamed. For now we have reduced feeds and rerouted the electrolytes to allow time for these areas to heal. It seems his little system could no longer tolerate full feeds and needed to heal. For forty-eight hours we have reduced feeds. We must wait to see the outcome. What we do know is this: what was being asked of James's heart was more than it could tolerate. It cannot do everything we need it to do in order to go to the next level. It is going to require some type of intervention (procedure or surgery) in order to move onward. The chances of him being able to survive intervention are not good. But as the doctor said yesterday, "this is James and he has already proved us wrong. He has moxie and we just don't know how much he can tolerate." My plan is to pray hard; let the doctors decide the most appropriate route, and have faith that he can take it!" It sounds courageous for me to say that, right? The truth is, what else am I going to say? I better have faith that he can take it.

As for Jacqueline and me, we too are wondering how much we can tolerate. I'm not talking about James. I'm talking about us as individuals. Jacqueline stays in Charleston week after week, day after day, visiting James in the hospital trying to be a mother. The problem is that she can't be a mother is the usual sense. She can't do all the things with James that a new mother generally does with a newborn. She said tonight she just wants to curl up next to him and go to sleep, only she can't do that. She wants to hold him without it taking a three-member team to get him situated in her lap and tubes constantly getting in the way. She wants to change his diaper without hurting him due to the tremendous amount of edema swelling a very sensitive area. Poor little guy! All in all she just wants to be mom to a healthy baby. Unfortunately, she can't right now, which would be enough to deal with on its own.

The one thing she felt like was a real contribution was the breast milk. This being taken away was more than she could tolerate. I had planned to work all week, but we had to back up and punt. Hearing the pain in her voice let me know that I needed to get my tail to Charleston to help take care of her. The thought of her being by herself and feeling left alone to take care of all this was more than I could tolerate. Jacqueline also called her mom and dad and for support as well. Our pastor and his wife also paid us a visit today. We haven't been able to spend much time with them so it was good to have a nice visit with them and catch up. What today did, was help both of us heal. We were able to talk about some things, begin to digest some things (pun intended), and heal up a little bit. We always feel better when we are together. Being apart from one another is one of the hardest things. We always feel like as long as we're together, we can take it.

We talked a good bit with parents and pastors about feelings, plans, kids, conditions, being apart, being sick, being healthy, we covered a whole gamut of things. Jacqueline and I have both felt at times like we were very angry. We weren't angry with each other. We sometimes just get angry with the circumstances. We get angry that we feel helpless. We get angry that we have to be apart from each other, our children, our church. Sometimes this situation is more than we can tolerate. Fortunately for us we are blessed with an overwhelming amount of support from church, family, and friends. God gives us the people we need to help us through each day. We aren't strong enough to tolerate the change at times; however, with a little help from God and each other, we are made stronger and allowed to heal. When talking about anger one of the things we were advised on was this. If we have a choice between being angry with God, or angry with each other, choose God, because He can take it. If I'm being honest, I must admit that I've been angry with God more than once. "I thank God that he can take it." I thank God that he knows how to make me better and heal me up. I also thank God for forgiving me for my shortcomings when I can't take it. Amen!

What We Need ~Nurse Mom
Monday, August 8, 2011 1:13 a.m.

Tonight is a quick report and basically a request for what we need through prayers. James needs one: his body to accept nutrition. His feeds have been reduced to five from twenty-six and his body is currently on TPN getting liquids. James's protein levels are low and his nutrition needs to improve in order for him to grow and get strong. TPN is not good for James's liver and we need to get him back on full feeds so he can grow and become nutritionally healthy. His liver was slowly improving, but the past few days his liver has started to get worse again.

And two: there are two cultures of bacteria growing in James's ventilator that produced a positive culture test. He is currently receiving three antibiotics to fight off these infections as well as any other infections brewing.

Please pray hard! As Frick told me this afternoon as I was crying with my hands over my face in the PCICU, "James is going to get through this Mom. God is going to show us again how strong James is and how he is a fighter. Trust me Mom. Trust me. He is a fighter. It is just going to take time." Again, please continue to pray. Thank you!

I Need a Plan ~Nurse Mom
Monday, August 8, 2011 3:09 p.m.

The kids are with me this week in Charleston. I am trying very hard to spend as much time as I can with them this week playing, hugging, and loving on them. I have to "make" myself play with them as I feel very sad most of the time. I look forward to the day when I feel like my old self again. Yesterday, J. J. and I spent the day at the waterpark with the kids and then Frack and I worked on her scrapbook we are making this summer. Her scrapbook is looking amazing! She is so artistic and creative.

Frack and I spent a few hours Saturday afternoon in the Emergency Room at MUSC so the doctors could check her out. She was complaining of her heart hearting as well as her throat. I needed her to know I would be here for her when she wasn't feeling well just like I am here for James. While we sat in the room waiting on the doctors, Frack asked me about James. She seemed surprised I was spending my time waiting for her in the "hospital" instead of James. I got up out of my chair and sat next to her on the bed. "I will always be here for you as well Frack, even when you are sick. Even though it seems right now I am with James more, when you are sick I will be right here with you. I love you just as much as I love James," I reassured her. She smiled and let me know she knew I loved her. Frack seemed much better when we left. The doctor let her know she had a very strong, healthy heart and lungs. Also, she smiled as we left knowing her mom loved her enough to stay next to her side when she said, "I don't feel good Mom. I am sick."

James's heart rate was around 200 this afternoon and he has another fever. I wish I had better news to report to you all but I don't. I have requested a care conference for this week with James's doctors to find out the plan. Plan? What a complex word and meaning for James. I am not sure there is a plan right now. I am waiting to meet with all of James's doctors to find out what we will do next to nurse him to health. I hope and pray there are options and other things to try. Especially with his body not taking nutrition now and his protein level being so low. We really need James's body to be nourished and as healthy as possible.

James white blood count increased this morning to 21,000 from 18,000 yesterday. The increase in white blood count indicates an infection. Two bacteria growths were found in the respiratory tube and are cultured positive. Other cultures have not come back positive yet but his increase in white blood cells indicates infection.

I am very scared and don't know what to think. It scares me not to know the next step for James. I am trying to stay positive but am finding it harder and harder, especially when things seem to continue to go wrong with his condition. The past few months I have found myself rubbing my cross necklace for comfort. When things are happening that hurt or make me sad I rub my cross to remind me of God's love and comfort for us all. This morning, I added a new symbol to my necklace. I added another cross charm a friend gave me during the first week we arrived in Charleston. It has the word "Miracle" written on the cross. I plan to rub this symbol continuously now along with my other cross to remind me of God's love, comfort, and strength. I know we need another miracle from God to help James. We have already received one miracle: James is still here for almost three months on the 17th of this month (also Frick's birthday). Wow! Seventeen is a very lucky number for J. J. and me and since Frack and James were also born on the 17th.

The good news is I still feel faithful. I still believe that God is in control and can heal James. I hope and pray the current issues (nutrition, fever, elevated heart rate, two dirty nine-letter-words) are just another speed bump in James's healing, and I hope and pray I can remain to stay faithful and find peace during this extremely difficult journey. I wonder what God's plan or will is as Frick says it is for James? I wonder how much longer it will take to heal James's body and bring him home as a healthy baby?

Thank you all again for all the cards, visits, gifts, love offerings, donations, meals, childcare, etc., you continue to send. I have no idea what I would do without all the love God sends to us through you all, our family and angels. I am going to try to keep you updated as much as possible so you all know what to continue to pray for to God. Your prayers are amazing!

Blessings to you all today. May God's plan for you fill your hearts and minds.

On My Feet Standing ~Nurse Mom
Tuesday, August 9, 2011 12:18 a.m.

Today has not been a good day for sweet baby James. Today is what we would call a bad day. J. J. is on his way tonight back to Charleston to spend the night with James in the hospital as well as help keep me on my feet standing. I called J. J. around 9:30 tonight to let him know he needed to come back to Charleston tonight and spend time with James. I honestly am not sure what is going to happen this week as James's health continues to get worse with a big, deep "dip" today. I hope and pray for the best outcome but have a feeling I may need to start preparing for the not-so-good outcome. How does a mother prepare herself to lose a child? How does a mother prepare herself to lose a sweet baby that she carried seven months and then sat by his bedside for two-and-a-half months? I am not sure how to answer those questions yet? I am sure though I will figure it out if need be. Tonight's journal is the beginning of me trying to figure it out if need be. You may want to prepare yourself before you continue to read on. This is your warning.

Tonight for some odd reason I felt a sense of peace. I felt peace knowing I have tried to do everything I could possibly do to help James. I rub his head, I visit him several times a day, I change his diapers, I even wipe his head with a wet, cold washcloth hoping to help him reduce his fever. I do everything I possibly know to do to help him feel better. This is just what a mom would do right? Some say I need to go home. Some say I need to leave the hospital more. They are probably right. But I know, if I do lose James to heaven, I need to feel at peace with myself that I did everything possible I could do to help him. Leaving the hospital and going home more would leave me with an empty feeling of not doing enough. So, I continue to stay in Charleston and visit James and sit by his side so I know in my heart I tried everything I could possibly do to save his heart. A mom gives everything she has to save one of her children. To Frick and Frack, I would do the same thing for you both as well anytime without a blink or thought.

So, how does a mom know when it is time to let her child go? How does a mom know when it is okay to whisper those hard, soft words to her sweet baby when necessary? "It is okay sweet baby. I know you are tired. It is okay for you to rest and join God." Is it time for me to allow James to rest and go join God in heaven? Is he tired of fighting? I agree with Doc Optimistic though tonight, James is "one heck of a fighter." He continues to fight through everything. He is continuing to fight tonight even as his condition gets worse.

James isn't doing well tonight with a high fever of 103, high heart rate, high ventilator settings, and he was put back on a maximum dose of dopamine when his blood pressure dropped. His body is swollen again and he was feeling miserable this afternoon so he started receiving morphine again to help keep him comfortable. Is it time for us to give James permission to stop fighting and let his little body rest? Are we ready to let him rest?

The doctors will meet soon and talk about James's condition once again and discuss any possible solutions to fix his heart. James's heart is severely damaged and we are not sure what choices we have. Several options, such as an open heart surgery to stitch the valves, have been mentioned as well as a heart transplant. Also, I am sad to tell you that we may not be able to do anything to help fix his heart, especially since he is malnourished now and has several infections currently. This breaks my heart to report this option to you but it is the truth. Sometimes, the truth hurts. Is it time to let James rest peacefully and not put him through anymore surgeries or infections? Oh God, only you know.

I expect to know more by the end of this week as we will have a Care Conference with all of James's doctors. I expect to know what the best possible solution is to help James: surgery, new heart, or final peace and rest. I have been thinking more about his options. I have not given up hope on healing his heart. I have just added an extra option of allowing James's heart to heal in heaven. Don't ever think I am giving up hope! Oh how my own heart hurts as I type those words, "allowing James's heart to heal in heaven." The idea of allowing his heart to heal with a feeling of peace from his mother makes me wonder how does a mother feel at peace with this option?

Tonight, I am still on my feet standing. It is a good thing I can still stand. I will continue to stand while I carry faith, hope, love, as well as peace. My next step is to fill my arms with peace knowing I have done everything within in my power to help James and continue to be a servant of God in the process. Don't get me wrong; this will be hard to continue standing on my feet especially if we lose James. The one thing I do know is if this time does come and we have to make the decision of whispering those hard, soft words to our sweet baby James, you all will be there to catch me when I fall and can't continue to stand. That, my friends, is what the community of Christ does for each other. The community catches each other when they can't stand anymore.

Thanks be to God for you all for catching me during this journey. Thanks be to God for the amazing nurses, doctors, RTs, and CTs at MUSC for their knowledge and care for my sweet baby. I continue to stand on my feet.

The Lord is my Shepherd; I shall not want.
He maketh me to lie down in green pastures:
He leadeth me beside the still waters.
He restoreth my soul:
He leadeth me in the paths of righteousness for His name' sake.

Yea, though I walk through the valley of the shadow of death,
I will fear no evil: For thou art with me;
Thy rod and thy staff, they comfort me.
Thou preparest a table before me in the presence of mine enemies;
Thou anointest my head with oil; My cup runneth over.
Surely goodness and mercy shall follow me all the days of my life,
and I will dwell in the House of the Lord forever.

Update from a Friend ~Becky Pickett
Wednesday, August 10, 2011 4:27 p.m.

Friends,

Jacqueline asked me to update the journal for her. Sweet baby James has not had a good day. His heart stopped beating earlier today; however, the doctors and nurses were able to get it restarted using CPR and medicine. J. J. is back en route to Charleston to be with them.

Please pray for this wonderful family as well as the doctors and nurses treating James. Only God knows the future for James, so we ask all to pray for God's love to provide comfort during this difficult time.

Part 3

LOVE

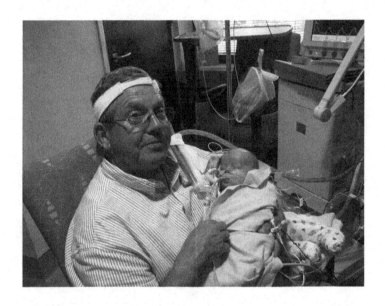

Love never fails.
1 Corinthians 8

L ove: an emotion of strong affection and personal attachment. Love is also a virtue representing all of human kindness, compassion, and affection; and "the unselfish loyal and benevolent concern for the good of another" according to Webster. The love a mother feels for her child is immeasurable. The love family and friends feel for each other is amazing!

CHAPTER 15

Life, Learning, and Love

Don't be afraid your life will end; be afraid that it will never begin.
Grace Hansen

Music ~Dad
Thursday, August 11, 2011 11:21 p.m.

I love music. I love all kinds of music. When I'm driving up and down the road, which has been quite a bit lately, I like to flip channels. I listen to one station until the Kia guy starts screaming at me, then I flip to another channel. Sometimes I play _Name That Tune_ with the girls at work. It drives them crazy, but I'm really good at it and like to show off. Some of the lyrics to some of my favorite songs hit me pretty close to the heart. All genres tend to evoke some type of feeling and say some pretty important things. As my heart breaks tonight, I thought I would share a few that really hit home for me.

When James was born, the song that played in my head more than any other was _I Hope You Dance_. We hope for so much for our children don't we? From the moment they're born we begin wondering what they will do with their lives. We wonder whether they will be interested in sports or band, drama, art, math or English. What type of personality will they have? Will they be laid back or aggressive? One thing that we all hope for is that they dance. We hope that they take chances, experience the fantastic, wondrous things that life has to offer. After we found out about James's condition another song began to play and replay more and more: _Amarillo Sky_ by Jason Aldean. "Lord I never complain. I never ask why. Please don't let my dreams run dry underneath this Amarillo Sky."

After finding out about James's heart condition and arriving in Charleston, Jacqueline and I both had a little bit of a hard time understanding. Internally we both wondered why this happened. Were we being punished? Was James being punished because of something we did? Could we have done something differently? Were we unfaithful to God? The mind races trying to figure out what we should have done differently. All of Job's friends thought the same way. But in the end, they were all wrong. Still, we want so bad to be in control. We want so bad to be able to change the outcome of this. All we really want is for James to have that opportunity to dance. I have these visions, these happy dreams for his future. I envision him bewildered by Christmas morning. I can even see the stocking with his name on it hanging alongside Frick's and Frack's. I picture taking him hiking in the mountains for the first time and Frick showing him how to climb rocks. I see Frack making him do cheerleading stunts like my sisters did with me. I can imagine him growing up like any other normal child, having his own personality and his own special place in my heart, just like Frick and Frack. The third song is fairly new by The Band Perry, *If I Die Young*. I guess this one makes the list for obvious reasons. Still, the sharp knife of a short life resonates and vibrates within my being until the tears overflow.

We have to change stations. The country songs are just too sad. The next station is the sports talk radio station. It seems that Butch Davis has been fired amid nine major NCAA infractions at the University of Non Compliance, I mean North Carolina. Now if we can just catch Roy Williams in the act then there's two more laughs for good measure and we're on to the next station.

Sometimes I come across the pop channel. Fortunately for us Justin Bieber and Britney Spears were left off the list. First up is the song *Stop and Stare* by One Republic. "Stop and stare, I think we're moving but we go nowhere, and you'd give anything to get what's fair, but fair ain't what you really need. Can't you see what I see?" It reminds me that we are all part of God's plan. Sometimes in James's room I stare at him. I read the numbers on the monitors and become hypnotized by the changes in heart rate, oxygen saturations, and blood pressure. The whole song captures these moments. This roller coaster ride makes you feel like you're moving. And you are moving up some days, and down others. But for all of our trial and error, steps forward, and steps backward, we end up moving nowhere. And we want what we feel to be fair for us. We want a different outcome than the one we're dealt with. But God knows what we really need. Only we can't see the plan as he sees it.

Then it's on to Christian Radio where I here Toby Mac sing, *I was Made to Love You*. I think about James as a creation in the image of God. We are all made for that purpose. So why was James made this way? He was made to love God. The amount of support and prayer that has gone up on behalf of James is incredible. It has us giving thanks to God. It has others giving thanks and sending praise. James has been a little testimony to God, but I see the potential for a huge testimony if he could just somehow make it through this. Then I hear *I Love the Way you Hold Me*. Actually I hear Frack singing it. If ever there was a baby that loved to be held it was Frack.

I held James for just the second time tonight. He loved it. He loves being held. His heart rate dropped almost 15 points while being held by me, Jacqueline, and Mama Peacock. Yes, Mama Peacock got to hold the baby. Holding the baby was one thing that was most important to Jacqueline. The day she finally held James was a beautiful moment in time. It's still a tremendous joy for her to be able to do that.

Last but not least we flip to the classic rock station. *Hotel California* is playing. We actually have a kids lullaby version of The Eagles. It was the first CD James listened to. There are two songs that must make the list. The first is *Let it Be* by The Beatles. First of all if you're making a list of music and you don't use The Beatles, then shame on you. They are The Beatles after all. "When I find myself in times of trouble mother Mary comes to me, speaking words of wisdom let it be." One of the easiest and hardest things to do in life is turn your problems over to God. The other song that resonates through the soul is the song *Time* by Pink Floyd. "Take it Away, the moments that make up a dull day." Time has become so precious with James. Every moment is significant. Every time he opens his eyes, I feel like I need to make it count. And with that, we have made it most of the way around the dial.

We did skip the R&B and rap stations. Maybe we will catch that one later. But most of you who are reading this don't listen to a lot of rap music so you wouldn't know what I was talking about anyway. What I can tell you that you will understand is this: the caregivers play music for James because it helps to keep his heart rate and blood pressure stable. Music has a way of speaking to us and calming us. It can also excite us, anger us, or move us in some other way. In the past three months we have been moved more than at any other time in our lives. In a lot of ways we have gotten more miles out of the last three months than the last three years. However, as I filled out a bank ticket today, I started to date it for May. It was August 10, but for some reason it's almost like time stopped moving forward for us on that fateful day in May when James was born. It doesn't even feel like we've had a summer, even though the weather has remained over 100 degrees for many days. I can't explain it other than to say it feels like we are stuck at this moment in time when our lives were immediately changed forever and our world came crashing down.

Nothing is normal anymore. It used to be that home was the safe haven and work was where the pressure was. Now, work is the safe haven and there is more pressure at home than I can bear. This life is hard right now. We were advised by doctors tonight to make some difficult decisions about how far they should go to save James the next time he codes. As a parent, how far would you go to save your child? How much would you put them through? These are questions that haunt me at 2:24 a.m. There are some out there that read this blog and have preceded us down this road. For some of them the journey didn't end well. I'm sure they are even more heartbroken than we are right now and we are pretty heartbroken. These folks continue to care. They continue to share with us and encourage us to keep going, even on nights like tonight when it feels like going on isn't possible. But it is precisely the moving on that allows you to arrive someplace else. Winston Churchill once said, "If you're going through Hades, just keep going." So this is what we will do. We will keep going. We will see it to its end. Like the Semisonic song, *Closing Time*, "Every new beginning starts with some other beginning's end."

The experts are thinking the end may be near for James. They might be right. But the end of this life marks the beginning of another for him and for us. But then again, if we get that miracle, if by some grace, he finds his way through the maze of surgeries well, that too means a new life for us.

There is a point to this. Much like your radio, we start at a station in life. Sometimes there is sweet music at our station in life but eventually a commercial hits and the Kia guy starts screaming at you. God has a way of moving you along to a different station. At every station you find joy and pain. Eventually all of it comes full circle and you start searching all over again for good music. I hope that my near future (by some miracle) ends up filled with music from Barney and Sesame Street. Maybe one day I can let him listen to the greatest hits from U2. Maybe one day he will listen to some new type of music that people my age can't stand. I hope I'm not the parent that moans about this new music and compares it harshly with the music from my day. I hope I will embrace the change. I hope I will embrace the new style. I hope I will let it be, and be thankful that he's still here for me to enjoy him. That's the kind of music we all could enjoy.

It may take a while to find sweet music, but it will be out there and eventually we will find it. Eventually we will find a new station in life that will play music in which we will find joy. Regardless of the outcome, we will be searching for that new station in life. I hope that you will continue to pray for us. We will need the strength that only Christ and prayer can provide. I pray for healing, for faith, for hope, and for love. Not only for us, but for some of those parents who have been down this road before. I pray for Frick and Frack who have been absolutely amazing through all this adventure. I'm so proud of them. And I pray for you, our friends, who care enough to check up on us through our CaringBridge site, inspire us to continue on with prayers and words of encouragement, and strengthen us by confirming to us that this site and our words by God's grace somehow make a difference. We give thanks to God for you. You have been and continue to be a blessing for us. Thank you to all. Thanks be to God.

Laying on of Hands Service Scheduled ~Dad
Thursday, August 11, 2011 11:45 a.m.

James has shown some minor signs of improvement. Currently he has a fever of 101, a heart rate 187, and good blood pressure. Ventilator support has been moved up to forty. A Laying on of Hands service has been scheduled for Friday, Aug. 12, at noon at the hospital in Charleston and at St. Giles Presbyterian Church in Greenville, South Carolina. As James 5:15 KJV says

> *"Is any sick among you? Let him call for the elders of the church and let them pray over him anointing him with oil in the name of the Lord."*

Please join us in Charleston or in Greenville for this service if possible. On behalf of the entire Martin family, thank you for your continued support and prayers.

I Am Desperate ~Nurse Mom
Thursday, August 11, 2011 9:53 p.m.

The past few days have been extremely hard for me. I cry quite a bit and find myself imagining my life without James. I imagine how hard my heart is going to continue to break if I lose James. Tonight, I lay my head directly next to his head on his bed, listened to his ventilator, held his hand, and cried big crocodile tears while I mourned. I mourned the fact that Doc Honesty may just be right after all. I may not be bringing James home friends. I lay next to James's head tonight on his bed and cried, watched his beautiful eyes look me over and imagined we were at home lying in my bed just like I imagined while I was pregnant and sick lying in the bed at home. His eyes were wide open and watched my face as tears flowed onto his bed sheets. I talked to him for a while as he watched me and listened to my voice. He fell asleep while I rubbed his little hand with my fingers. I told him I loved him very much and I was so sorry. I am so sorry he is having to endure this heart defect.

I told him about his nursery at home that is waiting for him, but also told him about heaven. I told James what I imagined heaven to be like if he decides to visit soon. "There are wonderful people waiting for you in heaven." I said. "You will finally get to meet my grandmother Helen. She would be waiting for you, along with Jesus, I am sure and will take great care of you in heaven." Oh how I dream of the day I can lay down with him in my bed at home and snuggle and talk to him just like I did with Frick and Frack. The sad news is this day may not come for me. I hope and pray I am able to handle this day if it does come. Burying your own child should never happen to a parent.

Watching James code in his hospital room yesterday afternoon and then receive CPR was a very hard thing for me to watch. Once again, I went into my safe place of calmness preparing myself to lose James. After he was given CPR and medicine, he came back with his eyes open looking around. What do we do now I wonder? What should I think? James continues to fight even when he is very sick. Even when the doctor thinks his precious heart is wearing down, he continues to fight. The doctor didn't expect James to live past this morning. When I saw him this morning I didn't expect him to either, as his color was purple and he looked pasty. Is it okay for me to tell James it is okay to stop fighting? I feel awfully selfish. I still want James to stay with me here on Earth and not go to heaven. I want him to go home with me and lie down on my bed and cuddle as I sing him sweet songs and watch his eyes watch my face. I want Frack to be able to organize his clothes in his dressers as she is so patiently waiting to do. I want Frick to be able to teach James how to throw a football as like he desperately wants to do.

During sad times like these past few days, I have to lean, not stand, as a friend posted on the CaringBridge guestbook. I was leaning and having a hard time standing, especially when I tried to walk back to the hospital this morning. I was especially quick to listen for my three little birdies whistling this late morning and wanted to hear them sing a song of joy. I am sad to say, the birds were not singing this morning. As

I walked past a cancer patient sitting on the bench outside the entrance doors to the cancer center I wanted to grab him and shake him and ask him if he had heard any birds singing. I wanted to beg him to please tell me he heard birds chirp so I would know not to worry. Still friends, I was searching for the signal of peace this morning. I was searching for a silly signal of birds chirping. The sounds were silent however. The silent sound of numbness came across my body as I walked to the hospital without the sweet music and sounds of birds.

Last night I felt the feeling of desperation takeover my body. I felt extremely desperate. I want to fix James. I have come to a point where I can't do anything else. The doctors say there is not much we can do right now. James is very sick. In order to perform a surgery, a long shot, James's condition will have to improve drastically. Then, the surgery is not any guarantee. I have done everything I possibly can do to help him, except one last thing. When in times of trouble and worry as I was feeling yesterday I turn to the Bible. I turned to the Bible yesterday and read my favorite book, the book of James. As James 5:14 states:

> *Are any of you sick? You should call for the elders of the church to come and pray over you, anointing you with oil in the name of the Lord.*

With this said, tomorrow around noon there will be two services offered. One service will be offered in Greenville, South Carolina, at St. Giles Presbyterian Church and another service at MUSC in Charleston. Just as the Bible states, in James we are calling for the elders of the church, of all churches, to come and pray. We are calling for the laying of hands on James. I am continuing to ask God to perform yet another miracle and heal James's heart and body. This is it for me. This is the final thing I know to do to help James. What a wonderful testimony to God. What a wonderful testimony to God to have the elders come and help pray and ask for God's healing on my sweet baby. What an amazing testimony for God to heal my sweet baby James.

God, I am begging you. I am begging you along with many others to heal James's heart and body. James is still alive and a miracle can save his life here on Earth. A miracle will allow me to take him home God and lay down in my bed with him, look into his eyes and continue to share your love and grace with him as well as the many, many prayer warriors reading this blog and traveling this journey along with us. Lord, please hear our prayers.

In closing, thanks be to God. Thanks be to God for creating an amazing little baby named James. Thanks be to God for the many, many countless hours of prayers you all continue to send to God in James's name. J. J. and I will be on the fourth floor tomorrow at the ICU waiting room by 11:30 a.m. greeting anyone interested in joining us for the Laying on the Hands service here in Charleston. Much love to you all!

Ignoring the Voices ~Nurse Mom
Saturday, August 13, 2011 4:32 a.m.

Today, I prayed, visited, and cried with lots of family members. Some were family by blood as well as family by Christ. During the Laying of the Hands service today in Charleston, I held baby James in my arms as we all gathered (approx. twenty people) in James room number eight in the PCICU. Doctor Optimistic and "Nurse Has Walked in my Shoes" allowed us all to gather in James's room to hold the service today. I laid James on a prayer shawl I received from a friend and I wrapped another prayer shawl on James's head. It was given to me by the pastor from a lady that worked at Palmetto Presbyterian. Her prayer group made this shawl for James and wanted the pastor to bring the shawl to us today.

During the service today at noon in Charleston, as well as in Greenville, I felt peace and comfort knowing we all were being faithful Christians once again asking God to heal James's body. We were being faithful Christians by asking the elders and others to come together and pray over the sick. We were being faithful by following the Bible. I wondered what the nurses and doctors working in the Unit were thinking today as they saw twenty people come in the back door and walk in James's room. I wondered what they thought as they heard us all read scripture and recite our faith and beliefs in Jesus Christ together in unison. I wondered if all the babies in the Unit could hear twenty people singing *Jesus Loves Me* to James as well as the other eleven babies in the Unit.

This morning, at 4:30 a.m., I lay wide awake and once again wondering. When I say I am wondering to myself, I feel like my silent thoughts and wonders become voices in my mind or voices in my head. Lately, these voices in my head have turned into guilt. The thoughts in my head are saying, "You should have called them back. Why can't you answer your phone when it rings? How come you haven't written your thank you cards? So many people are praying for you and why can't you just get up out of the bed and give them an update? Make sure you pump tonight because if you don't pump your milk will stop and you will not be a good mom. Call Frick and Frack and let them know you love them. Do something. Do something now to save your son. You are his mom. Why aren't you giving back? Why are you receiving?" Do any of you experience these voices? Do any of you experience these silent thoughts that turn into voices of guilt in your head? Oh how the guilt eats me up for the simplest things that are so, so silly. Oh how these voices and thoughts sometimes make me feel like I am going crazy. Am I going crazy I wonder?

As I cried and visited with three "sisters," a cousin, and Doc Mission today in the hospital cafeteria I asked them if they thought James knew I loved him? Once again, the silent thoughts and voices in my head brought this ridiculous comment out through my lips. One of the "sisters" told me this wasn't me talking. This was the devil putting these things in my head and not to worry and think these things. I have been thinking about her comment all day. I have been wondering.

So, with this post early this morning I want to get rid of all these silent thoughts and start ignoring these voices of guilt. I want you all to know I appreciate everything. I mean everything you all are doing for us during these times of troubles. I do read every post on the CaringBridge. I read every email you send, I read every comment and message you send to me on Facebook. I do hear every message you leave on my cell phone even if I don't listen to it for days. I see every text message you send and I feel the pouring of love you give. I want so bad to return all of your calls, respond to every one of your messages, but I am not able to do it. I am not able to answer my phone every time it rings. I want to make myself go to the post office and mail all the high school seniors their graduation gifts I have had sitting for a few months now. This weekend, some of them are moving on to college and I can't even find the strength to call them to say, "I am thinking about you and oh how I will miss you dearly." Know, I will miss you dearly! Some days all I can do is get up out of the bed and take a shower and put on my makeup. Some days all I can do is get up and get going and remain standing or "leaning" as I am doing lately.

I want so badly to finish sending out every one of you a thank you note for all the gifts and packages you send. I want so badly to call you all individually and thank you for everything you do as well as say to me. I am just not able. I am just so, so tired. I can't stop though. I have to continue getting up and I have to continue to keep going. I'm praying, praying, praying! Oh how I wish I could just stop and relax.

I ask you early this morning to please forgive me for the things I am unable to do right now. I want you to know that even if I am not able to send you a thank you note, I do appreciate everything. Without your love and support I am not sure if I would be alive right now. Without all of your love and support I am not I would be able to continue to get up in the mornings and even take a shower. It is your support and prayers that continue to fill my heart with hope, faith, and love.

I do promise you one thing, especially you J. J., I promise you I will be okay whatever the outcome is with baby James. Yes, I am sad. Yes, I cry often now but I will find the strength to continue. God will give me the strength to continue. I will find the strength to get up and even lean if I have to. Frick and Frack, I will love you always and yes, just as much as James. I will continue to be your mom and cherish every moment. Hopefully soon, God will fill my heart again with joy and I will be smiling just like I used to smile. J. J., I will never leave you. Yes, I may be angry and be mean to you at times, but always know I will never leave you. To you, all my family members by blood as well as Christ, I will forever be grateful to you for your support and prayers.

I will release the guilt and ignore the voices, especially the bad voices during this dark, very dark time.

Thanks be to God for you all. Thanks be to God for all your prayers today in Charleston, Greenville, and in Spirit. The next few days are very critical for James. We need him to start taking on nutrition again as well as remain stable with his heart rate. J. J. and I will be watching the next few days very closely trying to decide in faith, with God's help, about James's condition and future treatments. May God fill all of our hearts and minds with love and help us ignore the voices.

Let's Continue to Do What We Do Best: Pray and Worship ~Nurse Mom Sunday, August 14, 2011 4:44 a.m.

Good morning! Yes, good morning to you all. Today is Sunday, one of my favorite days of the week. Frick and Frack will be joining you all in Greenville this morning at St. Giles for worship, and I will be joining my friends in Charleston at Palmetto Presbyterian to worship and pray. When I talked to Frack on the phone last night she was excited to let me know she was going to Sunday School today. What an amazing gift to know your daughter still gets excited about going to Sunday School to see her friends and study God. Frick and Frack have been staying with the "Bird Family" since Tuesday of last week. Thanks be to God for these saints who open their home so freely to Frick and Frack and help provide a safe haven for them during these uncertain times. Once again, I can never show or pay back my appreciation to you.

I am up early this morning once again. I am unable to sleep again. My goal for this upcoming week is to get back on a healthy sleep pattern and schedule in order to give my body the much-needed rest and healing it needs through sleep. I just called James's nurse again this morning for an early a.m. update on James. He had a good night. He is resting peacefully and his white blood count is still the same, hanging around 30,000. We need his white blood count to decrease so we know the dirty nine-letter words are decreasing. I think it has been twenty-four hours since he has had a fever. This is a good sign. We hope and pray this means his body is trying to get rid of the infections. We need his white blood count to reduce to between 10,000-15,000 in order to be a candidate for the next surgery to re-stitch his valves. He could even maybe be added to a heart transplant list. I hold onto faith and hope we will see good signs soon. I hope and pray God will send me the signal of improvement in James's health to let me know I am doing the right thing by sitting with endurance and faith in the Lord. Friends, we are sitting back, waiting, and watching to see what James does the next few days. We are praying and waiting.

Friday, James restarted feeds, small feeds of three ccs, but they were breast milk feeds. James continues to be on a feed as well called Total Parenteral Nutrition (TPN). This feed is given through his port line in his arm. TPN feeds are not always the best as they can damage his liver. TPN feeds are like a "yellow liquid vitamin" given to James through an I.V. If James can get off of TPN feeds through his port line and go straight to breast milk feeds through his nose into his gut, this would be a huge success for him. Please pray for James's body to sustain full feeds again through his nose with breast milk and allow us to stop the TPN feeds through his veins so James's liver will not be damaged again. Yes friends, I never stopped pumping. I never stopped pumping James's "liquid antibiotics." I did restart my caffeine habit again though. I have been "pumping and dumping" so I could have caffeine again. I think this morning on my way to worship I will stop and have a Caramel Macchiato in your honor. I will stop and have a small cup of joy for my soul again as I continue to search for little bits of joy in these dark days.

Let's continue to do what we do best this morning. Let's continue to pray and worship this Sunday morning. I am getting ready to get up out of the bed this morning without J. J. having to "make" me like he did yesterday morning. I am going to stand, yes stand, this morning and do what I do best. I am going to shower, put my makeup on and entice my dad to take me to an early breakfast. What a joy for me to go to an early breakfast with my dad before I start to do what I do best: pray and worship.

I hope you are able to get up this morning and do what you do best. I hope you are able to stand and pray and worship our God. Pray and worship our wonderful God even when we experience dark times. Have a wonderful day filled with rest, Caramel Macchiattos, joy, worship, and peace!

Scars ~Dad
Monday, August 15, 2011 10:46 a.m.

When you were a child, who did you want to be when you grew up? For me, it was Roger Steinbach. I'm sure there are a lot of kids out there who wanted to be the quarterback of the Dallas Cowboys. Hopefully, at some point in time they grow out of that and realize that the Cowboys suck! For me, it came simultaneous to the Carolina Panthers entering the league. For my best friend growing up, he wanted to be Michael Jordan and play for the University of North Carolina. My dad was a huge Sonny Jorgensen and Ted Williams fan. Frack wants to be a veterinarian. Frick says he wants to be a doctor or a banker. As a parent I have great expectations for my children. I try in the way I live my life to inspire them. I demand more than average from them because I don't want them to have average lives. Average stinks in my book. You can't be extraordinary without the little extra. My children have done very well. If I'm being honest, they have thrived.

Now, before you start thinking me arrogant, please know that I take absolutely no credit for this. They have done well because of God-given talent and their mother. They have an excellent support network from our families and church friends. They attend a great school with terrific teachers who care a great deal for the children they teach, including mine. Still, when I look at Frick, I see no limits to his potential. When I look at Frack, I see pretty much the same thing. They're wonderful, talented kids with limitless potential. I'm willing to bet I'm not the only parent who sees this in the eyes of their children.

It's different when I look at James. I hear the doctors and nurses talk a good bit about the difficult road he could have facing him. I hear them ask me time and time again if it's worth it. I hear them ask, "What do you expect to gain from the next surgery?" The answer is, maybe a few more years. That's all I can expect to gain at a maximum. They tell me that even if he defies all odds, and makes it to a heart transplant, the longest living transplant patient has made it fifteen years. So, best-case scenario, he makes it to fifteen. He's going to be behind, and everything is going to be a challenge. So why put him through all this?

Today, I got my answer to this question. One of my friends from all the way back in high school came down yesterday and I got to meet her son Sebastian. He's ten years old and small for his size. He has a handsome pair of glasses and a glorious smile. But the best, most beautiful, thing is a scar right down the middle of his chest, just like James. He has two scars where feeding tubes used to reside in the exact same place that James's lines to his heart used to run. The scars are in exactly the same places as James's scars. It gave me cold chills as he lifted up his shirt to show me his wounds. It reminded me of the song, *By his Wounds*. "By his wounds, by his wounds we are healed."

I told Jacqueline my friends were coming. Last night she confessed she was a little afraid to see firsthand what it was that she was fighting for. She was afraid of exactly what she was going to see and hear. What we ended up receiving yesterday was a real gift from God. We received confirmation that no matter whether James makes it or not, he is going to be different. There will be challenges. It will be difficult. It will be worth every single bit of it. Sebastian's first question to me when he met me yesterday was, "Do you like football?" Not hello, not nice to meet you, but "Do you like football?" Do you know what this did to me? Anybody that knows me knows that football is my favorite thing on the planet! He went on to tell me that he wanted to play football but his mama wouldn't let him. It was then that Jacqueline's heart melted. The mama's friend said to him, "Sebastian there's many ways to be involved in football." What a perfect and wonderful answer. Jacqueline immediately fell for little Sebastian, his mom, her friend, and the rest of the family. Sebastian may or may not be able to do a lot of things. He may or may not be able to do complex algebra. He may not be able to quarterback the Dallas Cowboys, but he can smile. And boy does he smile. He has the kind of smile that brings joy to everybody in the room. He's the kind of kid that lights up a room with his eyes. He has the personality, to take a joke from his mama, and get the humor in it and play it up. He has this inquisitive nature that lets you know he's interested in you and what you have to say. He can figure out a video game in about five minutes and begin playing it pretty well. He has the ability to hound his mom for a PlayStation PSP. In short, he is absolutely magical. He is not perfect. There are a lot of things he can't do. But don't start judging his quality of life. That child is a beloved child of God. He is surrounded by a family who loves him and friends that know just the right things to say. Most important, he has scars. His scars are too similar to those James bears. It has been said that scars are souvenirs you never lose. The past is never far. James and Sebastian have a handsome collection of souvenirs. You don't have to look too far to realize that they will forever be different. But be careful not to set limits on them. We are all limited in ways. No one determines our ceilings except God.

Today, we will have another conversation with several members of staff about continuing on with James. They will ask us again if we really want to continue. They will talk to us again about his potential for a quality of life. I will smile graciously. I will remember the fact that he has improved over the last four days. I will remember we all have scars. We all have invisible ceilings and I know God determines my ceiling, not a team of doctors. I will remember Sebastian and say, "all things are possible," (thank you Donna). Thanks be to God!

James has made some small but meaningful strides over the last few days. The first two things we need to do are begin getting over the infection and begin taking on digestion. His white blood cell count came down from 33k to 28k. This is good. As white blood cells decrease it usually means less infection. Also, they began giving James three ccs of breast milk. It's not much but it's a solid first step. He seems to be taking it. In conclusion, the infection seems slightly better and digestion is working okay. So we keep going, one last time. We continue to pray for the miracle. So keep praying.

Update from the phone ~Nurse Mom
Tuesday, August 16, 2011 9:10 p.m.

Good evening from Easley. I came home today to spend the day with the kids and celebrate Frick's ninth birthday tomorrow. When I asked Frick what he wanted for his birthday he replied, "I would like to have the entire family together for dinner. Also, I want you to cook your homemade macaroni and cheese for me as well mom." What a request from a nine year old. It was a request to have his mom, dad, and sister together for dinner. I told him I would see him soon. Frick's grandmother and Paw are also here with us as well. Frick will enjoy lots of family for his birthday dinner. I normally try to cook the kids' favorite meal for their birthday so I better refresh my cooking skills since it has been five months since I have cooked. The two months before James was born I was on bed rest and never lifted a finger in the kitchen. And you all know what I have been doing the past three months.

I called James's "Nurse Ninja" several times today to check on him. Bless her sweet heart for having patience with me and my phone calls. James is stable today with a 7.35 blood gas and a heart rate running between 160 and 170. The great news is James's white blood count is coming down slowly. This morning his white blood count was down to 21,000. I think it peaked around 34,000 last week. Hopefully this is a sign of his body getting rid of the dirty nine-letter-words: infection. James has been fever-free for a day or so now, so let's hope and pray he is able to fight off these infections. Also, James's feeds were increased today from three to six ccs. Slowly, he is able to get more food. I am sad to say his feeds are formula again as the breast milk runs through him quickly and his body needs to absorb the nutrients. My milk supply is running low now since the demand hasn't been needed. I want to continue to pump for hopes of one day I may be able to nurse. I just don't know yet if the supply will last.

Being home is a good feeling. It is good to sleep in my own bed and have space. Frack and I worked on two more pages of her scrapbook tonight at the kitchen table. I think a hot bubble bath and relaxing is in my future. I continue to think about James and how he is doing while I am away. I had to leave James in God's hands again so I can be a mom to Frick and Frack. I knew I needed to be home for Frick and celebrate his birthday. He has given so unselfishly the past three months and does anything and everything I needed him to do. I could at least fulfill a birthday dinner wish from him don't you think?

Please continue to pray for us as well as James. Please pray for James's white blood count to decrease. We need his white blood count down between 10,000-15,000. We also need the swelling and edema to decrease again as James's waist measured forty-seven again. Yesterday, it went down to forty-five but was back up today. We will need to continue to pray for pee to reduce the extra fluids and swelling in James body.

Also, I am adding a new request to your prayers tonight. Please pray for God's will to be done with James. God has a plan for James and his life. Of course, as his mom I want James home with me and I want to rock him in his light green rocker waiting for him in his nursery here at home. I hope God's will and plan is to bring James home healthy and happy for us all to enjoy and testify to God's love and miracles. I am not sure what the plan is but I am learning and trying to strengthen my faith in God every day. Blessings to you!

CHAPTER 16

You Will Never Walk Alone

Never, never, never, never, ever give up. ~ Winston Churchill

Quality of Life ~Nurse Mom
Wednesday, August 17, 2011 11:59 p.m.

The past few days I have been thinking about what it means to have a good quality of life. I have been forming a mental picture in my head of my family, my three children, my life, a happy marriage, and being debt free. Well, the debt free part is a complete joke as I discovered a few weeks ago our medical bills are already over $1 million. Yes, you did read that right, over $1 million. Thank God we have insurance. I do not have any idea what quality of life my family will have in the future but I do envision a life of happiness full of love. I envision a life full of love and happiness. What does it mean to have a good quality of life? What type of life does God envision for us to have?

Last night I lay down in the bed with Frack and chuckled and smiled as she told me she thought my life was "perfect." "I wish I had your life Mom and we could switch lives," cried Frack. Perfect? I couldn't believe she described my life as perfect right now. What a strange word to use to describe my life currently. Frack just found out last night our pet cat, Max, was killed in our front yard by two dogs roaming the neighborhood the day after James was born. Frack asked her dad last night why she hadn't seen Max around the house in three weeks and J.J. thought it was best to tell her the truth. Max was dead. Max was thirteen years old, a beautiful blue-eyed cat, and a birthday present to me from J. J. on my twenty-second birthday. Frack sobbed and sobbed as she lay next to me holding her binky (her pink blanket) she was given as a present when she was born and wiped tears from her eyes. Last night, Frack wished to change lives with me as she felt like I was the lucky one. Frack envisioned my life better than hers last night as she cried over the loss of her beloved Max.

Today, we celebrated Frick's ninth birthday. What a day. Frick played this afternoon in the neighborhood with friends and ran in and out of the house waiting for his dad to get home from work so he could open his present from the family. We enjoyed a wonderful dinner consisting of barbeque ribs, macaroni and cheese, fried apples, rolls, and cookie cake topped with cookies-and-cream ice cream. Frick invited several of his friends and their parents in the neighborhood over to dinner to celebrate his special day. For a small moment today I felt like things were normal. For a small moment tonight, while talking with friends and enjoying fellowship over bread, I felt like I was normal. Frick was smiling ear from ear and running around the house and yard with his friends and sister. His life was filled with lots of smiles today and much happiness. Frick's ninth birthday was perfect and the "best ever" he told me as he closed his eyes tonight to go to dreamland. Frick couldn't envision his life any better today as he celebrated a wonderful birthday with family and friends.

I continued to call the nurses while I was away for an update on James. I learned James is continuing to have good days while I am away. Now, when I say good days that doesn't mean he is coming home tomorrow. I use the words "good days" to describe James still being alive continuing to make small, yes small, improvements. Tonight, James's feeds are on fifteen ccs and his ventilator was reduced this morning from forty breathes per minute to thirty-six breaths per minute. His heart rate was between the 140s and 150s and oxygen saturation was around eighty. The goal for James is to reach full feeds which is 25 ccs an hour. Once James gets to twenty-five, we can hopefully cut off the TPN feed. His feeds are supposed to increase every twelve hours by three ccs, so hopefully by Friday night James will be off the TPN feeds and on the goal of full feeds. His girth measurement around his waist today was still forty-six centimeters and continues to be pretty large. His day is filled with lots of rest and peaceful sleep. James doesn't envision any other life, as he doesn't know any different life than the past three months. All James knows to this point is resting in his hospital bed in MUSC, watching his mobile, feeling his head rubbed and listening to the machines, also known as "slot machines," beeping and going off every time a medicine needs to be refilled or a pressure is off.

As for my life these days, I live in fear of the phone ringing in the middle of the night. I fear the phone will ring and deliver bad news. Before I go to bed at night I make sure my ringer is set on loud just in case. If my phone rings I will hear it and answer the call. As for my life these days, I live with lots of guilt over the silliest things I do that seem to be wrong to me. Why didn't I mail those presents yesterday? Why haven't I thanked the ABC family for their gift? Why can't I get my act together and get back into work mode? Why didn't I return the phone calls? Oh there is lots of guilt I am trying to work through. There is lots of guilt filling my head with the silent voices I continually ask to go away and come back another day.

J. J. seems very concerned with me and my state of mind lately. He worries that I am trying to be perfect and fears I am trying so hard to please God with everything I do. I hate to admit it but J. J. is right. I think and hope that if I do everything I can to make God happy with me he will provide grace and heal James. I try to be perfect in God's eyes so he will take care of James and heal my precious baby boy in the hospital bed. What a silly thought I know. God doesn't envision me to be perfect. God knows I can't be perfect. This is why he sent his son to die on the cross to save us all from having to be perfect. We are allowed to fall short. We are allowed to make mistakes. By the grace of God, our mistakes are forgiven. We are forgiven by God's grace.

As I look at the cross I wear around my neck everyday I think about how heavy the cross can be to carry. I think about how Mary felt as she watched her son Jesus die on the cross. Standing by and watching your son die is absolutely heartbreaking. I wonder what Mary envisioned for her family? I wonder what Mary envisioned for her life, happiness, and love? Was it God's will?

I leave you tonight thinking about the quality of life. Who are we to say what one's quality of life should be? Who are we to envision what is necessary for a person? Who decides the general standard or grade of life? God decides. God knows exactly what he is doing with James. God knows exactly what he is doing with me, with you, and with us all. I remind myself all the time of a quote a youth sent to me via text message when I was walking home from the hospital and searching for the signal. The quote by Alexandra Stoddard states, "Slow down, calm down, don't worry, don't hurry, trust the process." I need to remember to continue to trust the process of God. I need to remember God is in control and he will love me even if I am not perfect. God has a plan for my life. God does envision for us all to have a life full of happiness and love. God wants us all to have a good quality of life, even James. I am just not sure yet if James's good quality of life is here on earth with us or if it is in heaven with our lost loved ones. The hard part for us all is to continue to listen and trust God's directions. The hard part friends, is living the Christian life as we walk through the shadow of death. The hard part is fearing no evil or fearing the ring of a phone call in the middle of the night. We will continue to pray as we are all called to do. Much love and happiness to you and your family tonight!

News from Charleston ~Nurse Mom
Friday, August 19, 2011 11:08 p.m.

We are all back in Charleston again as a family. J. J. arrived tonight with Frick and Frack around 10 p.m. J. J. is watching ESPN, Frick is listening to music on his iPod, Frack is trying to go to sleep with a stuffed animal and I am smiling. Things seem to be normal. Things are as normal as normal gets for us tonight and everyone seems to be happy again. This is our new normal.

James is resting peacefully tonight and had a good day. The amazing news from Charleston to report is the amount of fluid drained from James's tummy today. Around 7:30 p.m. a drainage tube was inserted in James's left side. When I arrived around 8:30 p.m., 300 ccs were drained from his tummy into a foley. Wow! I wish I took a before and after picture for you to see the difference. It was amazing! When we left tonight to go to our home-away-from-home, James's drainage tube held around 350 ccs of fluid. This amount is more than his daily amount of fluids put into his body in a day. I asked the doctor if I could be next. I would love to have the extra fluid drained from my tummy. James's tummy was almost flat when we left tonight and I could see him breathing as his belly moved up and down. Before the drainage tube was inserted I called James "Baby Buddha." Hopefully with all the extra fluid drained from James's tummy his ventilator rate will be reduced soon and we can begin to decrease the current thirty-four breaths-per-minute rate.

By the morning, I am happy to report that James should be on full feeds of twenty-five ccs. Even if it is formula and not breast milk, I will take it. The TPN feeds were turned off yesterday and hopefully will stay off as long as James is able to tolerate full feeds. Today, I noticed James's thighs looked bigger so I hope this means he is gaining weight and able to tolerate feeds. We are not sure how much he weighs but will try to weigh him this Sunday.

James's left thumb tip is turning purple. His tip of his thumb has been purple for almost a week now since he coded last Wednesday. I am concerned about his thumb and hope it gets circulation soon so he doesn't lose the tip. I tried today to rub his hand, keep it warm and prayed for the circulation to return back to the tip of his thumb. Please add this concern to your list of prayer request. I know the list is getting long but I do know God is listening as James seems to bounce back when things seem scary. All of your prayers are working.

Things for James are looking better. I caught myself smiling today and I still feel a smile on my face. I spent most of the day talking to James, listening to music and rubbing his head and hands. He was wide-awake most of the day. I even allowed myself to start reading a new book today called *Wrestling with Angels*. I am giving myself permission to restart doing things I enjoy. I am giving myself permission to take care of myself again and crush the guilt that tries to creep into my mind with silent voices. Tomorrow, I plan to go to the beach with the family for a few hours, play with the kids in the water, and read a few pages of my book. I plan to enjoy the summer I haven't had with the kids starting tomorrow. I plan to take time for myself and thank God for the small blessings I continue to enjoy every day. Even though my new normal is tough at times, God still provides the small blessings that I need to continue to count every day. Thanks be to God!

Smile ~Dad
Saturday, August 20, 2011 9:50 a.m.

Smiles have been hard to come by the past few weeks. Life has been difficult to say the least with most of us Martins being exhausted, stressed, and emotionally spent. We have been through a tough few days. It was nice last night to see doctors, nurses, and most of all Jacqueline, smiling when I made my way through the PCICU. When you see someone greet you with a smile it changes your whole demeanor. You know there is good news to be shared and these people are happy to see you. A smile is a priceless gift from God and can sometimes say more than a thousand words.

Last week I had to drive back and forth from Duncan to Charleston three times. James's white blood cell count was continuing to rise with no relief in sight. The downward slide was at its worst when his heart finally stopped pumping on Wednesday afternoon. His white blood cell count was at 32,000. His fever was almost 104. He was on the strongest antibiotics they have. Nurse Picturesque and Nurse Ninja were able to bring him back and get him going again, but we almost lost him right then. On Friday morning they couldn't get a blood pressure to register. His white blood cell count went even higher to almost 34,000. You could tell by the attention the nurses and doctors were giving him that everyone was on high alert. He could code again at any time. Pressure, stress, anxiety, everyone was feeling it. There was this overwhelming sense of helplessness. It's an awful feeling when you have done all you can do and it's still not working. It's still not enough.

Then, on Friday afternoon of last week, we had the "Laying on Hands" ceremony. We did exactly what the Bible tells us to do. The passage is found in book of James (go figure). This was important for Jacqueline and me. There's a reason we had him baptized on day three of his life. If James passes away, Jacqueline and I need to know that we have done everything we know possible to help him—both in this life and the one after. On Saturday, his white blood cell count still remained at 30,000. It was a little better but still extremely high. On Sunday, it was the same. On Monday, it dipped to 28,000. On Tuesday we saw it go to 21,000, Wednesday 19000, Thursday 16,500, and Friday 14000. Finally, his infection appears to be gone and his white blood cell count is back to normal. They inserted the tube to drain his chest and abdomen. His belly looks much smaller. His heart rate now remains strong in the 130s and 140s instead of the 170s and 180s. This means that it has more time to rest and recover. James is now on full feeds at 25 ccs per hour. His liver has made some nice strides and his bilirubin numbers are around six. It once resided higher than twenty. His kidneys are functioning well. His digestive system is performing a lot better than it has over the past two weeks. In short, what a difference a week makes!

Maybe the ceremony worked. Maybe the antibiotics worked. Maybe my little Jedi used the force. Maybe it was the overwhelming amount of love and support we have received over the last week. Maybe it was God hearing our prayers. Maybe it was the skills of all the doctors and nurses. Maybe it was the machinery and hospital equipment. Maybe it was the sanitary procedures they have performed at just the right time. Maybe it was God's will and God's time. Maybe it was all of the above under the control of a higher power. Hmm . . . yes, I think maybe it is all of these things.

In any case, I am grateful for a lot of things this morning. I am thankful that Liverpool beat Arsenal this morning and I got to watch it live on ESPN3. "You will never walk alone" (Liverpool's song). I am thankful that Frick had a great birthday and knows how to use the new iPod Touch. Happy ninth birthday little chip off the old block! I'm thankful that my Jacqueline is finally sleeping better. I usually fuss at her when she sleeps in. I felt a tremendous amount of relief when she called yesterday at 11 a.m. and told me she was just waking up. I know how it feels to go days on end without sleeping. I know about the worry, stress, fear, anger, guilt, and helplessness. I know about these feelings that come with a sick child. Then I remind myself I am only the father. I have no idea what it's like to be his mother. I only know that it's probably exponentially more difficult to go through. For her to be able to sleep means more than I could ever explain so I won't try. I'm happy Frack is getting to pick where we go to lunch today. Most of all, I'm happy that James has a vent rate down to thirty with orders to continue decreasing throughout the day. I'm happy his heart rate is at a healthier number and his vitals are all on solid ground again. I'm happy he has overcome these recent infections. I continue to pray and praise God for his ability to once again overcome. I hope and pray we can continue to make progress.

Today, we have plans to visit the beach. I'm going to be a clown and let the kids dunk me time and time again pretending to put up a good fight that they will somehow always win. Today, I look forward to listening to Jacqueline talk about the water and how it makes her feel. I will hear all about the beauty of seashells, the smell of the salt air, the feel of the warmth from the sun on her skin and sand in her toes. I will hear about the sound of the ocean, and how the only way to eat seafood is fresh from the ocean. "Seafood doesn't taste the same anywhere else. The only way to eat it is fresh at the beach," she will say. I will appreciate the time and that for a moment we are living again. For a moment, we are enjoying life again. As I sit in the Intensive Care Unit looking at my child that all but died last Wednesday, I'm amazed at how much I have to be thankful for. My blessings are too abundant to mention. Frack is thankful for her books. Frick is thankful for his iPod. I am thankful my team won. Jacqueline is thankful that James is once again making a comeback. So today we thank God for good writers like Margery Williams and Matt Matthews. We thank him for Steve Jobs, Apple employees, and the iPod. We thank doctors and nurses for their love, intelligence, and skill. We thank Luis Suarez and Liverpool nation. We thank God for smiles and for those people that make a habit of bringing a smile to others. We encourage everyone to take inventory of your blessings. Think about all God has blessed you with and give thanks. A funny thing will happen. Instead of having all the worry and heartache that life brings, all of a sudden you find your smile. And a smile is a wonderful thing.

CHAPTER 17

What is Normal

If you judge people, you have no time to love them.
~ Mother Teresa

What's Important? ~Nurse Mom
Monday, August 22, 2011 11:50 p.m.

For the past week and a half I look at James's thumb tip on his left hand every time I walk into his room. I hold his hand and try to massage his fingers in hopes of increasing the circulation in his hands. I drive the caregivers crazy with questions about James's circulation, purple thumb, and statistics. "What can we put on his thumb to help increase the circulation? Should we massage his fingers more to help his thumb? What are we going to do about James's thumb," I question over and over.

Last Saturday, J. J., Frick, Frick and I spent the morning shopping for school shoes and visited the Citadel Mall. It took Frick an entire month of looking at many different shoe stores before he found the "perfect" pair of tennis shoes. I have no idea when he became so peculiar about his shoes, but he wanted to make sure he found the perfect pair before purchasing anything. Frack also got a new pair of pink animal print flip flops from Target because Friday night at the hospital she broke her strings off her flip flops.

When we arrived back at the Ronald McDonald House we came through the kitchen area to walk upstairs to our room for a nap and rest before dinner. As I walked into the back door entrance I heard a strange noise that sounded like a child crying. J. J. and the kids continued to walk up the stairs to head to our room, No. 210, and I stopped to look and see what and where the crying noise was coming from. I noticed a boy and his mother sitting at the dining room area at the table close to the stairs. Have you ever wanted to look at someone to see what they were doing but didn't want to stare? I wanted to see so bad what was happening but didn't want to be caught staring. One particular reason I didn't want to get caught staring was because this boy's face is severely damaged. This little boy's face is distorted and disfigured severely. His family is from Turkey. They are here to get him help and evidently have been here on and off for a while.

I cannot even begin to explain to you what this little boy's face looks like because I cannot find the proper words to explain it to you. If I had to guess I would say his entire face looks like it was burned with third-degree burns, but I am not sure that was the case. I am not sure what is wrong or what happened to this young, sweet, spirited boy, as his family does not speak English for me to ask. The dad speaks limited broken English.

As I am walking up the stairs I glance at this sweet child of God and notice he is crying softly while his mother sits by his side at the table and listens. She watches him take small bites of a peanut butter sandwich. I walk into our room question J. J. "Did you hear the little boy crying?" J. J. answered my question with a quick yes and told me with a sharp tone in his voice he did not want to talk about it. I am too persistent to stop questioning with such an answer from J. J. I asked him again what he thought was wrong and he once again let me know quickly he didn't want to talk about it. J. J. responded back with a concern of why God allows so much suffering in the world to happen. Of course, Frick and Frack's ears perked up immediately and their attention was pulled away from their games and they began to question as well.

You all know me by now. You all know I cannot ignore a child who is hurting. Even if the child is not mine and it is not my business, I have a hard time walking away and ignoring the hurt. So, with this said, I walked back downstairs and approached the little boy and his mother. I knew I wasn't going to be able to communicate with them since they didn't speak English. Remember, they are from Turkey. I stood next to the little boy sitting in the chair, looked at his mother and opened my arms wide as to ask with silent sign language what was wrong. The little boy was still crying, tears were slowly falling on his face and a soft cry full of hurt from this child continued to ring in my ears. His mother pointed to the left side of his head to show me a freshly sewn scar with stiches. This little boy just had surgery on the left, as well as right, side of his head and was in pain. I stood lifeless. I stood lifeless as I didn't know what to say or do. All I wanted to do was say some comforting words to this child and his mother, but of course the three of us didn't speak the same language. The mother picked up her white, folded napkin and continued to wipe the tears off her son's unique face. I immediately put my hand around his shoulders and started to rub his back thinking this was the only way I could show my sorrow for him and his pain. I wondered how many people were scared to touch him in the past? I wondered if people were afraid to touch him since his face was different? Then as I looked up to see his mother, I noticed she began to tear up as well. Immediately, I went over and gave her a big hug. All I knew to do was hug them. I held up one finger again as to communicate with sign language and told them I would be right back. I ran upstairs, desperate to do something kind for this little boy. I remembered a good friend and youth sent us several boxes of Skittles candy as well as other goodies in a care package. I brought him down one of these boxes of skittles hoping this gift of sweets would help make him feel better. Candy always makes little boys feel better.

"What can we put on his thumb to help increase the circulation? Should we massage his fingers more to help his thumb? What are we going to do about James's thumb?" I questioned. I look back over these questions I hounded the caregivers over just days ago concerning James. I look back over these questions and feel silly. Here I hound the nurses over a purple thumb tip. I've watched this little boy for the past few weeks walk around the Ronald McDonald House with a unique face. My mind starts to race about James if he loses his thumb tip as the doctor said might happen. I worry about kids picking on James in school because his thumb tip is gone. How insignificant is a thumb tip when a little boy's entire face is distorted? This little boy's face is so unique it is hard for people to even look at him. His face is so unique it is hard for me to even look at him. Do you think kids make fun of him? Do you think he even has any friends to play with because he is different?

Even though J. J. can't talk about this little boy because it makes him sad to think about his pain, I can. I tell you this story because I find myself worrying about things like purple thumb tips all the time lately. I find myself concerned with things that seem large to me but are probably very small to others. I bet you the little boy from Turkey staying in the Ronald McDonald House would trade a missing thumb tip any day for a "normal" face. I am sure there are lots of other children in the world who would trade their defect for a missing fingertip. I may even trade James's heart defect for a chromosome defect. Who knows?

I decided to walk down to this family's room that afternoon and invite them to go with us to the beach. I knew they didn't have any transportation and figured an afternoon at the beach would probably be fun for their family. I talked to Frick beforehand and explained to him that I was going to invite them to the beach so the little boy could play. Frick understood completely what I was doing and agreed he would feel comfortable playing with this boy even if he was unique. I explained to Frick that I was sad because I wondered if anybody ever asked him to play. After I found the father to ask him if they wanted to join us for the afternoon, I discovered they were not able to go. They were waiting on a doctor to arrive that afternoon around three p.m. I saw the boy again today. I saw him playing in the hall at the Ronald McDonald House with the therapy dog, Cooper and the House Manager. The boy was laughing and running around as Cooper was lying on the floor getting some love.

It has been three months now since James was born and diagnosed with a severe heart defect. I have been living in Charleston for three long months while J. J. drives back and forth every week to work in Greenville. Even though James is very sick, the only evidence you can find that he is deathly ill (with the human eye) is his scars and purple thumb tip and fingers. He doesn't have a unique face. He has a beautiful face that looks at you with beautiful eyes. James has brown hair and perfect small lips.

I am not sure if James will make it. We are not sure if James will survive. The doctors and nurses do not think so as he is very sick and science doesn't prove to be on his side. As I rethink about the little boy with the unique face (probably twelve years old), I remind myself that nothing is guaranteed but anything is possible. I remind myself anything is possible with God. Yes, J. J., there are tons of people suffering in the world. We have been experiencing suffering now for three months with James's severe heart defect. But the good news is this: with the grace and love of God we are able to make it. We are able to overcome the suffering by leaning on each other when things get unbearable. The little boy's mother is able to wipe his tears with her white folded napkin. A best friend is able to continue to take care and love her child Chase, age five, even when he wasn't suppose to make it and live when born. Sebastian, a special little boy, is still dreaming of playing football even if he will never be able to take the field. J. J.'s Oregon Ducks, even ranked third, may win the National Championship this year since Auburn lost their star quarterback to the Panthers.

I have no idea why God allows suffering in the world. As a good pastor friend told me months ago, "God doesn't give us these things because he thinks we can handle them." God would never intentionally give us suffering. I think God watches how we handle the things we were given. So yes Frack, if James dies, I know you don't want him to die, but if he does, we will have a funeral. We will be sad and yes Frick, I will cry again because I am sad. But if James dies we will know God intended it. We will continue to hope and pray God's will is to heal James but we will know, and hopefully one day accept, God's will. All things are possible through Christ. Let's just continue to pray God's will is to heal James's heart as well as his purple finger. You know, I will still continue to think about the silly small things. Peace and grace to you all James's prayer warriors!

Hurt ~Dad
Tuesday, August 23, 2011 8:57 p.m.

"I focus on the pain, the only thing that's real. The needle tears a hole, the old familiar sting. Try to kill it all away but I remember everything." These words, written by Nine Inch Nails and performed by Johnny Cash, haunt me tonight. Tonight, the only sound I could hear was the sound of the TV. I watched it for hours. Every show I watched involved somebody hurting. It seems to be the one common theme that all TV centers around. I watched *Celebrity Rehab* with Doctor Drew. It's a show about famous people struggling with addictions. I found myself genuinely hurting for these people. They all had great God-given lives they somehow managed to screw up by drug use, alienating their families, and falling into the trap that becomes a self-fulfilling prophecy. They take more drugs to kill the pain. They alienate their families to do the drugs. They feel guilty for being weak and making the wrong choice. So they take more drugs to kill the pain. The hardest part for all of them was forgiving themselves. I found myself praying for these people. If they would only realize that it's the weakness, the tears, the admission of guilt, the heart-felt apology, the admittance of shame that endears them to people. If they could only see their families were dying to forgive them if only they could forgive themselves, then they could begin to recover.

It's hard to admit your flaws. It's hard to admit when you're weak. It's especially hard when you've always been told you need to be strong and you know deep down on the inside that you're not. And you're scared that just below the brave façade they will see the truth. They will see that weakness. I will tell you that after this weekend I am weak. I held up okay until this weekend. Since Saturday, I find myself inches away from tears. My little Turkish friend that doesn't really know me, Batuhan Itku, absolutely broke my heart. I can't think about him without crying. I've seen his face. It's deformed. It's still pretty severe, but nothing compared to the way it was before his six plastic surgeries. I have visions of him being picked on by other children, or worse, left out. Children are cruel. I'm sure he has endured ridicule from other kids. I've read his story. Schools have refused to enroll him. Parents of other children have asked for him to be removed or they would not bring their children back. People are cruel. Maybe it hurts me so bad, because I know I'm one of them. In elementary school, I was one of the cool kids. I was part of the "in crowd" that would have been right there in the mix ridiculing this precious child of God right along with the rest of them. And I am ashamed. If I could go back and change some of the things I said or did, I would do it. But I can't go back. We can never go back. One of the hardest parts of this journey is looking into the mirror. I ask myself the questions over and over again. What have I done wrong? What lessons am I supposed to learn from this? Why all this pain? I feel like if I can just confess the sin, learn whatever lesson I'm supposed to, or just do my part in some way that maybe God can put an end to the pain. This probably sounds a little desperate. This probably sounds weak. But I just want to fix it. If only I had some measure of control. If only there was a set of instructions to follow. I want a quick reference guide for the exam. I want God to give me the main ideas that I am to learn from this chapter. I'll go read up on them, pray about them, pass the test, and we can stop all this pain.

Then again, maybe I'm just opening my eyes a little wider to other people. I realize their pain and suffering is mine to share. I'm going through this with James. I have to go through it. I'm his father. But you don't. You, choose to live this journey with us because you're not afraid to carry that cross. Historically, I've been afraid to. Historically, I would look people in the eyes when they were telling me their problems and I was very good at saying the right things. I was very good at showing my concern, and for the moments we were together, I truly felt some of that hurt. But deep down, somewhere off to the side in places we don't like to talk about, I was thinking, I'm glad it's not me." I don't mean to sound disingenuous, because a part of me *was* concerned. But my eyes have never been opened to the heartaches of the world like they have these past few weeks. There's so much pain in the world. And I feel so weak because I've done precious little to do anything about it.Most of what I've done has been for very selfish reasons. I've done mission work, but mostly it's because I enjoy spending time with the youth group at our church. Mission work also makes me feel good about me. To quote Terrell Owens, "I love me some me!"

One thing I have never been eager to do is just share somebody's pain. To see that mother rub the scars on Batuhan's face as they both wept deeply, tenderly, was more than I could bear. I couldn't even talk about it. I can't fix it. I can't do anything about it. All I can do is sit and cry into a pillow helplessly. All I can do is weep with that mother and child. I remember a conversation I had with Doc Mission in Greenville. I told him I thought this cross was more than I could bear. He responded, "The cross is heavy J. J. The cross is always heavy." Way back then, a few weeks ago, I was only looking at my burdens. The only cross I was carrying was the one about my family, my situation. This weekend God opened my eyes and showed me that I have no idea just how heavy that cross really is. I have no idea how heavy that cross is for other people. Yet somehow, they are able to carry it. I know I'm weak because I know I could not carry it. I could not give up everything I own, leave my country, and endure rejection after rejection from doctor after doctor telling me there is no hope. I couldn't endure seeing my son rejected by schools, teachers, parents, and other children. I couldn't carry that cross. And to see someone else have to carry it breaks my heart.

There is so much pain in the world. Some of it is completely out of our control. Some of it is brought on by our own shortcomings. But how much less pain would there be if we embraced those that were different, forgave those that made mistakes (especially ourselves), and lifted the ones carrying the heaviest cross? Maybe we can lift that burden by giving a child a box of candy. Maybe it's by reading your baby brother a book. Maybe it's simply crying into a pillow and praying for God to ease another's pain. My prayer tonight is that we all find a way to ease the heartache of another. Help to carry their cross just long enough for them to rest for a moment and catch their breath. Find a way to show God's love and grace. It will renew their energy and give them the strength they need to carry their cross a little further or maybe they will help someone else carry theirs.

So tonight we pray for purple thumbs to get better, for many scars to heal, and for God to strengthen and maybe change our hearts so we can find ways to be blessings instead of burdens, and stop some of the hurt.

A Teaspoon of Hope ~Nurse Mom
Thursday, August 25, 2011 1:51 a.m.

Doc McNair Wilson, the famous cardiologist, remarked in his autobiography, *The Doctor's Progress*, "Hope is the medicine I use more than any other. Hope can cure nearly anything." Doc Harold Wolf, professor of medicine at Cornell University College of Medicine said, "Hope, like faith and a purpose in life, is medicinal." Can you tell I am doing lots of research and reading with my free time since I am quoting famous people?

Tonight friends, I received "a teaspoon of hope" from James's doctor. Tonight I met with Doc Optimistic after evening rounds and good news of James being a candidate for surgery next week was reported. Yes, James will hopefully receive his second surgery, surgery number two next week. An echogram, a sonogram of the heart, was taken yesterday and reviewed. Doctor Optimistic reported to me tonight that James's echogram showed improvement in his tricuspid valve and now we need to take advantage of the "window of opportunity" and perform the next surgery to help heal James heart. Thanks be to God!

James was born with severe mitral and moderate-to-severe tricuspid regurgitations. In simple "country girl" language, James's blood flow in both sides of his heart are not correct due to these two valves, in particular the mitral valve. The heart is divided into two sides. The mitral valve is in the center of the left side of the heart and the tricuspid valve is in the center of the right side. These two valves divide, each pumping one side of the heart, and are in the center of each side, which makes up the four chambers of the heart. The normal heart is a two-sided pump with four chambers. James's blood flow is going in different directions because his mitral and tricuspid valves do not close properly (all the way) and they leak extra blood flow by allowing the blood to flow back and forth. Mitral and tricuspid valves help control proper blood flow in the body.

James's mitral valve has not shown any improvement in echocardiograms to this point as the leaflets on the valve show a very large opening when they try to close. James's mitral valve is categorized as severe regurgitation with scientific expectations of little improvement. His mitral valve does not close all the way and allows a large gap for backward blood flow. Have you ever been to a waterpark with a lazy river? Imagine the lazy river, water flowing smoothly, wrapping around different corners and constantly flowing in one direction. Imagine the blood flow in a normal heart like the water flow in a lazy river. The water flows in a constant rhythm, in one direction, as the blood flows in a normal heart. The blood flow in a normal heart is supposed to flow constantly in one direction. The opening and closing of healthy valves in a heart helps blood flow circulate and flow correctly. James's mitral and tricuspid valves do not close all the way and the openings allow the blood to leak backwards and cause problems. James's leaking or regurgitating valves allow his blood to flow incorrectly in his heart like a child fighting the water flow in a lazy river by kicking and swimming backward against the slow, flowing water current. Incorrect blood flow causes problems with the body's lungs, as the lungs help oxygenate the blood, etc. This is an extremely lengthy explanation and I will save the explanation of the blood oxygenation and use of blood flow in lungs for another entry explanation, maybe.

Yesterday, the echogram administered showed less leaking in James's tricuspid valve. If you remember, early on in this trial or journey with James we asked for everyone to pray for improvement in James's tricuspid valve. The tricuspid valve, previously classified as moderate-to-severe, needed to show signs of improvement for us to have hope of helping James's heart. This is a great sign of less leaking and provides an additional "teaspoon of hope." Now, there is hope that James can live for a while by using only one side of his heart to pump blood instead of needing both sides. This will allow us more time to do additional surgeries and completely "reroute" and correct the blood flow. The hope is James's tricuspid valve can pull the load of pumping blood to the body for a while as he becomes a single ventricle heart patient using only one side, the right side, of his heart as a pump for blood flow. The hope is with the help of at least three additional surgeries, James will be able to live a healthy, prospered life as a sweet disciple of God. James will continue to live by using only one pumping side of his heart instead of two pumping sides for a while. Only one side of James's heart will pump blood by using the tricuspid valve since the mitral valve is severely damaged. James's right side of his heart and tricuspid valve will be used now to help pump his blood flow and the mitral valve will be "stitched" up, creating a single ventricle heart also known as surgery number two.

I mentioned above three additional surgeries. The surgery next week will not completely fix James's heart. He will need additional surgeries called "staged reconstruction" over the next few years. Surgery number two will come next week; surgery number three at six months of age, and surgery number four around three years old. "Staged reconstruction" will help reroute James's blood flow as he grows and continue to help his circulation. Keep in mind the plan can all change once Doctor Heart is in the operating room and opens up James's heart to perform what is needed. This is the current plan now. Doctor Heart will know what is best once he gets in and sees with his eyes what is happening.

So, I question why now? Why the sudden decision of surgery? We have been waiting patiently, well maybe not patiently, but waiting for three long months. Hope is the medicine, along with the tools (caregivers), for healing. God continues to provide us with teaspoons of hope to get through this trial and journey of healing James's heart. Today, we were given a teaspoon of hope. We need to remember we can never give up hope. We need to remember we can never give up our teaspoons of God's medicine no matter what we face in life. Reports of only two days to live, codes, compressions, CPR, and dirty little nine-letter-words cannot take away our teaspoons of hope in God. In the Christian life, we will face trials and temptations. When we successfully overcome these hardships in our lives we harvest maturity and strong character. I remind myself often to not resent this trial and trouble of a sick baby. I remind myself to continue to witness to you all God's love and grace as well as teaspoons of hope. I continue to be thankful to you all, James's prayer warriors, for continuing to pray for healing even after three long months. Thank you for your continuous prayers asking God to heal James's heart. Just as the first 18 verses of the Book of James summarize: God gives us patience, strength, and "teaspoons of hope" to face these trials. Thanks be to God! Let's continue to pray. Blessings to you all!

A Few Quick Clarifications ~Nurse Mom
Friday, August 26, 2011 12:45 a.m.

1. The CaringBridge website is a journal and written documentation of our journey with James. Some postings are sad. Some postings are happy. Some postings are preachy. All postings are truthful and come straight from the heart, and you may not want to continue reading if you feel offended, saddened, or embarrassed with the postings. There are other ways to get updates on James without reading the journals. If you enjoy reading the postings, please continue. Currently, there are 30,321 visits, so I hope a few of you are staying informed as well as updated.

2. There are many days where there is not different progress to report on James. Many of you have mentioned you get "worried" if you do not see an update each day. We do not want you to worry. There is no way we can field all the daily phone calls or emails with requests for daily updates on James. So, with this said, we try to update you with not only the current numbers from each day for our "number crunchers," but we also try to update you with stories, things, and events we experience as some of us get bored with just numbers all the time. We are all different.

3. We are not ashamed of anything we say or share with you all in this journal. This is the reason the website is open to anyone and is not password-protected. Hopefully, by reading our journal you will find strength and connect in other ways with your own life, whether it

be silently or out loud with others. We try very hard to not use actual names in order to protect friends and caregivers from being identified.

4. The website was created to keep you all updated on James, but it was also created as a therapeutic way for us to manage this difficult trial. Truthfully, this site was created for us. We never thought we would be in these shoes today, especially now three months away from home tending to a sick baby. Yes, none of us know how we would handle such a situation like this until we walk in the shoes. Our CaringBridge journals update you on how we are able to handle this difficult situation. It is hard to put yourself in another person's shoes so we journal and share with you thoughts.

5. We are not judging anyone by sharing stories or experiences in this journal. We are simply sharing things we see and hear. This is a humbling experience for us both and this journal is not meant to exalt us in anyway just to share James's stories. Sometimes it may be hard to hear or experience things that make you uncomfortable to face or see. The truth hurts. Sometimes it is hard to face, but remember, we are not judging others. We are just letting you know our journey and how it makes us feel. There is lots of good in the world. We report on it as well as the bad. Right now times are hard and trying, and we try to continue to thank God for helping us through this time. We try to praise Him with the good reports given on days.

6. Please keep all of your negative comments or advice to yourself about how we are handling things at this time. This is not the right time or place. We need to continue to concentrate on James as well as Frick and Frack right now and everything needs to be positive. We already have enough negative steps to overcome. Please continue to bring on the positive and hopeful comments.

Just a few quick clarifications so you know what you can continue to expect from this journal and information on James. We should have stated these expectations in the beginning, before now, but timing has never been my strength. We hope these journals could result in a book and the proceeds could continue to do additional good in the world through mission work for others. James had a stable day and there is nothing new to report. These are just a few quick clarifications with love.

A Strong "Will" ~Dad
Saturday, August 27, 2011 5:51 a.m.

Jacqueline's father talks about growing up as one of six brothers. The rules were simple: get up and get your shower early so that you had hot water. Get to the breakfast table early so you got the portion you wanted. The early bird gets the worm and the late risers better be ready to fight hard for the scraps. He instilled that same tough mindset in Jacqueline. He instilled that same willingness to fight for what you want. She doesn't back down very easily. It drives me crazy sometimes but I wouldn't have it any other way. I wish he had instilled that willingness to get up early, since she is not what I would refer to as "a morning person." As my Facebook status read once, (key word in the sentence being once), "Sometimes I wake up grumpy. Other times I let her sleep." But she is what she is and I better love her for it because God help us, she's not changing. Her *will* is just too strong.

I have absolutely no right to complain about being strong-minded because I have no room to talk. I'm pretty well set in my ways and will sometimes argue just for the sake of arguing. The late Pat Tillman used to sit with members of his football team at Arizona State. He would argue with people at the cafeteria table defending one side of a topic. One day, his good friend Jake Plummer came in, sat down, and agreed with Tillman on the subject, presumably to avoid an argument. Then Tillman did an odd thing. He switched sides and began defending the other side of the argument. Jake stopped between bites and said, "Pat, I just want to eat my food. The only reason I agreed with you is because I didn't want to argue. Now you've taken the other side. Are you just looking to argue? Are you simply looking for a fight?" Pat Tillman said, "Jake, to be honest, I don't even have an opinion yet. I'm trying to advocate for both sides and listen to the arguments so I can decide for myself." Pat Tillman was an interesting guy. He wasn't the easiest guy to get along with but everyone around him loved him because he was different. He was more strong-minded than most, more determined than most, and stuck to his values no matter what. How else do you explain him becoming a first-string NFL football player as a seventh round pick? How do you explain him giving up his high-paying NFL salary to go fight with the Special Forces in Afghanistan? He was the special kind of guy people gravitated to because he never backed down from a fight or what was right, no matter the sacrifice. He ended up making the ultimate sacrifice but not before making his mark on this world. I would like to think our family has a little Pat Tillman in us. I'm determined to do whatever I have to do. I'll make as many trips up and down I-26 as I have to. I'll make or miss as many days of work as I have to in order to see this through. In situations like this, I better have that kind of will. I'm going to need it.

Last night, Jacqueline and I spent a little time talking to a lady who has been in the Ronald McDonald House for seven months. Her husband can't go back to work because she couldn't take it here on her own. She couldn't stay down here by herself. It was just too hard. So they have both been in Charleston, not working, for seven months. Sometimes I forget just how hard this is on Jacqueline being in this shoebox every day, most of them alone. I look at Jacqueline and thank God she has the will to fight. Thank God she is strong enough to do what she has to do. Part of this comes from within. She has been raised to be an independent, strong-minded, pain in the tail. I mean that most affectionately of course. That's the thing about a strong-minded person. It's always a double-edged sword.

The other thing that gives us strength is our support network. We are blessed with a tremendous support network, church family, work family, and blood family. Everywhere we look we are blessed and surrounded with love. Undoubtedly, this gives us a lot of strength. I had a member of our family write an email that was a little critical of some of our blog entries. Part of me read that email and thought, "Oh no you didn't!" Part of me thought, "What? I don't understand." Another part of me said, "Yeah, I see your point." After talking on the phone, I began to understand more of where this person was coming from. This person felt like we were putting down human beings as a general group and that we were just in a dark place. Human beings weren't as bad as we were making them out to be. After reading back over the blogs I see this person's point. It wasn't the intention, but sometimes words have side effects. It would have been easier just to stay quiet and let it go. I respect this person for speaking out. I have been raised to stand up for what I believe. Jacqueline has been raised to speak the truth. We have both been raised and taught not to back down from the truth or what we believe. So when I received this email from someone with a similar set of learned behavior, I knew it was going to be "on like Donkey Kong." It was going to be a battle of wills.

A funny thing happened instead. I found out yesterday James will have surgery early Monday morning. After getting a few of the details, I began to call family. I started with blood family, then work family, then church family. I spoke with the person that sent the email but didn't bring it up. "Surgery is on Monday. I'll talk to the doctors over the weekend. They are inserting a melody valve via open-heart surgery. They may try and stitch the tricuspid valve. They won't know until they open James up and look into his heart." We finished the conversation, both of us told the other "I love you," and we ended the call. About ten minutes later the person called back and we began to address the email. It took less than two minutes to begin to better understand one another's point of view. We talked for twenty minutes, mostly about my family and how we were coping, all that we were trying to do with the CaringBridge website, and why. There was no fight. There were no raised voices. There was only a very nice dialogue that brought about a good bit of understanding. It was filled with love, compassion, and empathy. It was nice. It wasn't a battle of wills. It was a question of "What will we do next?"

This is soothing to me. Knowing that James is going into surgery on Monday morning is enough to focus on right now. I really can't worry about anything else. Based on what the doctors have told Jacqueline, we are preparing for a huge fight. I'm preparing for the kind of fight that takes days to resolve. Another family member met me at church the other day to let me into the fellowship hall. She said sometimes she and her husband wouldn't speak for three days because it becomes a battle of wills. Then somebody will ask her what she's fighting about and she can't remember. That's the kind of fight I'm prepared for. I'm prepared for the one that lasts several days. This conversation gives me hope. Maybe it won't be this huge Battle of the

Bulge. Everything doesn't have to end in a huge fight. Maybe this will go smoothly and James can recover. Things can go very differently than the knockdown, drag-out fight we expect.

That said, if it does come down to a fight that lasts days, I'm glad he has that strong will inside him. I know he has inherited it, I just hope he is ready to put it to good use. The next two days we will rest. Jacqueline wants a pedicure, a massage, and a good night's sleep. I need some down time and a good cup of coffee. James needs some good old-fashioned formula and fully functioning organs. We have two days to get our minds ready. Monday morning we will be prepared for peace, for death, or a fight. That said there is only one will that really matters, and that's God's will. I just hope and pray that my will and God's will are the same. Thy kingdom come, thy will be done, on Earth as it is in heaven. Peace to all!

James's Surgery ~Nurse Mom
Sunday, August 28, 2011 1:33 a.m.

J. J. and I just got back from visiting James tonight after we watched a movie together. James looks great. He is resting well and his heart rate is around the 150s. As soon as we walked into the room he opened his eyes and watched us as we talked to him and rubbed his hands and fingers. James opens his eyes now when we walk in the room and when we start talking to him. If you stand behind his head and talk to him he will try to turn his head around and see you. Since he is intubated he is not able to turn his head yet. But tonight I noticed he was trying to move his shoulders. I reminded myself that lying in a bed for three months has made his muscles weak. His drainage tube was turned on for fifteen minutes tonight and seventy-five ccs were drained from his body. We do not want his belly distended again before the surgery so they are turning on the drainage tube briefly every six hours.

James is resting up for his surgery on Monday morning starting at 6:30 a.m. Yes, 6:30 a.m. is very early. Frick and Frack will be arriving in Charleston tomorrow from the mountains with their grandmother and Paw. I am planning on spending time with them since they will be going back to Greenville for a few days. J. J. and I don't think it is wise to have them here in Charleston when we all will be on edge with the surgery. My parents, as well as J. J.'s parents, will be with us during James's six-hour surgery. We will try to post updates frequently on how the surgery is going, but we will not be able to call or email all who are concerned and praying. Please continue to pray for James. This is a very risky surgery.

James will have open-heart surgery on Monday and an experimental surgery will place a melody valve in his mitral valve to help stop the leaking valve. Also, the tricuspid valve may or may not be stitched. We are not sure. Doc Heart will wait and see what he thinks when he opens James's heart. This is not a typical surgery that is done on infants. We hope and pray the melody valve will help James's mitral valve stop leaking and correct the blood flow. We need the melody valve to correct the blood flow from the mitral valve and allow James's lungs to heal. Hopefully he will be extubated off the ventilator or breathing machine. During the open-heart surgery, James's heart will be stopped and he will be put on a heart and lung bypass machine to keep him alive. The surgeons will go back into his previous incision from the first surgery and try to scrape away some of the scar tissue before they place the new valve that normally lasts in kids and adults for 5-10 years.

We will be given a pager during the surgery and Doc Heart's assistant will send us frequent updates via pager during the surgery on how things are going during the procedure. Our family will be sitting and waiting as well as praying in the PCICU waiting room during the surgery. Please continue to pray for James and spread the word for prayer Monday morning starting very, very early. Tomorrow, J. J. plans to hold James and spend time with him during the day.

I am not worried about the surgery. I am relieved this day is finally coming as I have been waiting for months for this day. I do feel a bit of anxiety though as I think about the lengthy surgery and the details of the procedure. I continue to put my faith in God and know God knows what He is doing. Even though James's condition is uncommon and we are in unchartered waters with the correct treatment, I feel very confident that once again James is a fighter as he continues to fight. If this procedure works, I think of the possibilities that maybe one day another baby will be saved since we were faithful enough to take the risk and try this experiment and surgery. It is very unusual, though, for babies to survive with this type of condition. Remember, James was not expected to live long enough for me to get to Charleston from Greenville to see him alive.

Prayer is very powerful! Thanks for all the prayers you send up to God.

CHAPTER 18

Game Plan

> *"Always remember . . . Goliath was a 40-point favorite over David."*
> *~ Shug Jordan, Auburn Football Coach*

Game Time ~Dad
Monday, August 29, 2011 6:39 a.m.

I love Saturdays during football season. I wake up before everybody so I can get my chores done. When ESPN's *College GameDay* comes on, I am ready to go. My number-one favorite thing is watching my Wolfpack or my Ducks win their game. My second favorite thing is the pregame show. I love the build-up before the games. I love the storylines. I love hearing the interviews with the players prior to the game. I can almost tell which team is going to win by the interviews before the game. Winners have certain intensity about them. Winners have a certain confidence in their eyes. I remember back to my elementary and high school days when I played on teams. There was a nervous energy that comes out of the silence before games. I always had music playing in my head before the event. It helped to control the rhythm with which I played. On very rare occasions, I recall getting into a special zone. There is no place like it. Time slows down. There is a heightened sense of awareness. Difficult things seem easier, much easier. The only word I have ever heard used to describe it is the "zone."

Tonight, I have read a book to help calm my nerves. I've also listened to music that I would have listened to years ago in build-ups before a game. For us, it's game day. The time has arrived. I have stayed by James's bed to make sure he rested well, that he did not run a fever, and looks as healthy and ready as he can be for this surgery. It's go time. So, two songs have played in my headphones to get me ready: Roy Jones Jr.'s *Can't Be Touched* and The Caesars, *Jerk it Out.* "Can't be touched, can't be stopped, can't be moved, can't be rocked, can't be shook, we hot!" The other song starts out, "Wind me up. Put me down. Start me off and watch me go. I'll be running circles around you sooner than you know." These songs get me pumped up. And I have to tell you, I'm pumped up! I'm ready to get in the business of getting better or die trying. I'm ready!

Jacqueline has selected a different song for James. She chose, *For the Fruit of All Creation.* It goes, "For the fruit of all creation, thanks be to God. For the gifts to every nation thanks be to God. For the wonders that astound us, for the truths that still confound us, most of all that love has found us, thanks be to God!"

Jacqueline was awake, showered, dressed, and ready to go by 5:30 a.m. She said her prayers, kneeled over James, and humbly rubbed his hands and feet, making her last-minute peace to God, before James went into the operating room (O. R.). She is now ready.

The nurses put on their masks and MRSA gear. They washed hands, checked paperwork, and made last-minute arrangements as to who would be doing what during the transfer down to the O. R. The nurses, respiratory therapists, doctors, x-ray technicians, and anesthesiologists were all smiling. Interestingly, they all have their own little routines and prayers, yes prayers they go through for these kids prior to surgery. Each of the nurses on duty tonight came by separate times to wish James luck and let me know they will be saying their prayers for our family. They let us know when they will work their next shift and told us they look forward to seeing us all again.

The surgery will last six hours. James leaves in three minutes. We won't see him again until 4 p.m. this afternoon or maybe a little after. Surgery will end at approximately 12:30, but he will spend the next three-and-a-half hours in recovery. The doctor team has decided to stitch the tricuspid valve and put a melody valve in the mitral valve position. Here we go. Say your prayers. Wish all of us luck; it's game time!

Monday, August 29, 2011 9:02 a.m. ~Dad

We just got first page. "All is going well in the operating room. They started about 8 a.m. Baby James is very stable. Will send hourly updates until they are finished." Thanks be to God!

Monday, August 29, 2011 10:21 a.m. ~Dad

Surgery is moving along and the doctor has just come in to assist with valve insertion.

Monday, August 29, 2011 11:38 a.m. ~Dad

Valve is placed and will soon look at it with the echo. So far, so good. If echo shows good placement they will be done. If not, they may need to revise the position. Baby James is behaving.

Good news ~Dad
Monday, August 29, 2011 12:46 p.m.

Here is the exact text message from "Nurse Informer "(Doc Heart's assistant):

"They are now coming off heart lung bypass so Doc Heart, I am told, is happy with the valve placement. Yay! Depending on the amount of bleeding they will come over to the PCICU in about 1-2 hours. Will keep you posted."

They are preparing James's room for his return. We just found out one of the nurses we have grown the closest to has requested to admit James and is coming in on her day off to make sure he is taken care of. She is one of the charge nurses, and is recognized by her peers as one of the best. This is the type of care we are receiving at this hospital. How blessed are we? God is good, all the time!

Monday, August 29, 2011 2:26 p.m.

They have closed up James's chest. We are waiting on the doctors to come in the PCICU to let us know how the surgery went and how the valve is working. Will update you later today with report.

Praise God! ~Nurse Mom
Monday, August 29, 2011 3:25 p.m.

Just spoke with Doc Heart and James did well during his surgery. The melody valve seems to be working and there is just a small leak. Once he was able to see James's valves, the tricuspid valve's leak was not bad so he didn't do anything to it. We need James's heart to get used to his new blood flow and heal. J. J. and I are going in the unit in fifteen minutes to see James for the first time since this morning at 6:30. James's chest is closed and he is on a few new medicines. More details will come late tonight.

Please remember to thank God, the caregivers' healing hands as well as continue to pray for safety and recovery for James during the next 48 hours. This will be very critical for his healing. Thanks be to God!

CHAPTER 19

Jest of Love

"There were times of hardship when people forget the courage they need to keep fighting; and survive. But I think as long as we have something to believe in; to keep close in our hearts, courage will never truly leave us. We only have to reach deep in our heart to find it."
~ *Sakura*

"OUR" *Sweet Baby James ~Nurse Mom*
Tuesday, August 30, 2011 3:32 a.m.

"Beep, beep, beep." Tonight, or shall I say early this morning, the heart rate monitor machine was beeping loudly and constantly ringing in James's room. This rapid beeping reminds me of the morning I arrived in Charleston at the hospital, more three months ago, to see James after a C-section birth and airlift from Greenville Memorial Hospital. A lot has changed the past three months since Tuesday night, May 17. Three months ago James did not have a two-inch vertical incision along his chest. Three months ago I was living in Easley in my own house, sleeping in my own bed instead of sleeping in Charleston at my home-away-from-home charity house. Three months ago Frick and Frack had a normal life, and J. J. came home to his family, his entire family, after a good day at work. A lot has changed the past three months. Actually, if you break it down a lot has changed the last 103 days, fifteen weeks, or three months. Who's counting though?

It is now early in the morning and I am sitting with James in his room at the PCICU at the Medical University of SC (MUSC) and watching Nurse Full of Joy work her magic to help James heal his rehabilitated heart. He was doing well this early morning, under the circumstances, and remains stable. It has now been nineteen hours since James was rolled away for surgery. It has been nineteen hours since my sweet baby James's chest was cut open again. His heart stopped. His eight-pound, fourteen-ounce body was put on a heart and lung bypass machine in order for the surgeons, doctors, and caregivers to fix James's leaking or regurgitating valves. James continued to hold his own this morning after his long day filled with an open-heart surgery.

`For all the number crunchers I know you are probably dying for numbers. James's heart rate is in the high 180s. His blood pressure ranges from the 60s-70s/30s, and oxygen saturation is around ninety. His heart rate is higher because he was put back on the blood pressure medicine, dopamine, after the surgery to maintain a healthy pressure. James is paralyzed and will stay this way throughout the night so he will stay still and rest. He is also on a new medicine to keep him asleep so he doesn't wake up and realize he is paralyzed. Can you imagine waking up paralyzed and not being able to move or not know what is going on?

There seem to be ten medicines on a drip now going into his body with fifteen pump machines. Approximately five of the fifteen are flushes. Some of the ten medicines I recognize from three months ago: heparin, dopamine, epinephrine, milrinone, and fentanyl. Some new medicines I don't recognize: amiodarone, midazolam, cisatracurium, etc. There were lots of medicines administered tonight to Mr. James. Nurse Full of Joy worked very hard while continuing to keep a very close and watchful eye on James. She listened for his pulse in his cold right leg with a Doppler machine. Even though James was running a slight fever, currently 38.3, his extremities are very cold. Nurse Full of Joy will watch his stats tonight just like our prayers during this journey, faithfully.

"Doc Enigma" was on the floor tonight and was also watching James very closely. He is a mystery (hence his stage name) to me and I haven't figured him out yet. Doc Enigma is very attentive to his patients and very knowledgeable about correct care for James. When I seem to hound him, as I did the past few days about antibiotics and fevers, Doc Enigma stood his ground and politely explained to me his reasoning, even when I repeatedly asked the same questions to make sure I understood. Doc Enigma reassured me earlier tonight, saying, "Nurse Full of Joy and I have this covered." Yes, Doc Enigma, Nurse Full of Joy and you do have this covered. Thanks be to God for you both tonight.

Another echogram was taken tonight to take a look at James's rehabilitated heart. When I asked Doc Enigma how the leaking looked, he responded with, "What leaking?" The new melody valve seems to be working correctly at this point and the mitral valves have minimal leaking. Now we need to allow James's body to heal and recover from this extremely harsh surgical procedure.

James's body has lots of new wires, IVs, and tubes. He has two new R. A. lines in his tummy, measuring 10-15, to watch and measure the pressures in his heart. There is also an additional drainage tube inserted in his heart draining a small amount of blood into a Pleur-evac machine. The ventilator rate was reduced last night around 7 p.m. from thirty to twenty-six. I hope this is a great sign the blood flow is corrected with the new melody valve and James will soon be extubated and taken off of the ventilator machine. We have never seen James without the tape on his mouth because he was instantly intubated at birth so he could breathe.

Yesterday was a long day but it was a good day. We are one step closer to trying to fix James's heart and bring him home alive and healthy to Easley. Please continue to pray for God's healing and allow the caregivers to continue to provide excellent care to our sweet baby James. Yes, he is *our* sweet baby James. He is just not mine and J. J.'s baby, he is definitely ours. Without all of your support, love, care, and most important prayers, I don't think *our* sweet baby James's "beep, beep, beep" would be ringing in my ears tonight just as it did three months ago. God bless you all!

Win the Day ~Dad
Tuesday, August 30, 2011 3:41 p.m.

The primary objective for day one after open-heart surgery was to not lose ground; stay steady. If we can stay steady we will have won the day. We have been able to do that. We did have to increase support by upping the dosage of heparin by a very small amount. We tried to reduce the epinephrine but it was too soon. Thankfully we didn't lose ground. We took James back off the paralytic and he opened his eyes and looked right at me today as if to say, "I told you!" My good friend Mr. Youth Basketball player would say, "James goes hard in the paint." It means that he's not afraid and won't back down from a fight. I agree with you my friend, James does go hard in the paint and his dad is some kind of proud! But we are a long way from being out of the woods. Nurse Ninja has him today and reminded me the critical period was forty-eight hours post-surgery, not twenty-four. So, let's hope the next twenty-four goes similarly to the first twenty-four hours. James has held steady. His heart is holding its own. His vitals are as stable as the doctors could have hoped for so far!

So keep praying. Don't stop now. We won yesterday. Now we need to win today. Here's some excellent advice from Chip Kelly, Oregon's head coach: "Win the day!" Thanks to all for the prayers!

Four Miracles ~Dad
Tuesday, August 30, 2011 8:06 p.m.

James's heart rate has climbed from the 170s into the 190s. We have increased support on the ventilator. His blood pressure remains stable and we have not had to increase any of his medications. They do want to keep him sedated. He is currently awake, looking at his mom, listening to some very soft flute music that almost put me to sleep, and looking handsome. He isn't swelling. He isn't retracting. He looks to be fairly comfortable which is a good thing. They have increased ventilator support to keep him comfortable. They are also planning to increase the dose of versed to keep him calm and comfortable. Last, a little Tylenol® for the slight fever. If we get the fever down and keep him sedated, his heart rate should come down also. That is the hope. We don't really know what to expect because this is the first time this has been done. Let me repeat that for you. The doctors and nurses don't really know what to expect because this is the first time this has been done.

Miracle number one: James is still here. He is the first to have a melody valve inserted into his mitral valve. It has been used extensively in the pulmonary valve but not the mitral. So far, so good.

Miracle number two: The little girl in Bed One of the PCICU had heart surgery earlier. She was put on a bypass machine during her surgery. When they went to restart her heart, it wouldn't so they put her on an ECMO machine. They will preserve her organs and try again.

Miracle number three: The little girl next to James got up and walked yesterday. Yes, she had a nurse on one arm and her dad on the other. She walked approximately twenty feet. What's the miracle you ask? This little girl is walking around with a 100 percent artificial heart called the Berlin heart. It extends the lifetime of a future heart transplant patient and buys time until a matching heart can be found. Can you imagine? This little girl is walking around with an artificial heart. "The bionic woman ain't got nuttin on her!"

Miracle number 4: All of these kids are alive today because for some reason God has allowed them to survive the experimental, the temporary, and the downright impossible. For some reason he has granted all of them this day. But miracle four is not for them. It's for us. See, He gave us this day too. If you think about it, each day is a new miracle for all of us. This is the day the Lord has made. I will rejoice and be glad in it and thankful for it. Amen. Peace and love to you all. Sweet Dreams!

This is Frick ~Frick
Thursday, September 1, 2011 11:33 a.m.

James is doing well today. They went down on the ventilator by two points. He survived open-heart surgery. Mom and Dad are home for "meet the teacher." Frack and I go back to school Tuesday. Mom and I are going to play swoosh and wrestle with six figures. Swoosh is a game where u try to knock your opponent down. One time I knocked Mom of the bed.

This is Frack ~Frack

This is Frack. James was born on May 17, 2011. That is my birthday! I will plan his birthday when he turns one! He might come home. I hope. I got to sleep with mommy one night! I get to go to Toys R Us!!!!!!! Today is teacher day. I get to meet him or her. I miss Miss Wooten!! She was my teacher last year. James is doing good today. I am GLAD. I will dress him every day! I will see him this weekend YAY! I LOVE James!!!!!!!!!!!!!!!!

Recharging My Batteries ~Nurse Mom
Thursday, September 1, 2011 11:48 p.m.

Frack asked me tonight why couldn't we just go one day without saying James's name. Interesting. Frick told me this afternoon, "You are a better mom now. James has changed your life." As a look of surprise and shock fell across my face, Frick followed his comment with "I don't mean this as an insult Mom." Surprising. College football started tonight and J. J. is extremely excited for the big game this weekend between the Oregon Ducks and LSU. Not Surprising. As for me, I am trying to recharge my batteries after a long start to the week with James's open-heart surgery. Much needed.

Lately, the word James is used frequently in all my conversations and thoughts. Evidently, Frack is tired of hearing about James, even though she reminds me often she loves him and mentions every day she doesn't want him to die. Every day Frack asks me what will we do if James dies. Of course I tell her we hope he doesn't die but if he does die, we will have a funeral. Immediately, she asks me what will we do with all of his things in his room. Frack wants to keep everything in James's room. She is starting to show signs of being a pack rat just like her mom. Last night she put all of James's clothes in his dressers and organized his room. She was in hog heaven, getting a chance to decide what and where to put James's things. I thought allowing Frack the chance to have "control" and organize James's things may help her get the thoughts of him dying out of her head. She told me she "just couldn't help thinking about him dying all the time." It is quite interesting to me that she asks if we can go just one day without saying his name, especially when she thinks about him all day. I may have to seek a professional on this one.

Speaking of James, he had a good day. I talked to his nurse on the phone tonight and then called an hour and a half later to talk to the doctor. I have lots of numbers to report tonight for the number crunchers. James's ventilator went down two breaths this morning from thirty-four to thirty-two. Some of you may remember his ventilator setting was near 24 a few days ago. Yes, it was set lower. Last Tuesday night, James had a low gas level around 7.20, which is scary, so the rate went up to help increase James's gas level. The caregivers like the gas levels to be around 7.37/7.40. James was starting to wake up from surgery and started to breathe over the vent when he wasn't ready. With this said, the rate increased to thirty-four, which is okay considering he just had open-heart surgery four days prior. When he went into surgery he was on a rate of thirty breaths per minute. With this said, four days later James's breathing rate is only two breaths higher tonight.

The good news "Doctor Dear" happily reported to me tonight was James's CO_2 levels are the best they have been in a month. His levels today and yesterday were forty-two and thirty-seven. A month ago, the CO_2 levels were in the seventies. CO_2 levels for a healthy person average around forty. This is a good sign that we will hopefully be able to wean the ventilator rate down soon. We hope and pray this will happen, but James needs slow, baby steps moves.

Frick said today, "James has changed your life, Mom. You are a better mom now." Today was a day for both kids. I made sure today was their day. Boy do they deserve a day. Evidently, it has been a long time since I actively asked Frick to play with me. We played Super Mario Bros., enjoyed lunch at his favorite diner, met his teachers for the new school year and played Swoosh, his favorite "Mom and Frick" game. I won the Swoosh game by the way. It has been a long time since I won. He normally tackles me and takes me down. I guess from the eyes of a nine-year-old boy, I was a better mom today. I guess James has changed my life. James reminded me how lucky I am to have two healthy children. James reminded how much I took Frick and Frack for granted. Don't get me wrong, I still do love James, but Frick and Frack are healthy and today was their day. I made an extra effort to ask them to play with me. This was apparently something I did not do before James blessed our family. Frick always provides perspective to me exactly when I need it.

The past few days James's platelet count numbers have decreased. Platelets are new territory for me. I am not very educated yet on platelets and transfusions of platelets. I have lots of research to do now to educate myself. Yesterday, James's platelet count was down to twenty-one. The caregivers' goal for platelet counts is greater than eighty. With this said, twenty-one is very, very low. After a transfusion, actually two transfusions, James's platelet count tonight has increased to sixty-one. Doctor Dear said they were "robust" and hopefully they will continue to climb.

One may ask why the platelet count decreased, especially since yesterday platelet levels were twenty-nine and after the transfusion the platelets only went up to thirty-three. The platelets were continuing to decline quickly and get very, very low. Sorry, that is all I know about platelets at this point. I need to do my research to be able to speak intelligently. I do think platelet levels are what help control the clotting in the blood and bleeding. Give me a few more days to research and I will be more knowledgeable on this topic. I am not sure this is a big concern at this point yet since the platelet levels are "robust" at sixty-one.

The doctors' thinking behind the decreasing platelet levels explains James's body becoming septic after surgery. The dirty nine-letter-word infection has a new synonym called septic. Cultures were drawn Tuesday night but there were not any signs of new bugs growing yet. There were not any signs of a new dirty nine-letter word or positive culture growing. The doctors do think James is septic though since his platelet levels decreased so low. Further, his white blood count levels increased to 21,000 last night. Doctor Dear explained to me that James's immune system is extremely low and weak. I asked him if we could compare James's immune system to one of a cancer patient receiving chemo treatments? Doc Dear agreed that was a good comparison. The doctors expected the platelets to decrease as well as the white blood count to increase after surgery due to James's history, immune system, and of course his good looks. I had to throw a punch line in there for you to enjoy. You all know he has good looks.

His heart rate remains in the low 140s and oxygen saturation levels are mid 90s. James is on a pretty good dose of pain medicine but he still wakes up and looks around. The RA lines inserted into his heart measure the heart pressures. These two lines show a decrease in pressures from fifteen to eleven, which is a good sign. Hopefully, the doctors on the morning round will decide to do another echocardiogram tomorrow to take a look at James's heart with his new melody valve inserted into his mitral valve.

It is going to be quite interesting watching J. J. and Frick watching the college football game Saturday night. J. J. will be all excited and probably wearing his Ducks jersey from ten years ago. I threaten to throw that jersey in the trash every year and still have not done it. Frick will be wearing his purple and gold LSU colors as well sitting next to his dad analyzing every play. Fall is coming. College football is starting. What happened to summer?

During the past three-and-a-half months since James's birthday, evidently I have become a better mom. My batteries are recharged. I am ready to get back to hounding the caregivers and making James healthier. My batteries are recharging for a day for Frack when I don't mention James's name once all day. I guess I will have to rename that little bugger James, so if I use a different name for him then Frack can't say I said his name. I need to outsmart her on this one. My batteries are recharging to continue to love J. J., even if he pulls out his ten-year-old Oregon Ducks jersey and wears it in public. Most important, my batteries are recharging to continue to become a better mom and wife. Yes, James has changed me Frick. James has changed me for the better. I took so much for granted before James was born. I let work, busy life, technology, and many more things take over. I forgot how to actively ask you if you wanted to play. Swoosh it is tomorrow morning! J. J., I may even cook you and Frick a special dinner Saturday night for the big game. Frack, one day my love, one day we can go all day and not even mention James's name. We can mention your name all day long. Let's continue to recharge our batteries! Whatever it takes.

"On The Road" ~Nurse Mom
Saturday, September 3, 2011 1:09 a.m.

As I was on the road and driving alone tonight back to Charleston I started feeling sorry for myself. This is quite unusual for me to feel sorry for myself. The kids didn't want to come back to Charleston with me this weekend after all. They wanted to stay home. J. J. and I gave them a choice to pick where they wanted to stay this weekend and guess who got the short, unlucky end of the straw? I guess the kids deserve a calm relaxing weekend at home since they have been on the road the past three months visiting friends, family, and hospitals. Being able to sleep in your own bed is nice. Plus, Frick and Frack enjoy playing Super Mario Bros. together at home on the Wii upstairs in the playroom. They are trying to beat the game and win all the levels.

As I was on the road tonight I thought about how our lives have been turned upside down. Things are different now for the five of us living apart most of the time: J. J., Frick, and Frack are in Easley, and James and I are in Charleston. Frick compares our current lives now to a divorced family. He jokingly teases about J. J. and I "fighting for custody" over the kids. "No, they are with me this weekend in Easley. No the kids are with me this weekend in Charleston," we say.

Sometimes I do feel like my family is living a separated life residing in two separate cities most of the week three-and-a-half hours apart. Once again, I have to stop feeling sorry for myself. I need to pull up my big-girl pants and continue the grind of getting James healthy and home alive, even if my family is apart.

When I arrived at the hospital tonight I anxiously entered James's room, looked at his machines, and scanned the settings. I made it all day without calling the nurse on duty and asking about James. Of course J. J. called early this morning so I did get a morning update. Tonight James and I were talking and his right foot starting moving. James loves to move his right foot and kick off his sock. I tease J. J. about James being on the special teams as a kicker for a football team one day. A few years ago I used to joke J. J. about Frick playing on special teams as a kicker. A few weeks ago James kicked his foot so hard he kicked his sock half way down his hospital crib. For some unknown reason, James moves his right foot back and forth all the time. I like to think he is telling me he is okay.

After I scanned the settings on the ventilator I saw James's breaths-per-minute rate dropped to twenty-four. I took a double look to make sure my contacts were not fuzzy and blurry from crying earlier in the car. It's always hard to leave J. J., Frick and Frack behind in Duncan, South Carolina, at the gas station meeting drop spot on interstate 85. Isn't that what families do when they share custody on the weekends? Drop the kids off with the other parent at a designated meeting spot? Yes, James's ventilator rate was down to twenty-four breaths per minute tonight. He was breathing at a rate of 30-32 breaths with lots of pink lines averaging six to eight breaths over the vent settings. The oxygen setting is back down to twenty-one, as well, which is room air.

Monday when James was paralyzed for the open-heart surgery his oxygen rate was set on 100. The peep setting is on six again and the volume is set to fifty-five. I think normal volume is forty-five and normal peep is five. Don't hold me to these normal numbers though number crunchers, since normal isn't a word I keep in my vocabulary. Nothing seems to be "normal" for James anyway. Doc Enigma likes to use the word "common" instead of normal. So, for now I will try to use the word common. I like it!

When I entered James's room his nurse was watching his heart rate of 163. She had just changed his diaper and he was upset, so the nurse gave him extra pain medicine to calm him down. When James cries you cannot hear any sound since he has the endotracheal tube in his throat. James wasn't crying when I arrived, but his heart rate was around the 160s and didn't go down during my whole visit this evening. I looked quickly to see if he had a fever because normally, or shall I say commonly, James will have a fever when his heart rate is elevated. But he did not have a fever tonight. His temperature was 36.7 Celsius, which is 98 Fahrenheit.

Doc Enigma didn't seem to be concerned with James's heart rate so I didn't mention it when we talked. I did mention everything else though. You can imagine how detailed I try to be when I meet with the doctors. I feel like I hound the hades out of them sometimes with 50 million questions. Sometimes all I know to do is ask questions and keep up with the facts.

Platelet counts are still low. The platelet counts were back down to twenty this morning when James's blood was drawn and tested. Another blood work test will be done on his platelets at 4 a.m. I asked Doc Enigma about my new friends the "clotters" aka platelets, tonight. I am ignorant about platelets and their usage. The clotters need to increase to at least eighty, which is normal. There I go using that word "normal" again. When you cut your arm and start to bleed, platelets help your cut clot and our new friends help the arm to stop bleeding. Clotters surround the cut, clot and reduce bleeding. James doesn't show any signs of bleeding currently but our clotters need to increase since twenty clotters are very low. Even though cultures don't show any positive growths of infections yet, except in the respiratory tube, the low levels represent a possible infection in James.

James is receiving lots of medicines to help him recover from the surgery last Monday. The chest drainage tube is removed. This is a great sign. We still need to pray for pee. James's belly is bigger and the fluid needs to be removed from his mid-section in order for his lungs to work properly and remove the ventilator. Oh, what a happy day it will be when James gets off the ventilator machine. There is a gourmet burger restaurant in Charleston J. J. is waiting to visit to celebrate the day James comes off the ventilator. What a treat for J. J. on this day to see James's mouth without any tape. There are currently two drainage tubes in James: a peritoneal dialysis (P. D.) tube and a foley. The P. D. tube is not currently draining that much fluid and the foley is filling up with urine as the Bumex and other medicines help reduce and release the fluid retention in James's body. Doc Enigma hopes to reduce James's body size the next few days and make him smaller by releasing the extra fluid retention in his body coming mostly from his belly.

The left thumb tip is still purple and looks like a blister is forming under the nail tip. Also, James's right index fingertip is now purple as well. I try not to think about these purple fingertips because I get very upset at the thought of James losing the tips of his fingers. I know if that is all that happens to this child I should count my lucky stars right? Nope. I am having a hard time accepting the fact that the left thumb is purple and now the right index finger is purple. Aren't scars on the chest enough? God, please help James's fingertips. Please help them heal along with his heart, lungs, liver, and gut. Is this too much to ask for God?

I wish a happy Labor Day weekend to you all. I hope you and your family have a safe holiday weekend. If you are traveling and are on the road please be safe. Enjoy the holiday weekend as well as enjoy the college football kickoff. Hopefully, I will continue to have good news to report to you the next few days. Hopefully, James will continue to beat the odds and heal. Thanks for your continued prayers!

Give Thanks ~Nurse Mom
Sunday, September 4, 2011 1:42 a.m.

I just wanted to let you all know the good news I received today. James had another echo done today on his heart. The results from the echo were amazing and miraculous! His tricuspid valve and mitral valve are not leaking anymore. I asked the nurse three times today the same question over and over about the echo results to make sure I heard her correctly. Also, I asked the night-shift nurse again as well. Can you believe this report of good news? Can you believe the valves are not leaking anymore? Can you believe the tricuspid valve fixed itself without any repair from the doctors? Also, the mitral valve that was supposed to be "beyond repair" has now shown signs of zero leaking with the new melody valve in place.

I don't know what to say. Once again, I feel kind of speechless with this good news. I still think I am in shock as the good news of the valves has not sunk in completely yet. I wanted to make sure you all knew tonight so you could give thanks to God for listening and hearing all of our prayers. Please give thanks to God for this wonderful report. Also, the caregivers at MUSC are amazing as well and take very good care of James daily. Please give thanks for them.

With this said, James's body can hopefully start to repair and heal the damage done from the past. We need James to start taking on nutrition and full feeds so he can grow and become healthy enough to come home. He is currently on a setting of five ccs for feeds. We need the extra fluid in James's body to be released so his lungs can expand and he can breathe on his own without the ventilator. We need James's body to become infection-free, increase his new friends the clotters, and decrease his white blood count back to a "common" range.

Praise God for this wonderful report of the valves being leak-free and remember to give thanks for this miraculous testimony of healing.

Here is a link to see what the melody valve looks like working in the heart: *http://www.visibleheart.com/video/melody_valve.mov*. This link is a video of a melody valve working in a pulmonary valve though. Remember, James's melody valve was inserted in his mitral valve. Blessings!

CHAPTER 20

The Greatest of These

Love begins with a smile, grows with a kiss, and ends with a teardrop.
~ Anonymous

See ~Dad
Monday, September 5, 2011 10:54 p.m.

I was listening to the band One Republic tonight. It's one of those bands that you only listen to when you're in certain moods. I'm a little depressed today so One Republic suits me. The song was *Stop and Stare*. The lyrics say, "Stop and Stare. I think I'm moving but I go nowhere. And yeah I know that everyone gets scared. But I've become what I can't be. Stop and stare. You start to wonder why you're here not there. And you'd give anything to get what's fair. But fair ain't what you really need. Oh, can't you see what I see?"

When I'm a little bit down, One Republic seems to capture my mood pretty well. The lyrics hit me today. James has another infection. They can't find it and don't know what it is but his ventilator was moved back up to thirty. His platelet count is low. His white blood cell count was extremely high. He's not taking on digestion and they've stopped all feeds. He's swollen again. They put him on another antibiotic to help fight whatever infection might be causing these changes. James gets better. James gets worse. James gets better. James gets worse. Stop and Stare. I think I'm moving but I go nowhere. Every time we have setbacks like this it scares the mess out of me. They tell me that he has little-to-no reserves left for setbacks. Then they tell me he has an infection they can't find. Then they shower me with this good news saying, "He's stable." How stable? He's a week removed from

open-heart surgery. He has an infection they can't identify. He can't
digest food. And oh, by the way, his white blood cell count is up to the
number it was when he coded the first time.

I'm angry. I'm furious with the nurse who didn't have time to talk
to me this morning because she was too busy taking care of my child.
"Yeah I know that everyone gets scared, but I've become what I can't
be." What I can't be is angry with Nurse Ninja. After all, if it weren't
for her, James's fate would already be sealed. It was her and Nurse
Picturesque that brought him back the day he coded. Thank goodness
I was smart enough to bite my tongue and not say anything stupid
(for once). It's not her I'm angry with. It's not any of the nurses or the
doctors. It's not James, or God, or fate this time. I'm not angry with
anybody. But I am *so* frustrated by the circumstances. I'm so tired of
being in between. I want James to either get better or die trying so we
can get home and start living again. I feel like our whole family is in a
time warp. I want Frick and Frack to have their mother back at home.
I want my wife home.

Just the other day Frick joked that it was like we were divorced.
I understood where he was coming from. Jacqueline confides in me
all the time that she feels alone. She wants the kids and me with her
in Charleston. She says she's going crazy. I understand where she's
coming from. I went school shopping today for the kids. I got them
the required items: pencils, notebooks, folders, crayons, glue sticks,
erasers, sanitizer, Kleenex, dry erase markers, etc. I think I did a pretty
good job. But that's not my job. That's mom's job. Please understand,
I'm all about women's rights, and I know that this sounds chauvinistic,
but that's not how I mean it. Mom always takes the kids shopping
for school supplies. She loves it. It's a day she looks forward to. It's
tradition in our house. I missed her today. It just didn't feel right with
me doing the school shopping.

"Stop and stare, you start to wonder why you're here not there."
I've wondered all weekend if I should be here or in Charleston. This
is the first weekend since James was born that I have not traveled to
Charleston. Frick and Frack were tired of travelling and begged not to
have to go to Charleston again. They simply wanted one weekend to

stay home and play with their friends before they went back to school. So, I stayed. But every time I've talked to Jacqueline she has told me how lonely she feels. I don't feel right not going to see James. But Frick and Frack, they have wants too. So I don't know what I'm supposed to do. I start to wonder why I'm here not there. It's not fair. It's not fair to Frick and Frack that the house feels broken. It's not fair to Jacqueline to feel all alone. It's not fair that I'm their husband and father and I don't even know what I'm supposed to do or where I'm supposed to be. And nothing about this is fair to James. I'd give anything to get what's fair.

But then again, there are the last lines of the chorus. It feels to me like words from God. "Fair isn't what you really need. Oh, can't you see what I see?" I can't begin to know or understand God's plan. I don't have his vision. I don't know why we're going through all of this. I'm sure other families in our position have felt this way also. I'm sure there are moments when they, like me, get frustrated. I don't understand. I don't know why this has happened. And part of me, a very shameful selfish part of me, just wants this to be over with. Don't get me wrong. I want James to live long and prosper. If someone could confirm that eventually this would be his outcome, I would probably handle this a lot better. But God has made no such promises to me. The only thing I know is that he has a plan and my family is playing their part. I hope that honesty will get more brownie points with God than my selfish shortcoming of impatience. But what husband and father wouldn't want this to be over quickly? We are all suffering. And we want our suffering to be over as quickly as possible. This is taking its toll on all of us so when you pray tonight, say a little prayer that gives the five of us a lift. Help get us all through this difficult time. Pray that we get through this as expeditiously as possible. Your prayers always give us a lift. I can't imagine where we would be without the blessings and support that we have been given but even with the support, it's still hard. Still, I'm thankful for the many blessings great and small that all of you have given. Lunch with friends today was a much bigger blessing than I let on.

I had lunch today with two friends. One of them brought his daughter. She has grown a foot over the summer and has matured right before our very eyes. The other friend was driving his new Audi and talking about the office that his firm had moved into. We talked about their lives and how they were moving forward, the good the bad. It reminded me that while we have been seemingly stuck in a time warp since May 17, everyone else has continued to live his or her life. Time just seems to be passing us by. As I looked at that beautiful grey convertible, and thought about their lives moving on, I got a little bit jealous right up to the point where he handed me the keys. Normally, I would have turned his offer down, but not today. Today I needed a lift. And today my friend God and some German engineers gave me five minutes to enjoy. I began to remember that in the future, there would be happiness. It may not be right now, but my family too will have our moments. We have to trust God. We have to be patient.

Fair isn't what I really need. I need to wait and see what joys God has set aside for us. Let me see what he sees. Pop Pop Bob says, "The sun doesn't shine on the same dog's, um, on the same dog every day." And sure enough it didn't shine on me much today, although maybe a few minutes during lunch. But I'll have my day because God is good, all the time. I'm sure he's looking down on me and saying, "Oh J. J., can't you see what I see?"

Number Watching ~Nurse Mom
Tuesday, September 6, 2011 11:30 p.m.

Tonight is a quick update for you all on James as I am very tired and trying to get to bed before midnight most days. My sleeping habits have been way off lately and I am trying to get myself on a schedule, if possible. Feeling run down, I continue to endure the emotional stress of patiently waiting for healing and number watching.

Cultures still do not show any positive signs of dirty nine-letter-words, yet James's body does show signs of another infection. The bad news is James's white blood count is still high, today at 30,000 and his new friends the clotters are still low today, around fifty-three. Pray for decrease in his white blood count with average numbers ranging between 10,000-15,000 and James's clotter friends to increase as well.

Hopefully, in the morning the drawn blood will show a decrease in white blood count numbers. This will be a sign of James fighting off infection. He is still swollen and his PDA drainage tube is cut off and on every six hours (I think) so he doesn't lose vital nutrients in his loss of fluid. TPN feeds and trophy feeds are equal to full feeds but his stools are extremely loose still. James needs full feeds to get healthy and to rebuild his immune system. TPN feeds are not the best since it is given through his veins, but I guess I will have to take it for now since James's stomach cannot handle full feeds through his nose. He is only getting two ccs currently through his nose because of his stomach issues. A baby gram (ultrasound) was taken this afternoon of James's left and right arm PICC lines as well as of his neck to see if he has any clots or issues forming that might cause the high white blood count numbers. As of tonight, I did not hear of the results.

I am tired and emotionally exhausted. I miss J. J., Frick, and Frack! I just need to continue to hang on until Friday night and they will be here in Charleston. We will all be together! Good night. Prayers for an infection-free body for James please.

Wake ~Dad
Saturday, September 10, 2011 11:09 a.m.

It's game day again. No, not for James this time. It's ESPN's College GameDay and he and I are watching it together for the first time this morning. My Wolfpack are taking on Wake Forest today, thus the reason for the entry title. Well, that and the fact that James has been wide-aWAKE since I arrived make it a good coincidence. We have talked a lot and he looks good. He's breathing comfortably, his color is good, and I'm happy to see him and spend some alone time with him after a two-week hiatus.

James had bad blood gas last night so they increased his ventilator settings. In talking with the respiratory therapist, I learned James had a lot of mucus before his gas last night. He sounds better now and his numbers have improved. His vent is now on thirty-eight breaths-per-minute. His white blood cell count has also risen. They are back up around 34,000, up from 26,000 the day before. We just can't seem to get James infection-free and his immune system is temporarily shot. They have stopped feeds for the time being until they can figure out what's going on. Once again, we have taken a step back, at least in the short run.

The big picture, however, is much more encouraging. This heart valve appears to be working beautifully. His body is getting higher oxygen saturations and one of the fingers on his right hand that we were in fear of losing has made a comeback. He still may lose the tip of his left thumb and the tip of his right index finger, but the middle finger healed up nicely due to improvements in both circulation and oxygen saturation. Also, James's kidneys are working pretty well. He has been able to urinate and get a good bit of the edema off of his body. His tummy and chest are still a little swollen but he is making progress on those fronts. The big picture for James is certainly a lot better than it once was. His recovery will take a long time because of the hits his body has taken, but we feel that the open-heart surgery was a step in the right direction. Now, we just need to get James back over the hump. We need the other parts of his body to begin doing their jobs. We need for James to do for James. We aren't seeing that happen yet, and that is the troublesome part. The doctors and nurses have told us time and again this will be a long process. This will take time. When we see vent settings increase it's disheartening. They remind us that James will tell us what he needs and when. They remind us to remain patient.

The number one thing we need is prayer for James to take on digestion and nutrition. This would be the one thing on which James's fate hangs at the moment. If James can take on nutrition it will help strengthen his organs. It also allows the body to hold on to electrolytes and even more important, proteins. Proteins help hold fluid within the blood vessels and prevent fluid from seeping into the tissues. This will allow us to remove the tube in James's belly that helps drain extra fluid. Digestion will also help reduce edema on his stomach and chest, which will allow the lungs to better inflate. It will enable us to lower the ventilator support. Ultimately, it should allow him to get off the ventilator but at this point we expect that to take months. However, as of now he is not taking on nutrition and they are stopping his feeds.

We had hoped to be further along than this, but so far James just won't tolerate it. We need your prayers for this to change. This is now priority number one.

The doctors just finished their rounds with James this morning. One of the doctors went to medical school at Wake Forest. I was about to kick him out when he informed me that N. C. State was going to win today. Upon hearing this good news I decided not to throw him out. He's obviously a good, smart doctor. I can now relax knowing that a very smart overachiever has informed me that my team is going to win. This is good!

Even though James had a few setbacks this morning the mood in the unit is pretty positive. It's James's nurse's birthday. Doc Optimistic is back on call all week. Jacqueline, Frick, and Frack are having a big, hot cooked breakfast at the Ronald McDonald House, and I'm able to watch College GameDay with my baby boy. James is wide-awake and breathing comfortably this morning and his color looks good. Doc Optimistic went to finish his rounds and then is coming back to look at some fluid gathering on the outside of James's lung. He seems pretty content with where James is at the moment. A nurse reminds me that James's body is still adjusting to all this new oxygenated blood that it's getting and encourages me that it takes time for all of these things to work out. She told I should relax, kick back, hang out with James, and we should watch some good games together. I love this nurse! I can now tell Jacqueline that I'm under a nurse's orders to watch college football and I won't be telling a lie! Things are looking up!

The plan for today is to give James some x-rays, give him some blood, and give him six ccs of feeds per hour in a new feeding tube. All this and perhaps a little college football is just what the doctor ordered. Seriously, it's from his lips to God's ears! Peace to you all. Enjoy the games everybody!

P. S.: James is still wide-awake looking at his mobile. I've never known him to stay this awake for this long. I think he feels pretty good.

"Tick Tock" ~Nurse Mom
Monday, September 12, 2011 2:41 p.m.

As I drove the kids to school this morning I felt a small reality hit as Frick and Frack jumped out of the van to enter the school doors. I realized the season of summer was gone. Where were the last four months of May, June, July, and August? Time seemed to slip away and move on as a new fall season draws near. I am not living in the month of May anymore. It is now September, almost four months to the day of May 17 when my family's life changed and time seemed to stop. Tick Tock.

Last night Frack and I enjoyed cooking a Hodgepodge dinner (tuna sandwiches, macaroni and cheese, corn on the cob, peaches) reading books, and tucking small bodies into bed at bedtime. Also, Frick and I searched for three blue herons, four snapping turtles, and five raccoons in a science book while lying in his bed before bedtime. We prayed, "Dear God, thank you for Mama, Daddy, Jack, Julia, James, MeMe, Pop Pop, Grandmother, Paw, all our aunts, uncles, family, friends, pets and prayer warriors. Please continue to help us make the right decisions to live a good life in Jesus's name." Time continues to move on, life's activities continue and time doesn't stop.

"How is James doing today," I asked "Nurse Gifted." Several positive changes were made this morning by Doctor Optimistic and his team to help James's health improve slowly. Tick-Tock. Nurse Gifted reported to me over the phone the ventilator setting was reduced down to thirty breaths this morning, the fenoldopam medicine drip was cut off and feeds were increased to five ccs along with 9.5 of TPN feeds. Praise God for these small but positive changes for James! The fenoldopam used during the past open-heart surgery two weeks ago is no longer needed. This medicine was used to help James's heart squeeze properly. Tick-Tock. James's white blood count was still elevated around 27,000, and the clotters were around thirty this morning as well. A blood infusion will be given again today to help increase the clotters. Doc Optimistic doesn't think James has an infection anymore even though his white blood count continues to stay high and elevated.

James was on a grocery list of antibiotics for the past two weeks, a total of four antibiotics, in order to stop any infection lingering in his body. Blood cultures taken at least a week ago did not grow or show any positive growths with infections. With that said, a positive culture did grow from the ventilator secretions in the tube. This culture always shows positive though. This positive growth does not mean James has a respirator infection. The bacterium that grows from the tube-released secretions may just be a sign of the bacteria colonizing in the tube since James has been intubated now for almost four months. There is lots of water, which accumulates at different times, in the respirator tube and creates a haven for bacteria growth. Antibiotics have been stopped as the caregivers think James's body is not fighting infection anymore. They think James is stressed from the past four months of sickness, an extremely low immune system, two surgeries, as well as a blood clot in his right side of his neck. J. J. and I agree with this opinion. James's body must be stressed from everything he has been through in order to fix his sick heart. Tick-Tock

"What do you think about James?" Doc Optimistic asked J. J. and me Saturday afternoon. "James's body did not get sick instantly," I responded. Doc Optimistic gave us time to speak our opinions of James's body. This is one of my favorite things about Doc Optimistic, that he values our opinions as parents and actually listens. Even though James's heart seems to be functioning well with the new melody valve replacement in his mitral valve, I think it may take time, lots of time, for his body and organs to recover from the past three-and-a-half months of functioning with a sick heart. Also, we do not know how long James's heart was sick while I was carrying him during the seven months I was pregnant. We do know James's mitral valve was defective and did not develop correctly. Doc Heart was able to see this congenital heart defect while James's chest was cut open. He was the one who replaced the defected mitral valve with a melody valve during the open-heart surgery (surgery number two) two weeks ago. Tick-Tock

Time is such a precious commodity I take for granted. Just the other day it was the month of May, the season of spring. I was lying in the bed, bored, and angry at the fact I was stuck on bed rest and not able to get up and work in my yard. Just the other day it was the month of May and I was wishing for my sick pregnancy to end and waiting for the birth and delivery of my healthy, sweet baby James. Now it is the month of September, a new season, and how I wish I could rewind the clock to May and continue sleep while I wait on the delivery of a healthy baby. God did not intend on James to be delivered healthy. God did not intend on us having a healthy baby now. Even though James is still sick, the good news is James's heart is functioning much better today than almost four months ago. Through God's grace as well as the power of prayer from James's Prayer Warriors, James's heart is functioning much better today. Now, we just need time, yes time, to continue to "tick" and "tock" and allow James's body to digest nutrition and heal his stomach. We need James's stomach to accept full feeds again (approx. 32 ccs an hour), to allow James's stressed and malnourished body to build up his low immune system. We need time to reduce the ventilator settings and for James to be removed from the ventilator. Even if it takes time for James's lungs to recover, and it takes additional time for me to bring home a healthy baby, I can wait. Just yesterday, four months ago, I was lying in the bed not waiting patiently. So for now, I will wait patiently. For now, I am patiently waiting for a time of healing. I am waiting on God's time for James to recover and continuing to research for my own happiness and well as my family's happiness again.

There is a time for everything, and a season for every activity under the heavens: a time to be born and a time to die, a time to plant and a time to uproot, a time to kill and a time to heal, a time to tear down and a time to build, a time to weep and a time to laugh, a time to mourn and a time to dance, a time to scatter stones and a time to gather them, a time to embrace and a time to refrain from embracing, a time to search and a time to give up, a time to keep and a time to throw away, a time to tear and a time to mend, a time to be silent and a time to speak, a time to love and a time to hate, a time for war and a time for peace. What do workers gain from their toil? I have seen the burden God has laid on the human race? He has made everything beautiful in its time. He has also set eternity in the human heart; yet no one can fathom what God has done from beginning to end. I know that there is nothing better for people than to be happy and to do good while they live. Ecclesiastes 3: 1-12 NIV

Thanks for your continued prayers. Thanks for your strength and patience along with endurance of prayers for James's slow recovery. Let's continue to remember our creator and remember everything has its time and is good in its time. Thanks be to God! Tick-Tock.

GI ~Dad
Wednesday, September 14, 2011 7:12 a.m.

This morning James is having some tests run on his digestive system. Jacqueline requested these tests to see if there was anything that a specialist could recommend that would help James absorb nutrition better than he currently is. Up until Saturday and Sunday of this week, he has not been able to tolerate feeds. This is now priority number one for James. He must be able to absorb nutrition. If he can't, his long-term prospects of survival become dim. The good news is this: starting on Sunday, they started him back on 2 ccs of formula per hour. He tolerated it for a day so they bumped him up to 5 ccs on Monday. Yesterday, they increased it to 10 ccs per hour and he continued to absorb it. This is good news for us and a step in the right direction.

James has also been able to handle more of the breathing efforts on his own. They have been able to reduce the amount of ventilator support over the last three days. On Saturday, his vent rate was set on thirty-eight breaths per minute. Over the last three days, they have been able to reduce this down to twenty-six breaths per minute and he has tolerated these changes.

Taking on nutrition helps with everything. It will help to heal his organs and make him stronger. Protein helps the blood vessels retain the fluid instead of leaking into his tissues. These leaky vessels are what cause edema. James has made strides on the amount of edema resting on his body. This is one reason the doctors reduced ventilator support. His liver and his kidneys are improving. His lungs have gotten a little healthier, though they still have a long way to go.

If the GI (Gastro-Intestinal) specialist can find anything in the tests, we might be able to treat it and make another significant step toward coming home. Wow! At one point, this road didn't even seem possible. Yet here we are, almost four months later and a heart that seemed incurable now seems to be functioning well. His body appears to be responding to the treatments and conditions continue to improve. Thanks be to God!

There is another reason I titled this entry GI. With Sept. 11, fresh on everybody's minds, it's a good time to remind everybody to say a little prayer for those GIs defending us far away from home. I can tell you firsthand how difficult it is to be away from your loved ones. I also now know what it's like to have a son in a dangerous place. The lucky part for me is that I can drive three hours and see them. I can't imagine what it would be like for us if we were half way around the world. I will tell you that I wouldn't wish it on anybody, much less someone who volunteers for it. Our men and women serving overseas deserve our prayers and our thanks. Don't forget those folks during this time. Have a great day. Thank you for your continued prayers!

Prayer warriors needed ~Becky Pickett
Wednesday, September 14, 2011 3:28 p.m.

Friends,

Just got off the phone with Jacqueline. The doctors called her and she is headed back to Charleston now. James is not doing well today. His heart rate and blood pressure have increased. She asks that we pray for James's heart rate and blood pressure to stabilize and go back down. Also, please pray for Jacqueline as she travels back to Charleston. She was trying to have a couple of days off in Easley with Frick, Frack, and J. J. She will get back with an update as soon as possible.

Heartbroken ~Jacqueline
Thursday, September 15, 2011 6:37 a.m.

This morning, I am heartbroken. James passed away last night around 7 p.m. while I was holding him. J. J. and I are back at home in Easley. We were very anxious to pack up and come back home. We arrived home this morning around 5:45 a.m. so we could let Frick and Frack know about James death before they woke up in the morning. As of now, we are not sure about the funeral arrangements but we will post the arrangements as soon as we have a chance to make them.

Thank you for all your prayers and love over the past four months. James's death is going to be very difficult for us but as always we are going to try to stay faithful. I feel very numb. A parent should never have to bury their child. As always, blessings to you!

Home ~Jacqueline
Sunday, September 18, 2011 8:59 p.m.

(Spoken at the funeral from the pulpit at St. Giles Presbyterian Church)

Welcome family, friends, prayer warriors and saints. Welcome to our church home, St. Giles. Today is a very difficult day for me as you all know and can try to imagine. I felt called and needed by God as well as James to stand up today and personally speak in honor of *our* sweet baby James. Since James was born, he hasn't been able to speak so I, his mom, also known as Nurse Mom, for the past four months have been his voice and tried to speak for James to you all . . . especially through James's CaringBridge online blog. James's funeral would not be perfect and complete if I didn't stand up at this pulpit and speak to you all honoring James's strength, as well as determination during the past four months. Also, part of my healing as Nurse Mom requires me to report to you today about the place we call home.

Home is the place where your journey begins, not where it ends. Today, James is home. James is home in heaven with Jesus. James is home playing, being held, listening to music and eating with many angels right now. James is with angels such as Emerson Rose, a sweet precious baby who journeyed to heaven from MUSC in Charleston; Neil, a baby boy who now celebrates twenty-seven years in heaven, a dear close friend's mom, "Me Me," and of course my favorite cook, Grandmother Helen. Grandmother Helen has prepared fried chicken for everyone to feast and celebrate James's arrival home in heaven.

During the past eleven months I constantly thought about Jack and Julia (also known as Frick and Frack) and I thought about James coming home. From the moment I told J. J. I was pregnant, while the four of us sat at a Cracker Barrel restaurant during J. J.'s lunch hour, I thought about home for James. Frack and I immediately started to talk about what we wanted to do with the baby's room, the nursery at our home in Easley. Frick and I talked about how he would be driving James around when he was sixteen and James would be eight. While I sat by James's bed in the hospital for the past four months, four long months, I thought about bringing James home. I thought about how much I loved my four Js: Jack, Julia, James, and J. J. and how I mourned the fact I was away from my precious family. While I sat by James's side in the quiet noise of beeping machines, I would envision standing at this very pulpit, my church home, holding James in my arms. I dreamed of the day I could stand in front of you all, right here, holding my sweet baby James and show you the miracle of life. I dreamt of standing in front of you here in my church home testifying the power of prayer, the power of prayer for our, yes *our*, miracle sweet baby James.

Even though I stand here today without James in my arms, I am still standing. I stand here today because I want you all to remember the fact that even during the most difficult times of our lives, we can continue to stand. Please remember even when we face our worst nightmares, whether it be your mom or wife being away from home for four months taking care of your sick brother and child, losing a job, having a girlfriend or boyfriend break up with you, struggling with a drug addiction, sending your parents or grandparents to heaven or even burying your child, please remember with the love of God and the power of his helpers we will find the strength to continue to stand.

Even though James's home has been different from what we imagined and envisioned, (even months pregnant and four months in Charleston), James is in the best home possible: heaven. James is in heaven. I want you all to remember the strength and determination you felt over the past few months, especially since May, and remember that with God all things are possible. All things are possible even if the outcome is not what we wanted.

Remember God is good, even when we are in the valleys. Remember God is good even when the darkness seems to creep up and the sun doesn't shine and the three little birds don't sing. Remember we must continue to stand in God's glory and help others. James is no longer with us in body on this Earth, but he will always continue to be with us in our hearts. I plead to you to continue as Prayer Warriors for others in need. I plead to you to continue to always remember the power of prayer.

Today, I am going to end my voice for James with lyrics from a song I hold dear to my heart titled *Back Home by J. J. Heller,* "Don't let your eyes get used to darkness. The light is coming soon. Don't let your heart get used to sadness. Put your hope in what is true."

Fried Chicken ~Dad
Sunday, September 17, 2011 6:47 a.m.

Jacqueline's Grandmother, Ms. Helen, used to fix the best fried chicken anybody ever put in their mouth. Anything the woman ever fixed tasted like ambrosia for the gods. She had that gift. I remember the first time I went to her house for Thanksgiving dinner. She put on a spread that would have fed an army base, and I meant to taste a little bit of everything. I remember sitting at the table completely oblivious to people trying to talk to me. My focus was on that food. It was so darn good! I remember Ms. Helen would make her way around talking to everybody, asking if everything was okay. I remember her massaging my shoulders and saying, "Honey, is that all you're gonna eat?" Before I could swallow that mouthful, Uncle Andy had already responded, "That's his third plate Ms. Helen." Everybody laughed. She smiled real big and said, "Eat all you want honey. I love to see a man eat well and enjoy his food." I think I literally ate myself into a coma. I had a big old fat nap with a smile on my face. That was Thanksgiving and it was wonderful. However, the meal she was most known for was fried chicken.

Ms. Helen passed away a few years back. I knew in that moment that I would never have fried chicken that was as good as hers for the rest of my life. That is reserved for her. Ms. Helen and her fried chicken will always hold that special place in my heart. There will never be a Thanksgiving for the rest of my life that I don't think about her and send thanks to heaven for her gift to me: three plates full of it! I will never eat fried chicken that tasted that good. And I will never eat fried chicken that I don't think of Ms. Helen and give thanks for it.

So it is with James as well. James will always have this special place in my heart that belongs especially to him. No one will ever replace it or take it away. I thank God that I have two other healthy children to love on and raise. However, neither of them will take the place of James. James was only here for four months, but my life is forever changed by him. I think about him being in heaven. I'm comforted in thinking that Ms. Helen is there with him watching over him. We now have two angels watching down over us.

There are a few memories that James has given me that I will never forget. I will never forget his baptism, the "Laying on Hands" ceremony, or those happy days when he beat the odds and made it through those surgeries. Perhaps the memory I will use to honor him with will be the Michigan versus Notre Dame game every year. I know that may sound crazy to some of you, but those of you who know me know how much I love college football. Did you see the Michigan vs. Notre Dame game? For years they will talk about the first night game at Michigan. It was Michigan vs. Notre Dame. There were three scores in the last seventy-two seconds. The game was brilliant and it was an instant classic. I got to watch that piece of history with my little man James. Every year that Michigan plays Notre Dame, that game will belong to James in my eyes. That day will always belong to him, and I plan to honor him in some small way every year.

Of course with James's passing come the unanswered questions and I do have a few. I struggle a little bit with why all of this had to happen, and what was the purpose? Why was James brought into this world for such a short period of time? Why did he have to leave so soon? What gifts was James able to bring into this world? What purpose did this short life have? Was his purpose great enough for us to endure this pain that we're in now? I think maybe the answer is that it's not the amount of time that each of us are given, it's what we do with it. There is a poem called, *The Dash*. It talks about a tombstone and how the dates of birth and death don't really matter. What really matters is the dash in between those two dates. He left so soon because his job here was finished and God called him home. Jesus lived to be thirty-three years old, at least that's the number I've heard. Methuselah lived 969 years. James lived 120 days. I guess since he wasn't supposed to make it through two days we can call James an overachiever! Each day is a gift from God and we should consider them as such. As for James's purpose, I don't pretend to have all the answers, but I do know a few things. People have told us many times that the CaringBridge site has been a lift. People have reached out to let us know that we have no idea how many lives James has touched. James held on much longer than he expected to.

Jacqueline's and my eyes were opened to a wonderful charity called the Ronald McDonald House. How many times have I gone into McDonalds', ordered a couple of McDoubles or a Big Mac and never once given to this wonderful charity? The next time you visit a McDonald's don't ignore that opportunity to give your spare coins to these people. At a time when we needed to focus solely on James, they took care of almost everything else. We didn't have to worry about finding a place to stay, meals, all of the other stuff. We were allowed to focus exclusively on James because of the work of volunteers and staff at the Ronald McDonald House. A friendship between two churches over 200 miles apart was started because of James's life. Palmetto Presbyterian embraced us from day one during our time in Charleston. They prepared meals, visited, sent notes, gift baskets, signed the guestbook on the CaringBridge site. They took us in as one of their own. They opened up their homes to us. The pastors of St. Giles and Palmetto Presbyterian are even talking about a possible pulpit exchange on one Sunday as part of this kinship that has developed through James. When we found this out, Jacqueline looked at me and said, "James is still working." I just cried.

There is so much good that has come out of this short life. Jacqueline and I have been blessed by too many to mention or remember them all. As I write this, I'm looking at a poster board entitled, "St. Giles Loves the 5 Js." On the poster board are quarters and dollar bills given by members of the St. Giles youth. There are eighty-five gifts on this one poster board with the names of individuals moved to be a blessing to James and us. How humbling is that? Most of these gifts were given by youth. I was able to reunite with a dear high school friend and college friend. We get so wrapped up in our day-to-day lives that we lose touch. Then when something like this happens you find out that people don't walk, they run back into your life to let you know they're still there. Thank you Derek and Brent and families for that!

I think that somewhere in all of this is a point. We are called by God to be a blessing to others. In a lot of ways, James was able to give so much in his short time. He gave us memories, inspired the CaringBridge site, and by God's grace touched all our lives in different ways. In return, you have found a way to return the favor and show us God's grace by the many ways in which you've given back. I see my community of faith all acting in a Christ-like fashion. My blessings have been overwhelming. The outpouring of love and support make me ask the question, "What if we treated everybody like we've been treated these past few weeks all the time?" Our lives would be incredible. This world would be amazing. I thank James for showing me how good people can be.

So I end this by asking you these questions. James's gift was his ability to reach out, touch, and inspire without ever leaving his hospital room. Helen's gift was the ability to make you feel welcome and provide the best food you have ever tasted. I truly believe that her cooking hands were a gift from God. The question is, "What is your fried chicken?" What is your gift to the world that God has given to you? Are you using these high callings faithfully? If so, are you seeing glimpses of heaven in the joys that you're bringing to others? Are you seeing glimpses of heaven in the joys that this brings to yourself? If you're not using your gifts, do you feel like it is time to start? Whatever your fried chicken is, whatever God has given you in talents to give to this world, be sure that you give three plates full of it on a daily basis. Never forget that in life and in death we belong to God. He has richly blessed us to be a blessing to others in his name. We are asked to receive this high calling faithfully. As we prepare ourselves every Sunday to go out into our mission field, we do so by greeting one another and saying, "The Lord be with you." And then the person responds, "and also with you."

So mission partners, Prayer Warriors, friends, family, coworkers, loved ones, the Lord be with you!

A bird sitting on a tree is never afraid of the branch breaking, because her trust is not on the branch but on its own wings. Always believe in yourself.
~ Anonymous

Epilogue

It has almost been two years since James passed away. Twenty three very long months filled with grief and happiness yet hope and thankfulness for his 120 days of life. We made it through the first round of holidays and anniversaries of both his birth and death. I would be lying if I said it was easy, but the holidays were not as devastating as I predicted in my head for them to be without James. I am grateful for friends and family who have made these days a little brighter.

For the first month after James's death, my front door was not only closed, but it was locked. I found myself hiding at home and isolating myself from the world. I missed church a few Sundays and seemed to disappear from everyone and everything. It was easier for me to stay at home than confront the world that continued to go on during the darkest months of my life

Hiding away at home in my house with the door locked made my house seem very dark. It did not allow my light or lamp to shine in God's glory. Doc Mission called many times during this dark time and told me he missed me at church that Sunday. It was calls like this from many friends that helped me begin to get up and stand up again.

After many prayers, questioning, and dreaming in the weeks and months after James's passing, I decided to reopen my front door and walk back out into the world. After losing a child, reopening the door to the world can be a hard thing to do. The small, simple things we use to do in life now become challenges. I found doing things outside of my comfort zone. My house became challenges and at times brought anxiety. Comfort zones were never a problem for me in the past. I used to be comfortable in most situations. I am told this is a normal feeling upon losing a child but dealing with the feeling is far from feeling "normal" especially for me an extrovert.

Those first few days, weeks, and months were dark and hard. I tried to keep busy, searching for my new normal. Many days, I found myself looking at picture after picture from those several months. I found myself listening to the same music over and over. Frick wonders how many times I can listen to the same song over and over. Now, she listens to those same songs over and over. There is not a day that goes by I don't think about James and his short life. There is not a day that goes by I don't think about what I can do now to help make a difference in our community.

I started spending my time dreaming of ways to give back to those who so graciously gave to my family. I visited the Ronald McDonald House on holidays and helped prepare meals. I began selling Thirty-One products in order to donate insulated tote bags to the House for women to carry their breast milk across the street to the hospital. I got involved in heart walks, speaking engagements, and charity fundraisers to support causes James would be proud of. Best of all, I have gone back to college to obtain a degree in Special Education so I can teach children with special needs. This new adventure allows me to continue to shine my light and help other children and parents in need. I started a website, *threelittlebirds.org*, to remind others to always listen for the three little birds. The website allowed me to publish this book and tell James's story to the masses. Whether you have lost a child or not, I hope his story shines light on your life like he did mine.

Losing a child is the worst thing a parent can go through; but what you do following that death is crucial to regaining your life. One might find it selfish to move on, but we cannot ever stay stuck in time. Although my world stopped for those months I was in Charleston, life moved on outside. Today, my life must continue to move forward, and James is still a part of it. His spirit surrounds everything we do, new friends we make, and he has made our family stronger. Losing James has been so difficult, but it is with our community that my family and I are where we are today. We take baby steps when healing, but we are indeed moving forward. Thanks be to God and always remember, *"Three things will last forever—faith, hope, and love—and the greatest of these is love."* 1 Corinthians 13:13 NLT.

I love hearing from anyone who has similar stories, unique stories, or has found faith, hope, and love through their own journey. If James has touched your life, I would love to hear that too. Please write to us at *jmartin@thethreelittlebirds.org.*

Blessings,
Jacqueline

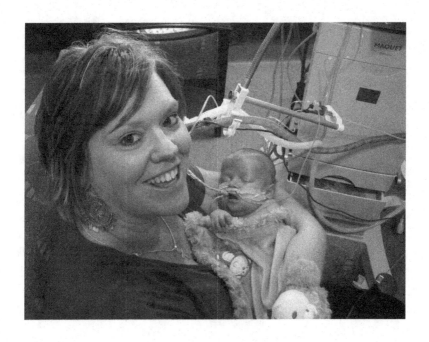

ABOUT THE BOOK

Three Little Birds: Faith, Hope, and Love is a raw and true story written during the life and loss of Jacqueline Martin's third child, James Robert. This story is meant to inspire and counsel readers, especially those facing a difficult journey of their own. James was born prematurely and with a rare congenital heart defect on May 17, 2011, and passed away on September 14, 2011. Three Little Birds: Faith, Hope, and Love is a testimony to the power of prayer and provides proof that God made sure Jacqueline and her family did not have to face this painful journey to physical and emotional wholeness alone.

Jacqueline's story speaks about her personal experience as a mom and about her attempt to live her life faithfully as a Christian while she managed the toughest trial of her life during a "parent's worst nightmare"—losing a child. Living life as a Christian means living life to a higher calling. Jacqueline's story is about taking a parent's worst nightmare and turning it into something extraordinary by improving the lives of others one baby step at a time. Imbued in Jacqueline's writing is the Martin family's message of faith, hope, and love in a direct metaphor for the three little birds. The three little birds are represented by her three children, as well as the greatest gifts of God.

Everyone endures hardships in their lives and receives tests of their faith during these difficult times. These tests of faith enable us to continue to count as well as remember our blessings. They seem to hide the world's nature and beautiful colors, silencing the chirping and singing of birds. During difficult times, community and help from others allow us to continue standing and to get through the trials. With the help of others, the world's colors shine brightly and open our eyes to different experiences, trials, and journeys in our life as well as the journeys of others.

ABOUT THE BOOK

Thank you to all of our Fund & Follow Supporters!

May this book be a blessing to all who read it. God Bless!
—*The Showalter Family*

Emerson Rose Heart Foundation—*Jason & Susan Smith*

May the memory of sweet baby James and the love of his family
bring you faith, hope, and love. He will never be forgotten!
—*Jim, Becky, Jessica, and Olivia Pickett*

In memory of Cassie D Boyd who demonstrated
faith, hope, and love to me—*Dave Boyd*

With all our love—*The Schillizzis*

For I know the plans I have for you. *Jer. 29:11*
—*Scott, Lisa and Ben Campbell*

"May the Lord give his richest blessings upon
this book and those that read it."
In Honor of Kimberly, Erik and Matthew Moyer
—*Jeff and Debbie Moyer*

In memory of sweet baby James, our special angel!
—*Curtis and Debbie Rogers*

Keith & Joanna Chandler
The Dawson Family
The Hamann Family
The Harris Family